FROM GUM WRAPPERS
TO RICHIE RICH

From *Nuts* #4, illustrator Hy Fleishman, Premier Comics, September 1954.

FROM GUM WRAPPERS TO RICHIE RICH
The Materiality of Cheap Comics

Neale Barnholden

University Press of Mississippi / Jackson

The University Press of Mississippi is the scholarly publishing agency of
the Mississippi Institutions of Higher Learning: Alcorn State University,
Delta State University, Jackson State University, Mississippi State University,
Mississippi University for Women, Mississippi Valley State University,
University of Mississippi, and University of Southern Mississippi.

www.upress.state.ms.us

The University Press of Mississippi is a member
of the Association of University Presses.

Copyright © 2024 by University Press of Mississippi
All rights reserved

Library of Congress Cataloging-in-Publication Data

Names: Barnholden, Neale, author.
Title: From gum wrappers to Richie Rich : the materiality of cheap comics /
Neale Barnholden.
Description: Jackson : University Press of Mississippi, 2024. | Includes
bibliographical references and index.
Identifiers: LCCN 2023056026 (print) | LCCN 2023056027 (ebook) | ISBN
9781496851611 (hardback) | ISBN 9781496851628 (trade paperback) | ISBN
9781496851635 (epub) | ISBN 9781496851642 (epub) | ISBN 9781496851659
(pdf) | ISBN 9781496851666 (pdf)
Subjects: LCSH: Comic books, strips, etc.—United States—History and
criticism. | Graphic novels—United States—History and criticism. |
Comic strip characters—United States—History and criticism.
Classification: LCC PN6725 .B36 2024 (print) | LCC PN6725 (ebook) | DDC
741.5/973—dc23/eng/20240226
LC record available at https://lccn.loc.gov/2023056026
LC ebook record available at https://lccn.loc.gov/2023056027

British Library Cataloging-in-Publication Data available

To Leigh

Yes, indeed

CONTENTS

Acknowledgments ix

Introduction: Comics and Books 3

Chapter 1: Back to "Back to the Klondike":
   Book History and Cultural Salvage 19

Chapter 2: "I Will Give You Bodies beyond Your Wildest Imaginings":
   Watchmen and the Editorial Construction of Value 49

Chapter 3: Money, Money, Money: Reading Ri¢hie Ri¢h 82

Chapter 4: Trash Culture: Dubble Bubble Funnies and
   the Theory of Premium Comics 113

Epilogue: Comic Books and Their Readers 148

Notes 154

Works Cited 155

Index 169

ACKNOWLEDGMENTS

This book comes out of long conversations with three people: my partner Leigh Dyrda, my friend Reg Wiebe, and my mentor Cecily Devereux. Many, many people supported me in many ways during the creation of this book, but without those three, it never would have happened at all. Thank you.

Thanks to my parents, Nancy Newman and Michael Barnholden, and my brothers, Kris and Dan, for all your support (including actual comics) over the years. Thanks to my children, Clare and Tristan, for your patience with trips to the comic shop.

Thanks to Julie Rak for the excellent advice and encouragement.

Thanks to my friends, in particular Marcelle Kosman, Matt Rea, and Matt Schneider.

Particular thanks to Bart Beaty, Roberta Gregory, Gerald Saul, Judith Logan, and Sîan Echard for favors and kindnesses, big and small.

A very special thanks to Brandon and Danica of Variant Edition Comics and Culture for their many special orders over the years, and particularly for granting access to their copy of the Carl Barks Library. This is where I tell you to go buy some comics at Variant Edition.

Finally, thanks to everyone who has, over the years, helped me eat the bubble gum.

FROM GUM WRAPPERS
TO RICHIE RICH

Introduction

COMICS AND BOOKS

The US Senate's Subcommittee on Juvenile Delinquency began their 1953–1955 "investigation of the mass medium of communication" with research into "so-called comic books" (US Congress 2). Defining the scope of their investigation required the subcommittee to ask, "What are 'comic books'?" The subcommittee found the term to be a misnomer, as many were "neither humorous nor books" (2). Instead, they made a material turn:

> [T]hey are thin, 32-page pamphlets usually trimmed to 7 by 10½ inches. Most of them sell for 10 cents a copy. They are issued monthly, bimonthly, quarterly, semiannually, or as one-time publications. They are wire-stitched in a glossy paper cover on which, in the crime and horror type, there has been printed in gaudy colors an often grim and lurid scene contrived to intrigue prospective purchasers into buying them. The inside pages contain from 3 to 5 stories told in pictures with balloon captions. The pictures are artists' line drawings printed in color, intended to tell part of the story by showing the characters in action. (2)

The subcommittee's description of the pamphlets, with a curious mention of wire stitching rather than the more common stapling, delineates the physical form that most American comic books would have through the twentieth century. Even with the use of stitching and gluing rather than stapling, and with fluctuations in size and quality of paper, "comic books" as such have continued to be much the same physical object into the present.

Comic books, the physical pamphlets, were a key element of mass communication in 1953, and so in the twenty-first century they stand out as a survivor from an older media landscape. Kiene Brillenburg Würth argues that the innovations of digital media are "rematerializing" print media by making their particularities more visible. In academic studies of comics, the focus is often on how digital comics are distinct from physical formats, which are further distinct from each other. The scholar Aaron Kashtan contends,

> for example, that *Watchmen* is not the "same" text when read as twelve individual comic books, or as a perfect-bound trade paperback, or as a digital file on Amazon's Kindle Fire—and that they are all different media through which the art form of comics can be delivered. (*Between Pen and Pixel* 25)

Watchmen is an apt example of comics studies' neglect of materiality: despite *Watchmen* being the subject of a very large number of academic studies, very few acknowledge that the story was originally published as twelve individual comic books—and there are precious few analyses fleshing out Kashtan's contention about how to read the text as twelve comic books.

This study begins with a physical description of the classic American comic book of the twentieth century in order to focus attention on the physical bodies of comics. In particular, the material objects containing comics change how readers can understand both the value of comics and the meaning of value within comics. Value here means both the semiotic portrayal of what is valuable (and what is not), and also the way that texts construct their own value—in all cases referring both to a fixed, monetary value and to a less precise sense of value as importance. To demonstrate, four comics—Carl Barks's story "Back to the Klondike," Alan Moore and Dave Gibbons's series *Watchmen*, the *Richie Rich* line as published by Harvey Comics, and the product *Dubble Bubble Funnies*—are analyzed in terms of the relationship between their fictional narratives and the materiality of the objects in which those texts are embodied. As N. Katherine Hayles argues, "materiality" is "the interplay between a text's physical characteristics and its signifying strategies" ("Print Is Flat" 67). The first two of these comics present an increasing value of the text juxtaposed with stories where value is a more complex notion; the next continues this tension by portraying an avatar of ludicrous wealth in an enormously cheap context; and the lessons learned from those three allow us to finally approach the most difficult case here, the inextricably inexpensive *Dubble Bubble Funnies*.

Carl Barks is the epitome of the comic book artist salvaged from the trash heap of mass consumerism; this can be seen by looking at the bibliography of any of his stories, but his 1953 story "Back to the Klondike" presents a special meaning as it travels from anonymous, cheap pamphlet to lavish hardcover. The story interrogates the meaning of the miserly Uncle Scrooge McDuck as he goes to vicious lengths to collect a debt; the narrative ultimately suggests that his sentimentality over his past is inexpressibly more important to him. This moral becomes complicated as the value of Barks's story literally increases, and as paratextual framing changes the story from being presented as an exceptionally complex Disney comic to a great work of art. Restoring materiality to the story of the proverbial "Good Duck Artist" suggests new ways to consider the role of book history in comics stories, and presents a fresh view on a well-studied part of the American comics canon.

Watchmen by Alan Moore, Dave Gibbons, and John Higgins, published in 1986–1987, may seem an unusual subject in a book about cheap comics, since unlike the work of Carl Barks it was never cheap and never had to be salvaged. Instead, it epitomizes the formative "quality graphic novel" trend of the 1980s, and examining this case study reveals less Barks-style fan uplift and more the other half of the cultural capital equation: publishers, in this case largely DC Comics, and their actions to turn esteem and quality into expensive products. Rather than ascending from cheap to expensive, the book history of *Watchmen* is a history of DC Comics' shaping *Watchmen* into an avatar of quality, with the relative cheapness of earlier editions becoming the foundation for increasingly deluxe editions. This sits uneasily with the text's representations of value, especially the value of comics themselves.

If *Watchmen* and Carl Barks's *Uncle Scrooge* have taken different paths to represent the materiality of "good" comics, Harvey Comics' character Richie Rich and extensive *Richie Rich* line of comic books reveal a very different history. Beneath a bibliography of excess, the stories about Richie Rich complicate the simple idea of the character to reveal a business/literary history that nonetheless ends in obscurity. A different material approach, distantly reading the circulation of Richie Rich stories, explains the character's afterlife as a satirical icon unmoored from the actual fictional narratives about him. While Richie Rich has essentially always remained a character in cheap comics, a book history approach nonetheless suggests a way out of the paradox of a character widely remembered differently than his stories would suggest. Value is once again at issue: despite the panoply of values in his stories, Richie Rich has come to stand for a rancid and off-putting valuing of money, which is deeply ironic given his publishing history.

Finally, all three of these examples have been circuitous approaches to a vexation for comics studies itself, a vexation unavoidable in bubble gum comics. If Carl Barks is the epitome of work saved from the trash heap, *Watchmen* stands for the levels of quality to which a company can elevate a work of art, and Richie Rich is a character trapped in the gutter by the materiality of his circulation, bubble gum comics are a case study difficult to even address seriously. Their disposable materiality, inextricably linked to academically distasteful consumerism and commercialism, leaves bubble gum comics as nearly unsalvageable in the paradigms of value by which most studies of comics have proceeded. A serious attempt to understand *Dubble Bubble Funnies* reveals a profound ambivalence about consumption and waste related to the troubled boundaries of food/junk and wrappers/trash, as seen in the very small comic narratives that briefly interrupt our consumption of gum. Pud, the hilariously wasteful central character of *Dubble Bubble Funnies*, is sometimes the hero and sometimes the butt of the joke, and ultimately as necessarily ambivalent about consumption as are all of us customers. All four of these postwar American comics represent value in ways that are deeply complicated by their materiality; this book is about cheapness because it is about value—in particular, material values that necessarily include the value level of "cheap."

The signification-focused field of comics studies is in need of rematerializing. Rhetoric abstracting comics from their materiality is common in critical and popular discourse: editor Leslie Cabarga's remark in a collection of reprinted comics, that "[w]hat's great about this book is we get to see the artwork in all its glory, unencumbered by off-register colors and bad printing" (10), makes explicit the subtext of many academic studies of comics. Rather than an encumbrance, such material features as off-register colors, bad printing, low-quality paper, advertisements, ephemeral seriality, and circulation in commercial contexts are an important part of understanding comic books and their associated forms, particularly in their history as a kind of book. Comics have a material existence that needs to be understood not simply as a sign of comics' regrettably cheap production but as part of the history of reading.

What does it mean to consider comics as a part of book history? It rewrites the history of comics from the development of the narrative form to the development of print formats. It turns the familiar procession of funny animals, mature superheroes, and memoirs into an unfamiliar history of a print format that figures itself in terms of both books and magazines.

The stapled pamphlets described by the Senate subcommittee—standard American comic books—have their origins in three specific technological developments. The first is the late modern industrialization of European print culture and the resulting rise in very cheap, large-run print periodicals. Philip Gaskell describes the period from 1800 to 1950 as the "machine-press period" of printing (230) after the inventions that made it possible for industrial presses to produce cheaper products. The "dime novel" of mid-nineteenth-century America, an ancestral format for comic books via its descendant the pulp magazine,[1] was notable partially for its cheap price, as the name implies (K. Davis 35), as was the "penny dreadful," a booklet format that serialized long stories and sold for a penny in contemporary Britain. While the nineteenth-century shift toward large numbers of cheap periodicals is a trend within print culture, it has also been argued that the shift toward ephemerality defines the early modern period (Eisenstein 88–89). Comic books, as an extension of magazine formats as well as the newspaper, would represent a late stage of this shift toward cheap, less durable printing of fiction.

The second development allowing for comic books to take their current form is the emergence of pulp paper, another nineteenth-century innovation. The development, between 1840 and 1850, of paper made from wood pulp rather than fabrics, accelerated the machine press's ability to print cheaply (Katz 217). As Rob Banham notes, "paper made from esparto grass and wood pulp is not as strong as rag paper, but these substitute materials allowed virtually unlimited production of low-cost paper which greatly reduced the unit cost of books and other printed items" (274). According to Robert Kirkpatrick, the price of book-quality paper, one shilling and sixpence a pound in 1800, had reduced to two pence a pound by 1900 (5). This also led to an ensuing explosion in the amount of wastepaper generated by societies that used newsprint (Strasser 91). The developments of the machine press and pulp paper functioned to ensconce print in a culture of mass consumption.

The final nineteenth-century technology of particular importance to comic books was the wire stapler.

> The stabbing of pamphlets was superseded in the later nineteenth century by wire stapling. Wire staplers were first introduced in about 1875 in default of satisfactory book-sewing machines. . . . [U]nfortunately the staples soon rusted and became brittle. Consequently the book-stapling machines were generally replaced by sewing machines by the late 1880s; the stapling of pamphlets, however, had come to stay. (Gaskell 234)

Staples would play a crucial role in physically and culturally distinguishing comic books from unbound print formats such as the daily newspaper. Stapling would also align comic books with the sphere of pamphlets, autonomous and somewhat more permanent collections of paper, while at the same time confirming their status as ephemera compared to publications bound by sewing or gluing.

Although it was technologically possible to create comic books by the 1870s, the actual print format would emerge in a later cultural and commercial context, one growing from nineteenth-century periodical culture.

Richard Noakes has noted the early nineteenth-century history in British periodicals of "comic journalism," in which "cartoons" and "vignette illustrations" were stock elements (96). "Cartoons"—a reference to the preliminary sketches, used as models, of early modern fresco painting, called *cartones* in Italian—were typically humorous and appropriate for the publications that included them, which described themselves as "comic papers" and "comic weeklies" (Noakes 98). This adjectival use of the term "comic" would eventually result in the phrase "comic book."

Thierry Smolderen has suggested that the visual culture of the late nineteenth century was the "crucible of comics" in that "new ways of seeing" enabled by cultural and technological change provided imitative examples for cartoons. Rather than treating such phenomena as X-rays, the kinetoscope, Japonisme, daguerreotypes, and the microscope each as an "autonomous sphere, each with its own structure of interpretation and expertise, cartoonists set about integrating these innovations into the common language of visual signs" (48). While Smolderen is interested in the effect of such cartoons on all visual culture, Lynda Nead has noted turn-of-the-century Western culture's heavy visual engagement with motion (for example, Eadweard Muybridge's protofilmic photographic motion studies). The eventual arrival of the sequence in comics in approximately the same period finds a powerful resonance in Nead's discussion of the "strip" of film and the use of film to reveal the human body in motion, scientifically and pornographically (171–97). In parallel, Eike Exner argues that the changing cultural understanding of sound in the same period led to the comics' distinctive audiovisual device, the speech balloon. The visual style of the comic "strip," including the key element of a sequence of pictures, emerged out of the complexity of late Victorian visual culture.

In the late nineteenth-century Anglophone world, weekly humor magazines such as *Puck* and *Judge* were called "comic weeklies" or "comics" for short (R. Harvey 17). In such magazines, the sequential cartoon stories were called "comic series" (Groensteen 93). In Great Britain, this development led quickly to autonomous publications of reprinted cartoons—for example, *Comic Cuts*, a name that drew on the "large cuts" or centerfold illustrations of earlier comics weeklies (Noakes 94). The term "cuts" is presumably derived from "woodcuts," since "the infrequent periodical illustrations of the 1860s and early 1870s were woodcuts" (Johanningsmeier 331). In America, newspapers of the 1890s—notably publisher Joseph Pulitzer's *New York World* and publisher William Randolph Hearst's *New York Journal* (Reitberger and Fuchs 12)—began to imitate the comics weeklies by including a full-color Sunday supplement of such cartoons, using color as a consumer inducement over the black-and-white weeklies (R. Harvey 17). According to historian and artist Jerry Robinson:

> The drama began in 1893, when Pulitzer bought a Hoe four-color rotary press in an attempt to print famous works of art for the Sunday supplement of his *New York World*. This effort was not successful, and the press was used instead to reproduce large drawings. (12)

Pulitzer began to publish a color humor supplement in 1894 (Nasaw 108). The anecdote about Pulitzer's rotary press suggests the importance of relatively lavish color reproduction in the concept of the comics supplement, as well as emphasizing that comics were an alternative to already valued works of art. Historian Robert Harvey points out that this innovation followed a history of newspaper supplements and even color newspaper supplements, but was specifically new because it focused on comics, even though most were single, captioned images (18). Hearst called his rival eight-page inducement—which first appeared on October 25, 1896 (Nasaw 108)—a "Comic supplement," and "most of the other major daily newspapers followed in his footsteps: there was a rash of 'Comic supplements' and 'Comic sections' nationwide" (Groensteen 93). The comics supplements would provide the immediate frame in which the regular newspaper comic strip would be created in the mid-1890s.

In the United States, imitation and competition between newspapers in the 1890s led to recurring cartoon narratives. Richard Outcault's *Hogan's Alley* series of cartoons, beginning in 1895, had the prominent recurring character the Yellow Kid—and Christina Meyer has argued that the Kid's reappearance in (and eventually outside of) the strips was a key part of his success while enacting a profoundly capitalist "logic of sprawl and proliferation" (77). Eventually, the recurring form of single-image cartoons became sequential within each installment, producing tiers or "strips" of "comics," possibly first used as a regular feature in Rudolph Dirks's December 1897 *Katzenjammer Kids* (R. Harvey 28; Reitberger and Fuchs 12). The precise date of linguistic slippage between "comic supplement," "comic strips," and "the comics" is unclear, but as Groensteen notes, by the early twentieth century the adjective "comic" migrated from the "comic journalism" of the 1850s to become a noun for cartoons, regardless of genre (94).

The early comic strips were still embedded in the context of newspaper publication and would remain so for decades. Although the "strip" development led to the 1907 advent of "Bud" Fisher's *Mr. A. Mutt*, "the first successful strip to appear in daily instalments" (Reitberger and Fuchs 15), the strip, about a racetrack gambler, appeared in the sports pages of the *San Francisco*

Chronicle rather than a distinct "comics" section (McDonnell et al. 45). While the Sunday papers had comics in a particular section, comics in the daily newspapers were generally scattered throughout the paper (Walker 28) and did not begin to appear on a regular schedule until Fisher's strip (Holtz 14), which developed the familiar "open-ended seriality" as an extension of the strip's relationship to sporting events (Gardner 42–45). Despite the existence of comics sections, the "comics" were not yet autonomous.

The comics supplement's flourishing was driven by competition with the comics weeklies and with other newspapers. From 1896 until 1929, these supplements were exclusively packaged with newspapers but were also physically and conceptually distinguished from the rest of the newspaper, to the extent that some supplements had different titles than the newspapers they came with. For example, Hearst's Sunday comics supplement—called a "color comic weekly" in advertising (Robinson 26)—was titled *American Humorist* (Nasaw 108). Pulitzer's *New York World* supplement was, by 1900, called the *Funny Side* (Robinson 47). In this stage, the "funny papers" were distinct from the "news papers" not due to a material difference but because of their content: they contained "the funnies" (synonymous with "the comics") instead of "the news." The phrase is also evocative of the "story papers," another name for the more respectable "penny dreadfuls" in the United Kingdom, and the "illustrated weeklies," the illustrated weekly newspapers following the model of the *Illustrated London News* after 1842 (Korda 19).

The earliest reprints of comic strips drew the comics away from the newspaper sphere by taking the material form of a book: printed pages were folded into signatures and then bound within covers to create more expensive, durable, and autonomous objects. While a 1911 collection of *Mutt and Jeff* strips "in an 18 × 6 inch landscape book, available by sending in six coupons clipped from the [*Chicago American*] newspaper," is often positioned as the first comic book (Sassienie 13), the term and the object are slightly older: a 1902 advertisement for cardboard-cover books reprinting newspaper strips described them as "comic-books" (Goulart, *Great American Comic Books* 8). Comic books, in this sense of books reprinting comic strips, have continued to exist ever since. Variations arose such as the Whitman Publishing Company's Big Little Books, first created in 1932, in which "the text was based on the narrative of the comic strip sequence being adapted; the pictures were actual panels from the strip" (Goulart, *Great American Comic Books* 16). It also seems probable that in this period comics supplements were sold second-hand as autonomous objects.

Although the name "comic book" came from the format of book reprints, the modern form of the comic book came from experiments with the Sunday supplements. In 1929, pulp publisher Dell Publishing (Wright 3) released *The Funnies*, a tabloid-sized Sunday newspaper supplement that was stapled and sold as a separate item from the newspaper (Sassienie 13). Eastern Color Printing of Waterbury, Connecticut, was a printer of comics supplements for several East Coast newspapers (as well as *The Funnies*) and became the site of key innovations in the 1930s. Sales employees at Eastern Color conceived of using supplements on their own as premiums—inducements offered with the purchase of an unrelated product—and, according to Bradford W. Wright, discovered that

> the standard seven-by-nine-inch printing plates, used to print Sunday comic pages about twice that size, could also print two reduced comic pages side-by-side on a tabloid-sized page. When folded in half and bound together, these pages would fit into an economical eight-by-eleven-inch pulp magazine of color comics. (3)

The size of the resulting magazine is significant, because as Wright implies, contemporary pulp periodicals were approximately the same size (Lefévre 76), giving the products a cultural legibility as well as the ability to be displayed in the same retail space. In the early 1930s, Eastern Color created premiums in this magazine format for companies such as Gulf Oil's *Gulf Funny Weekly* (Goulart, *Comic Book Encyclopedia* 181) and Proctor & Gamble's *Funnies on Parade* (R. Harvey 17). Eastern salesman Max Gaines eventually conceived of selling the pamphlets directly to children (Wright 2). In 1934, *Famous Funnies*, originally a premium for Woolworth's department stores, appeared on newsstands (Ryall and Tipton 13).

Despite physical autonomy from the newspaper, these early comic books reprinted newspaper comic strips and had yet to take their final step toward being an original format. However, one product was already there: in the late 1920s, much smaller pamphlets—"pocket-sized pornographic [comics] stories featuring celebrities in hard-core action" (Gluckson 143)—began to circulate through American "newsstands, cigar stores, second-hand bookstores, bars, and burlesque houses" (146) from an unknown origin. These "Tijuana Bibles"—also called "Eight-Pagers," "Eight-Page Bibles," "Bluesies," "Jo-Jo Books," or simply "dirty comics" (Gluckson 143)—are mysterious but, according to Bob Adelman, contain the first comics stories originating in the pamphlet form (28).

In a gradual transition over the late 1930s, mainstream comic books began to rely on original material, though they were still subordinate to comic strips. David Hajdu cites representative publisher Malcolm Wheeler-Nicholson of National Allied Publications, who told a writer, "I see these magazines more or less as brochures to interest the newspaper syndicates in an idea. It's much easier to sell a comic strip if you can show it in already published form" (quoted in Hajdu 20). According to illustrator Creig Flessel, Wheeler-Nicholson ran out of sample strips and began soliciting original work (Hajdu 21), with the result that National Allied Publications' 1935 *New Fun: The Big Comic Magazine* #1 was "the first comic book consisting entirely of original content instead of reprints of newspaper strips" (Meskin and Cook xxii). Four months later, *New Fun* would be retitled *More Fun* and boast in a first-page editorial that "everything between these covers is BRAND NEW, never before published" (quoted in Goulart, *Great American Comic Books* 47). While reprinting continued as a practice, the idea that comic books were primarily subordinate to the "real" business of newspaper comic strip syndicates would wane over the 1930s, although the cultural place of comic books would remain secondary to the more respectable comic strips for a very long time.

After the newspaper strip syndicates, pulp magazine publishing (named for the lower paper quality and resultant pricing) was the more relevant industry context. Ron Goulart suggests that original comic stories began to appear in pulp magazines as early as 1934 with *Spicy Detective*'s *Sally the Sleuth* and *Spicy-Adventure Stories' Diana Daw* (Goulart, *Comic Book Encyclopedia* 284). Wright notes that many early comic book publishers were pulp publishers and branded their comic books in the manner of pulp magazines (2). Many early comic books are extremely physically reminiscent of pulp periodicals, not only in their size but in their cover design and layouts. The similarity of branding suggests that comic books were initially seen (at least by publishers) as a variety of pulp magazine—like the Western, the Romance, or the Weird. The specific materiality of comic books emerges out of the context of pulp magazine publication as much as it does out of comic-strip premiums.

After the 1938 appearance of Superman in National's *Action Comics* #1, American comic books saw a glut of titles and an almost total transition to original material. Despite the fact that by the 1940s most comic books neither were reprints of comic strips nor featured characters originating in comic strips, and that a substantial number of the most popular comic books were not comedic in nature, the name "comic book" persisted. Furthermore, the "book" half of "comic book" persisted despite comics books' more obvious status as magazines. Many comic book publishers were magazine publishers, comic books circulated using the newsstand distribution system already in place for magazines, and, as Michael Feldman notes, in the United States comic books were legally magazines for the purpose of mailing (17). It does appear that this status required a certain amount of noncomics content, namely stories written in text.

The ideas of books and magazines, often in seeming contradiction to each other, are frequently invoked in comic book paratext after the familiar physical form had stabilized in the 1940s. While earlier language had been inchoate—a 1936 advertisement for the forthcoming *Detective Comics* referred to it as a "narrative-cartoon magazine in the comic field" (Goulart, *Great American Comic Books* 54)—American comic books from the 1940s and later are more likely to refer to themselves as magazines or books, for example in the phrase "The World's Greatest Comic Magazine," an intermittent part of the *Fantastic Four* logo since 1962. Despite their magazine status, comic books from the 1950s and 1960s also frequently make paratextual reference to "book-length" or "novel" stories (that is, stories taking up the entire pamphlet). One example is the blurb on DC Comics' *Showcase* #61, promising a "book-length" story. Some comic books do both, as on the cover of *Fantastic Four* #12 (March 1963), where the world's greatest comic magazine presents a book-length epic. The language is strongly reminiscent of pulp magazines, periodicals that regularly advertised their presentation of complete novels. These invocations of bookness, sitting alongside claims to periodicalness, should also be seen in light of comic books' efforts to present themselves as worthy of the cultural acclaim bestowed on books, an argument made overt in the editorial that appeared in Timely's *Venus* #4, cover-dated April 1949.

In this polemic, the editors liken the cultural position of comic books in 1949 to that of the novel in the eighteenth century, invoking the pronovelistic stance of man of letters Samuel Johnson to associate twentieth-century critics of comic books with "the people who called Robinson Crusoe 'slop.'" While comic books were physically and legally a kind of magazine, they could aspire to the status of being, like the novel, a kind of book. This editorial is a reaction to the positioning of comic books as worse than other media: in American culture, comic books have long been associated with harmful, poor-quality material. Sometimes this referred to their physical quality: the same issue of *More Fun Comics* in 1935 that proclaimed "all new material" also boasted that "all the pictures, type, and lettering are clear and legible . . . no eyestrain" (quoted in Goulart, *Great American Comic Books* 47). At other times it was simply their cultural positioning: in a chart of "everyday tastes" printed in a 1949 issue of *Life* magazine, comic books appear (along with pulps) as the only named "low-brow" reading materials (Travis 349). By far the greater focus of anticomics discourse was their supposedly immoral contents, with a particularly consequential moral panic beginning in the late 1940s—the context for the *Venus* editorial. On the other hand, even a figure fairly removed from this debate, fan and creator Jules Feiffer, would argue in 1965 that "comic books . . . are junk" while acknowledging short-lived exceptions (186). In another representative incident, the dust jacket for a 1966 hardcover of Charles Schulz's *Peanuts* comics sardonically pronounced a collection of Snoopy the World War I Flying Ace strips to be "the war novelist's war novel," mocking the notion that a literary narrative could look like comics. While the physical format of comic books stabilized, their cultural place would undergo significant shifts in the context of the widespread belief that comics were undeserving of the qualitative status of literature.

The Association of Comics Magazine Publishers was formed in 1948 in response to a Supreme Court decision (*Winters v. New York*) ruling that the regulation of violent content in the media "ultimately remains the responsibility of the media industries and their self-regulatory bodies" (Nyberg 39), bodies that had not previously existed for comics. The subsequent failure of the ACMP to self-regulate led directly to critiques of the industry by politicians, lawyers, psychologists, and journalists, most notably surrounding the Senate subcommittee hearings mentioned above. Historian Mariah Adin offers the case of the Brooklyn Thrill-Kill Gang—in which four teenage boys, readers of comic books, committed assaults and eventually a murder for no obvious reason during the summer of 1954—as an example of how discourse about juvenile delinquency seized on comic books as a particularly odious example of media influence:

> What made comic books distinctive from these other forms of mass media is that they were a genre whose audience (by and large) did not include adults. Even worse, unlike television, which typically sat in the family living room, or public movie theatres, comic books were cheaply accessible, easily hidden, and therefore often existed outside of parental purview. (106)

While many historians (see Nyberg, Hajdu, Adin, and Beaty) have complicated the historiography of the "Great Comic Book Scare" of 1947–1955, all agree that the resolution, in which the American comic book industry largely agreed to regulate itself with the Comics Code Authority board of approval, represented the producers of comic books agreeing that they were ultimately "specialty items for adolescent boys and collectors" (Hajdu 330) rather than literature. As we will see, even companies that did not participate in the CCA, such as Dell, contributed to this consensus.

In the 1960s, cartoonists began producing comics outside of the mainstream comic book industry. The "undergrounds" were known as such because of their resemblance to and association with "underground" independent newspapers such as the *San Francisco Free Press* and the *East Village Other* (Danky and Kitchen 17): for example, Berkeley's feminist newspaper *It Ain't Me, Babe* published a 1970 one-shot comic of the same name, the creators of which went on to make *Wimmen's Comix*, an ongoing underground. The underground comics (or "comix" to further differentiate them from the "straight" industry) enabled creators to circulate their work outside the strictures of the Code. The size and format of comix varied wildly, from photocopied zines to magazine-format comics to comic books. The underground distribution system, in which publications were sold wholesale rather than on a returnable basis, inspired the "direct market" in the 1970s, so called because periodicals were purchased directly from the publisher rather than a distributor (Hatfield 22). Charles Hatfield notes the appearance of increasingly ambitious comic book stories in this period, particularly in the "alternative" comics industry of independent direct-market publishers that followed the undergrounds, and traces the origin of the "graphic novel" concept to this market situation: the graphic novel "owes its life to the direct market's specialized conditions" (30). As Emma Tinker notes, the phrase "graphic novel" first appeared in 1964 in a fanzine essay by Richard Kyle, but it is most often traced to cartoonist Will Eisner, "who used it in 1978 to describe his *A Contract with God*" (1171).[2] The development of the "graphic novel," the most notable change in the cultural place of comic books, was due to the two "economic and institutional factors" of the direct market and challenges to the Comics Code Authority (Weiner 3), but perhaps even more importantly, against the backdrop of widespread American cultural devaluing of the comic book format.

Although the origin of the concept and phrase is controversial, the key moment in the popular uptake of the "graphic novel" in America is usually taken to be the appearance of three works in the mid-1980s: Alan Moore, Dave Gibbons, and John Higgins's *Watchmen*, published in a collected form in 1987; Frank Miller's *Batman: The Dark Knight Returns*, collected in 1986; and underground cartoonist Art Spiegelman's *Maus: A Survivor's Tale*, volume 1: *My Father Bleeds History*, also in 1986. While all three of these texts were originally serialized, fans, publishers, and journalists seized on the concept of longer-form, more expensive, and more complex storytelling, even if this was somewhat deceptive: the term's "adoption by comics creators and publishers' marketing teams in the 1980s represented little more than the lucrative repackaging of comics to appeal to an audience more comfortable with book-length works of fiction" (Tinker 1171). As Hatfield points out, the term "graphic novel" continues to be more of a marketing category than a genre: "[A] graphic novel can be almost anything: a novel, a collection of interrelated or thematically similar stories, a memoir, a travelogue or journal, a history, a series of vignettes or lyrical observations, an episode from a longer work—you name it" (5). In Hatfield's words, the primary significance of the "graphic novel" is that it is "a recognizable commodity within bookstores" (30). In a sense, the significance of the "graphic novel" is precisely the expansion of comics from newspaper and magazine formats sold on newsstands to a book format sold in bookstores.

The graphic novel has a marker of distinction that the comic book does not. In the words of Julia Round, the phrase "graphic novel" invokes "notions of permanence, literariness, and artistry" (14). As Douglas Wolk points out, the label "implies that the graphic novel is serious in a way that the lowly comic book isn't," which he notes makes the concept "open to being co-opted" by creators and publishers (63). The branding of comic books as "graphic novels" is the taste-creating strategy of the petite bourgeoisie described by sociologist Pierre Bourdieu: "What makes middle-brow culture is the middle-class relation to culture—mistaken identity, misplaced belief, allodoxia" (327)—the last term meaning the application of old categories (in this case "the novel") to new situations (more expensive reprints of comic books). Robert Hutton also uses Bourdieu's work to explain that "this shift could be described in Bourdieu's terms as a change from a committed mode of production centred on characters and brands to an autonomous one centred on individual artistic expression" (40–41). Nevertheless, Paul Lopes's earlier work cautions against ascribing only one strategy to the eclectic format of the "graphic novel": Lopes perceives both a "highbrow" strategy of literary merit (exemplified by *Maus*) and a "middlebrow" or even "lowbrow" "popular genre" strategy as seen in *Watchmen*. The use of Bourdieu's ideas illuminates how clearly the use of the "graphic novel" is an attempt to position certain comics within a larger field of cultural production; that is, as worthy of critical acclaim and existing as expensive commodities (allowing the conversion of cultural capital to capital). Intriguingly, collections of comic *strips* originally printed in newspapers (or increasingly, on the internet) are often classified as works of the humor genre rather than "graphic novels" despite their physical similarity to the "graphic novel."

Scholars Paul Williams and Christopher Pizzino have ably charted subsequent events: essentially, as comics were "novelized" by fans, publishers, and academics, some comics works were isolated at worthy of being treated as those persons constructed the idea of the novel: "the textual fantasy offered by the discourse of the art-novel" (P. Williams 155). While Pizzino correctly cautions against the assumption that comics have attained "full legitimation" (198), even more compelling is the shared point that by constructing some comics as transcending the commercial world of most comics, the paradigm that (almost) all comics are not worth considering is bolstered. In other words, the conditions of some comics' entry to academia, and the construction of the discipline of comics studies, were that other comics, associated too deeply with consumerism, would be disavowed. Furthermore, in this operation, the material aspects of even canonical comics become a matter for fan collectors rather than scholars. While the reality is more complicated, Williams's and Pizzino's descriptions of the dominant trend in comics studies hold true.

In the present, comic books and newspaper comic strips continue to exist, but they now exist in a culturally subordinate relationship to the graphic novel, to the extent that some distinguishing language is necessary. Although fans also call comic books "issues" (language borrowed from magazines) and "floppies" (in contrast with sturdier collected editions), and the term "booklets" has also been used, I use the word "pamphlet" to distinguish this physical format from the other forms in which comics appear. The "comic book," as a physical object (a pamphlet of comics, folded and affixed) never substantially changed: *Action Comics* #1001, July 2018, meets the Senate subcommittee's definition as closely as does its ancestor *Action Comics* #1, printed eighty years earlier. Despite this, many elements of comics' complex cultural place are illuminated by studying the history of comic books as a material print format.

The rise of comics to the status of academic subject has coincided almost exactly with the rise of book history, and the methods and concerns of book history have become part of the interdisciplinary set of ideas influencing comics studies. Robert Hutton, for example, analyzes the history of *Maus* precisely in terms of its physical history, citing Casey Brienza's call for more research into the production of comics (Hutton 30). Padmini Ray Murray's 2013 call to embrace the "cultural materialist" approaches (1) of publishing studies and book history notes these approaches as a way to "facilitate a fuller understanding of what it means to . . . create, publish and read a comic" (342). Murray's call has power because, although book history methods are present in comics scholarship, auteurism is still the predominant mode of comics criticism, and stories rather than editions are the common units of study. Murray also indicates that, as with book history's conception of the book as a commodity, this approach would centralize the comic book as a commercial object—moreover, a very modern form of consumerism that was disreputable at the time and remains distasteful to many scholars. While Hutton applies an admirable material approach to one of the most acclaimed comics works, and Murray has provided an impressive amount of work on labor in the comics industry, the old materiality of cheap comics, and how comics did and did not get out of that strata of value, require more study. In comics studies, the binary opposition between art and commerce is easily mapped onto the fields of academic and fannish study, but the material history of comics has a role to play in the academic consideration of comics as items of commerce in twentieth-century America. Considering comics to have value distinct from their status as art raises the question of how comics construct value in and around the text, and how these values are changed by their status as commercial products.

Chapter 1

BACK TO "BACK TO THE KLONDIKE"
Book History and Cultural Salvage

Carl Barks, the American cartoonist who wrote and drew Walt Disney comic books in the middle of the twentieth century, is an unusually dramatic example of the "salvage" paradigm of comics' place in popular culture. While his work was originally released without his name and circulated as cheap periodicals for a mass audience of children, his cartooning has been rereleased as expensive art objects organized around the principle of recovering the work of the great auteur Barks from its original commercial context.

In the 1953 story "Back to the Klondike," aged tycoon Uncle Scrooge is losing his memory, and a doctor prescribes capsules that restore his memory of a cache of "at least five hundred pounds of pure nuggets" (*Uncle Scrooge* #142, 5.1) that he buried fifty years earlier at White Agony Creek in the Klondike. Taking Donald and his nephews Huey, Dewey, and Louie to the Yukon, Scrooge announces his intention to collect a thousand dollars owed to him by "Glittering Goldie, the star of the North" (6.5), a character with whom he had a romantic history. After a lengthy hike over the "Chilcoot Pass" [*sic*], the characters arrive in the vicinity of Dawson City only to find that someone is living in a cabin over Scrooge's old claim. A "**little old lady**" (18.2) uses her pet bear Blackjack to menace the four as they try to dig out the gold, leading to a sequence of traps being sprung on both sides. The old lady turns out to be Glittering Goldie, and she and Scrooge agree to a contest to see who can dig "more gold in ten minutes" (30.2), with the winner retaining Goldie's money. Goldie digs up Scrooge's old cache, and Scrooge bewails that he should have taken more memory capsules. Because it confronts Barks's most famous creation, miserly tycoon Uncle Scrooge McDuck, with different ways to think about value, the history of the story "Back to the Klondike" exemplifies how the materiality of comics embodies the shifting tensions between value within and around comics.

In 2012, Fantagraphics Books began to publish the Complete Carl Barks Disney Library, a series of hardcover volumes "reprinting Barks' classic stories, with fully restored original coloring and fascinating historical and critical essays by a hand-picked group of Barks experts" (Fantagraphics). The volumes are released biannually, with each collecting several months' worth of artist and writer Barks's work for Disney comics between 1942 and 1967. Each cover balances the words "Walt Disney's" and "by Carl Barks" respectively above and below the name of the central Disney character and story title featured in that volume. In the second volume, the front and back cover feature several invocations of value. Scrooge McDuck himself appears above the title—"Walt Disney's Uncle $crooge: 'Only a Poor Old Man' by Carl Barks"—gleefully diving into a pile of golden coins; below the title, forlorn criminals the Beagle Boys sit around a table in their prison uniforms. A pull quote from film director George Lucas's introduction proclaims that these stories are "a priceless part of our literary heritage." On the back cover, the description of this volume indicates that the story "Back to the Klondike" "reveals how Scrooge amassed his vast fortune of one multiplujillion, nine obscquatumatillion, six hundred and twenty-three dollars and sixty-two cents—only to lose his true love!" All these ideas of value—the ironic "poor" of the title, Scrooge's pile of money, the impossible fictional numbers that describe his fortune, and Lucas's characterization of these stories as priceless—are pragmatically overruled in my copy by a price sticker that happens to rest directly atop that fantastic description of Scrooge's unbelievable fortune, indicating that the volume retailed for Can$35.99.

The understanding of comics as a formerly cheap and disposable consumer object is still embedded in comics studies, often as the unspoken contrast to the valued work a scholar is currently discussing. In this paradigm, the figure of the great cartoonist is important: a significant part of comics studies is based around the search for the rara avis, a genius who rises above their context to greatness (Yezbick 30–31). For example, Daniel Yezbick nominates George Carlson to join the ranks of those recovered from the mass of creators who "worked desperately and anonymously within or outside of the established systems of labor, distribution, and consumption that controlled and defined the history of comics for much of the last century" (30). In this conception of comics, their present (high) value is an exception to their past (low) value as cheap commodities, a rejection of a system that prevented comics from being seen as literature (or as art). The criterion of "great literature" is emphasized as appropriate, with the acknowledgment that the mass of comics do not meet it.

Carl Barks is the classic example of an unknown commercial artist recovered by connoisseurs and academics—the value of *his* comics has increased enormously since they were first published. Bart Beaty calls Barks the "central" case of "retrospective credit" assigned to forgotten auteurs (*Comics versus Art*, 8–9). As Beaty puts it,

> Barks, the creator of the best-loved stories featuring Walt Disney's Donald Duck, worked for most of his career in total obscurity, his published work credited to Disney and his true identity known only to his publisher and editors. The efforts undertaken by a small group of fans to first identify and later lionize the specific contributions of Barks to the development of the American comic book form demonstrate the importance of authorship in the development of comics as an art form. (*Comics versus Art*, 9)

Since he began writing and drawing Disney comics in 1942, Barks has gone through three distinct stages that are paradigmatic for the historic "appreciation" of comic books. Originally he was anonymous and solitary—a secret, inchoate auteur, his work "adulterated" by other commercial hands, most notably an unknown number of colorists. He wrote and drew stories of Donald Duck and Scrooge McDuck, but the final product was circulated to the public as a corporate creation.

In the next stage, which overlapped with the previous for the majority of readers, fannish appreciation of the 1950s and 1960s referred to Barks—without knowing his name—as "the Good Duck Artist." The concept of "the Good Duck Artist" belongs to organized fandom and circulated throughout fanzines, private correspondence, and personal interactions. It is easy to imagine that anyone who read multiple Disney comics at the time could have realized that (despite Disney's corporate policy of anonymity) some stories were distinct from others. At the same time, the idea of "the Good Duck Artist" suggests a connoisseur's investment of attention and time, and it implies a rigorous dedication to parsing the mass of Disney comics. There is a correlation in this period between fans who studied Disney comics closely enough to form these distinctions, fans who labored to communicate with each other about their connoisseurship, and fans who eventually broke the publisher's policy and discovered Barks's identity.

The identification of Carl Barks, the actual person, as "the Good Duck Artist" can be imagined as incarnating the concept of "the Good Duck Artist." Unsurprisingly, most interactions with Barks as an individual centered on praising him and inquiring about his inspiration, methods, contexts, and personal life—in other words, on appreciating the man and trying to focus on the meaning of the comics. Barks himself commented on his feeling that when people praised "Barks" they were describing some person other than himself (Ault 107).

From the 1970s to the 1990s, Barks the Good Duck Artist was publicly celebrated. This took the form not just of interviews and fan mail but also of reprints, critical appreciation, and institutional awards. Barks, along with Jack Kirby and Will Eisner himself, was an initial inductee into the Will Eisner Comic Book Hall of Fame in 1987, a moment when comics were palpably in the process of becoming both art and literature and thus required artists and authors—and Barks, like Kirby and Eisner, was both, a genuine *cartoonist* in the appreciative sense of the term.

In the third phase, which overlapped with the previous but has taken place mostly after Barks's death in the year 2000, his work has been the subject of academic criticism and art-book-style reprints. Unlike Yezbick's George Carlson, Barks had the good fortune to live through several decades of fame and become an actual participant in his own critical discourse. In the present, the appreciation that he received in life has continued but has taken on a more curatorial tone. Because of the artist's death, it is possible to conceive of his *complete* works with some finality.

From the point of view of a reader encountering and evaluating Barks, one very significant thing has changed between the 1940s and the 2020s. Barks's work was originally seen as a positive contrast to the work that surrounded it. Implicit in seeing Barks as the Good Duck Artist is the idea that the other Duck Artists were Not Good. In the twenty-first century, however, while Barks is openly lauded as a master, there is a sense that his work is more valuable than that of others from the receding past, who are best forgotten. Now a reader is increasingly less likely to find Barks's work anywhere near the work that originally defined his value by contrast. The connoisseur judgment, which has not changed except to shift context, is now emphatically that Carl Barks is good *as comics in general* rather than specifically in terms of Disney's duck comics.

The key story "Back to the Klondike"—where we learn the origins of Scrooge's fortune—has reappeared several times in North America, and "Back to the Klondike" is also generally praised as a prime example of Barks's strengths by fans and scholars. The publication history of this story reveals the details of Barks's cultural history between anonymous artist and celebrated auteur.

DELL PUBLISHING, 1953

"Back to the Klondike" was originally published in *Four Color* #456 by Dell Publishing. *Four Color* #456 is a pamphlet, made up of eight folio sheets of approximately A4-size newsprint paper with a cover on one sheet of glossier stock, held together by two staples. It has a retail price of 10¢ and is dated March 1953. On the cover, the title of the comic book reads "Walt Disney's Uncle Scrooge Back to the Klondike," with the three phrases on different lines. The words "Four Color" do not appear, even in the copyright information on the inside page. The number "456" only appears in the copyright information. Comics historians have retroactively created the title *Four Color* and repositioned Dell's numbering system (presumably originally intended for retailers) to suggest a continuity.

In fact, *Four Color* does not remotely resemble the way most American comic books were or are numbered. It was an anthology series, which might bear the name of Uncle Scrooge one month, Popeye the next, and Dick Tracy the month after that, never directly stating that they followed each other. Each issue contained *only* stories about one particular character. Furthermore, not only are comics in general, much like magazines, notorious for cover dates that do not indicate when they appeared on newsstands or were sent to stores, but *Four Color* is known for a particularly eccentric periodicity. "With *Four Color*, you never knew what was coming. You never knew *when* it was coming. They came at you three, four, five times a month" (Duin and Richardson 177).

As the copyright indicia on the inside cover indicates, *Four Color* #456 was printed by the Western Printing and Lithographing Company for the Dell Publishing Company. Despite this, the largest name on the cover is "Uncle Scrooge," the second largest is "Walt Disney," and the "Dell" logo is significantly smaller; Western is not referred to except once in the indicia. Carl Barks's name appears nowhere in the pamphlet. All three names on the cover, along with the title, are located in the top third of the cover, which is a feature of newsstand distribution and display techniques. By researching the history of Barks, Disney, Dell, and Western in this period, one learns that the priority suggested by this branding is distinctly rearranged. While Barks and not Walt Disney is actually the writer and artist, the credited company Dell itself also had comparatively little to with this object. Like all Dell comics in this period, the object was produced at Western's facility in Poughkeepsie, New York. Western's comics production was more or less autonomous from Dell, as Western handled production and editorial work. The fact that Barks and Western are the least-heralded creator names in *Four Color* #456 indicates the significance of branding over attribution.

Just as the name Walt Disney is a brand that promises a style and quality of story, the name Dell associates this comic book with a corporate presence, though again Western is arguably more significant to understanding the object. William Lyles (14–15) reprints a useful map of Western's Poughkeepsie facility. The two-story building was divided between hardbound books (on the second floor) and paperbacks and comics on the first floor. As can be seen on Lyles's map, the production of comics differs from paperbacks only in the bindery (since the comics are saddle-stitch stapled and the books are perfect bound, two quite distinct binding methods requiring entirely different machines and labor). Dell, a prominent brand in the "paperback revolution" that had swept American culture in the 1940s alongside comic books, had their products as the result of near-identical processes in the same physical space. The production lines of Dell paperbacks and Dell comic books make a circle through the Poughkeepsie building, ending up in the same truck loading zone/railroad depot. This was also where type and photolithographs, for the production of further printed matter, arrived from Western's typesetting facility in Racine, Wisconsin, via a shipping network that had trucks "stopping midway in Ohio to exchange loads with trucks coming from Poughkeepsie" (Lyles 13).

These details may seem irrelevant, and perhaps we will never know the unknown location in Ohio where this chiasmus took place. However, they emphasize the great degree to which industrial processes were necessary to promulgate the comic book. Speaking of a slightly earlier period, Christina Meyer reminds us that the "rapid and extensive dissemination" of media across America was made possible by "modern transportation infrastructure" (79), which is also true in this case. The highway system's role in the circulation of midcentury comic books might further resonate with the fact that Western's Poughkeepsie facility was a converted Fiat automotive plant (Barrier 19) to emphasize that comic books were as enmeshed with American industry as cars. Furthermore, the production line detailed here should remind us that while comics and paperback books share almost the same production and distribution process, they also shared distribution networks and ultimately shared retail space at newsstands. *Four Color* #456 is not really a work of art by Walt Disney, nor was it really produced by Dell Comics, or even Western alone—but it is also not a work of art attributable to Carl Barks alone. *Four Color* #456 is an undeniably industrial, as much as it is a corporate, product.

To step further back from *Four Color* for a moment, the naming of publishers suggests histories that emphasize the status of comics in 1953. Dell Publishing had originally been a magazine publisher, of cheap pulp magazines in the 1920s. They had begun to publish comic books in the 1930s, a very early participant in the comics publishing fad. For Dell, this would be repeated analogously with their entry into the "paperback" publishing trend of the 1940s, at which they were enormously successful. Dell was hardly exceptional in any of these trends, except perhaps in the degree of their success. Rather, this corporate history reveals the mutual origins of magazines, comic books, and paperbacks as trends in a publishing corporation's history (K. Davis 94; Marcus 16; Lyles).

All three kinds of print existed in the same distribution system (although at the time *Four Color* #456 was published, pulps had begun a precipitous decline that would end in collapse before the end of the 1950s). Publisher Dell used the American News Company for distribution. While the American News Company owned a great many newsstands, their primary business was selling returnable periodicals and books to other newsstands. By "returnable" I mean the business model in which unsold merchandise was marked as such (typically by having covers removed), returned via the same distribution system that had delivered them, and "pulped" back into paper. The system was enormously popular, and Dell's partner succeeded at it to the extent of being monopolistic: the ANC was found guilty of restraint of trade during a 1950s federal antitrust lawsuit. It was rare and notable for a company to use an independent distribution company before that point; it was also rare for a company to *not* overprint their merchandise on the premise of future pulping. The example of Bantam Books is useful, since their policy of underprinting was exceptional to the general rule (K. Davis 252). This is the invisible system lying behind *Four Color* #456's smallest but perhaps most significant cover element: the 10¢ price. The system of returnable periodicals; the practices of the ANC; the industrial efficiency of Western: all served to create this comic book, but also to keep the price of this comic book down, within reach of the purchasing power of the millions of Americans, children and adults, who read it regularly. All of these practices are also ironically why *Four Color* #456 is now worth a considerable amount more than ten cents. It was, in short, an ephemeral industrial product in a culture and a business context that made it cheap and disposable.

The copy I consulted in Rare Books and Special Collections at the University of Alberta is no longer in very good shape. It has a variety of flaws that can be enumerated in the language of collectors. The cover has flaking at the edges. In the interior pages, the paper is tanning from the outside in ("foxing"), well on the way to browning. The pages have become brittle and begun to crumble. As Paul Sassienie has explained, both the turning of white paper to brown and the stiffness are a result of the industrial manufacture of pulp paper, since at the moment of its creation, the natural binder lignin begins to react to the acid added to the mixture, a process accelerated by exposure to oxygen (133). It could be worse; as D. B. Wardle explains, any metallic impurities in the paper can assist in "the conversion of the sulphurous acid [in polluted air] into the much more active sulphuric acid" (4). More precisely, the chemical, as opposed to mechanical, process of making pulp paper runs less risk of this kind of acidification, so newsprint (apparently generally made chemically) is both better at preservation than many kinds of paper and generally on the low end of the scale of quality—especially compared to handmade paper or the acid-free paper now popular in publishing.

The quality of *Four Color* #456, and of the original "Back to the Klondike," is poor. In addition to the inevitable physical degeneration of individual copies, the tension between art and industrial process is evident throughout. The coloring is subpar. On nearly every page, one of the four colors is "out of registration" with the others. *Four Color* was created using the standard four-color process, in which the white page is imprinted with cyan, yellow, magenta, and black ink, creating different colors through their overlaps.[1] Registration refers to these inks' spatial relationship to each other, so being out of registration or register means that the inks do not overlay each other exactly. In *Four Color* #456 these are often quite visible, resulting in blank space on one side of a page's shapes and a spilling over on the other. Since black is one of the four colors, it's not really accurate to say that the colors are out of sync *with* the line art. Nonetheless, because we typically read the black lines as the norm, that's how it appears. This discrepancy rarely covers more than a millimeter of space, but is quite noticeable, particularly because it often spills over the border of each panel into the gutter. This reveals that the gutter and panels are themselves a creation of coloring, making up only one of the four layers of visible marks on the page. A variety of other printing errors, from apparently random blotches to spotty solids to faded lines, distinguish the coloring of *Four Color* #456. As a result, the coloring process, which was not undertaken by Barks but rather by Western's even more anonymous colorists, is extraordinarily visible in *Four Color* #456.

"Back to the Klondike" takes up the first twenty-four pages of the interior of *Four Color* #456. It is followed by the eight-page Barks story "Something Fishy Here." In the original *Four Color* #456, the inside front and back cover as well as the reverse of the back cover each display a one-page story by Barks. The two stories on the inside covers were printed in black and white despite being on the reverse of the full-color cover. The story on the back cover is also colored. Whatever role the coloring plays, the fact that *Four Color* #456 also includes two stories in monochrome creates a contrast within the book.

This both emphasizes what the four-color process looks like and circulates another version of Duck stories in which the lines are prominent—these two stories strongly resemble what comic art looks like after it's been inked but before it's been colored, though it isn't clear how widely this would have been known to readers. Rather than implying an artist distinct from the colorist, these black-and-white stories change how we read the other stories, specifically in that they inform any reader that rather than being an integral part of the comic, color is optional. A reader observing the color stories and looking for the outlines of a black-and-white comic is looking backward through the process and into something like Carl Barks's work. The final product is far from being the work of only one creator. In contrast to later printings, in *Four Color* #456 there are no advertisements at any point.

GOLD KEY, 1966

"Back to the Klondike" was reprinted under the Gold Key imprint of Western Publishing in 1966. As the name implies, Western was the successor to Western Printing and Lithographing, which had inherited Dell's licensed titles in the early 1960s. The 1966 printing is a 25¢ collection entitled *The Best of Uncle Scrooge and Donald Duck* #1. Despite this apparent canonization ("featuring two famous Disney classics," as the cover boasts), Barks also went unnamed in this printing.

This edition of the story literally reprints the original: the registration of the four colors is different from the 1953 copies. Somewhat surprisingly, the inside covers reproduce the original strips from 1953, although this pamphlet also includes unrelated stories from elsewhere in Barks's career: "The Ghost of the Grotto," "Billion Dollar Pigeon," and "Tralla La." "Something Fishy Here" does not appear. Although this printing of the story announces its "classic" status, in practice it removes the original and places it into a canon of other works, all by the unmentioned Barks.

However, the effect of placing "Back to the Klondike" among other stories is worth noting. "The Ghost of the Grotto," which begins on the recto side of the last page of "Klondike," doesn't involve Uncle Scrooge at all but rather chronicles Donald and the three nephews as their kelp-gathering business in the West Indies draws them into an adventure/mystery concerning the mysterious armored figure who has guarded Sir Francis Drake's treasure beneath a grotto for centuries. In the end, "the law says that gold belongs to the man who guarded it," and Donald declares: "a rash on ye whole business" (51.7), although in notable contrast to the previous story, Donald never had a legitimate claim on the treasure, nor did he know there was a treasure at all when he set out, learning about it only on the third-to-last page of the story. Furthermore, his motive in most of the story is to recover his kidnapped nephew and/or seek revenge against a troublemaker. All of this characterization contrasts the character with the absent Scrooge in "Back to the Klondike."

"Tralla La" has Scrooge harassed by endless demands for charity and oversight, and, pushed to a nervous breakdown, he declares his desire to "go to someplace where there is no money" (54.8); this turns out to be Tralla La, a pastiche of James Hilton's fabled Shangri-La. In that mountain paradise, Scrooge's discarded nerve tonic bottlecap becomes the foundation of a rudimentary economy that corrupts and destroys the community. While Scrooge orders his planes to drop enough bottlecaps to devalue the items, he instead orders too many and nearly destroys the ecology of the area as well. Despite this story's remarkable cynicism about the meaning of money, the following story involves Scrooge losing a messenger pigeon carrying a million dollars, who returns with two million dollars, having unwittingly provided the seed money for an oil operation in Venezuela; Scrooge's exuberance that "it just goes to show that brains like mine can't help making money" (77.7) sits uneasily with his fleeing storms of "money" in the previous story—and with the punch-line panel of Scrooge paying his pigeon a grain of corn.

Money plays such different roles in these stories, from punch-line plot device denied to the hero to blankly malevolent force, that one might almost be forgiven for imagining that different authors, since none are credited, must have written all four stories. At the very least, these "famous Disney classics" complicate the idea a reader might get from "Back to the Klondike" alone about what money means.

The 1966 printing includes several notes written on panels. Panel 1.4's notation "30030-611 / U.S. + D.D. #1–668" reappears with the addition of (17) at 17.8, which becomes (25) at 25.8. These signatures only appear in the first half of the magazine, since they were presumably used to assemble the printed sections in order for stapling. The industrial process is still extremely visible in this object.

GOLD KEY, 1977

"Back to the Klondike" next appears in the United States in a comic book titled *Uncle Scrooge* #142, cover-dated July 1977, in an object physically similar to the 1953 book. Unlike *Four Color* #456, *Uncle Scrooge* #142 is traditionally numbered, and on the cover: issues 141 and 143 appeared in the months surrounding it, implying some level of serialization and a sequence, both of which are curious given that this is a reprint of a story that was then twenty-four years old. The numbers do, however, argue that this title and character have a history. Unlike *Four Color*, *Uncle Scrooge* is an installment of a sequential chronicle of one particular character.

This is a comic book bearing the logo once again of Walt Disney. The 1977 "Back to the Klondike" has been recolored, for the most part dealing with the registration problems and blotches I described above. There has been recoloring of another order: Scrooge's overcoat in the interior pages is red, which brings this story into harmony with the majority of portrayals of Scrooge, though *not* the original of this story, in which it is green. The cover has been reused from 1953, though flipped into a mirror image, and on the 1977 cover Scrooge's coat is still green. This apparently trivial matter of Scrooge's color becomes significant if we think of it as part of establishing a "uniform" for Scrooge: not only does he wear the same thing, but it is recognizable as part of his look. It is curious that the one place the coat wasn't recolored was the cover, the most public face of the book.

Other differences between 1953 and 1977 present themselves. The 1977 book is approximately five millimeters shorter and a centimeter narrower than the 1953 book. The artwork has been reused but recolored (which is to say that three of the four colors have been redone), including the cover, which means that all the art has been slightly shrunken from the earlier printing. This is only a surface-level indication of what should be quite obvious looking anywhere outside the story: *Uncle Scrooge* #142 is a different object than *Four Color* #456. For one thing, it costs 30¢, exactly three times as much as its 1953 equivalent. For another, *Uncle Scrooge* #142 is also eight quarto sheets held within a glossier cover—but *Uncle Scrooge* #142 only includes "Back to the Klondike" and none of the four other stories present in the 1953 book. Instead, *Uncle Scrooge* #142 has advertisements.

The role of advertising in 1970s comic books has received study. In 1977, Judith S. Duke noted that "despite the fact that the trade magazine *Advertising Age* says the largest advertising vehicles in the children's publishing industry are comic books, most of the industry's income comes from single copy circulation" (118). A table that Duke provides conveniently covers the major American publishers in the first half of 1977 (immediately preceding the publication of *Uncle Scrooge* #142). Gold Key's figures don't list subscriptions, but going by the publishers that do, it would be surprising if Gold Key's major source of income was not *also* single issues sold by retail outlets. According to Duke's industry information, Gold Key had the second-lowest price for advertising among the major publishers, at $4,950 per four-color page, and they are solidly in the lower price range, charging a fraction of Marvel's and DC's rates (around $16,000). Gold Key's monthly "single issue" sales average around four million issues for the same period; advertising rates are not exactly proportionate to circulation. Surprisingly, then, for a relative afterthought to the business of comics, these advertisements have a pronounced effect on the story. Even more interestingly, some of them use the comics form.

The following products are advertised in *Uncle Scrooge* #142: Hostess Cup Cakes and Twinkies; the *Starstream* series of science fiction comic book adaptations; a business in which the reader can go door to door selling "personalized metal social security plates"; the "Handy Andy" toy tool set; the Mickey Mouse club of comic books and books; Hostess Cup Cakes (again); and a lengthy assortment of novelties and posters from the Gandalf Products Company. As Jennifer K. Stuller has noted, the advertisements in comic books can suggest the publisher's perceived audience, particularly in gendered terms (238). The products advertised in *Uncle Scrooge* #142 skew toward a preadolescent male audience. In the ad for Mickey Mouse comics and books (the ones published by Whitman and Golden Books, also divisions of Western Publishing), two cartoon boys enthuse over the "puzzles, stickers," and "new stories" to be found at "your favorite store," while a cartoon girl holding a book with distaff mascot Minnie Mouse on the cover adds "and cut-out doll books" (Barks, *Uncle Scrooge* #142, 17).

The Whitman/Golden Books ad takes the form of a single splash-page panel, where three children are reading products presumably analogous to *Uncle Scrooge* #142. They are all drawn in a style markedly unlike that of the main story. Most of the ads in this issue also use the form of comics, though only one, by using multiple panels, can be said to have a sequence. The first ad for Cup Cakes and Twinkies shows two baseball players about to eat their respective Hostess products out of their gloves, on either side of the page in what is not quite a splash panel because there are no panels at all. Although there is no dialogue, and the figures (especially the real baseball players, one of whom is Reggie Jackson) are drawn in a notably realistic style, the advertisement seems to be designed to run smoothly on the inside cover of a comic book, where in 1953 and 1966 another Uncle Scrooge comic appeared.

In his study of television, Raymond Williams concludes that the distinction between broadcasting and earlier communications systems is that while, previously, "items were discrete" (a book, a pamphlet, a meeting at a particular time and place), in broadcasting, "the real programme that is offered is a *sequence* or set of alternative sequences of these and other similar events" (81, italics in original). Williams immediately blurs the lines of this distinction, acknowledging that "some earlier kinds of communication contained, it is true, internal variation and at times miscellany" (81), giving as examples the magazine and the modern newspaper. Importantly, in addition to unrelated news items, this miscellany effect includes advertising and different modes of representation such as drawings and photographs. To Williams, broadcasting (radio and then television) inherited this tradition from print and from live occasions (83). While much of Williams's commentary is specific to broadcasting, it is worth considering the way that the overall "flow" of a comic book includes elements beyond the story. Underscoring this point, many comic book advertisements, such as the famous Charles Atlas ads, include elements of comics.

The flow of a comic book issue can be seen clearly with the second Hostess ad in this issue. On page 21 of *Uncle Scrooge* #142, we see a one-page comic: "Iron Man" in "A Dull Pain!" In it, we see the Marvel Comics superhero Iron Man foil the plan of "the Monotony Man," a character who has "the monotonous touch" and seeks only to make life dull. This dullness is visually represented by the increasingly gray scale of the artwork—panel 21.3 is entirely in shades of gray, which incidentally very closely resembles Barks's method for showing nighttime sequences in "Back to the Klondike." In "A Dull Pain!," one character in the background of 21.3 says "There's no hope," while in the foreground a boy with a baseball bat mopes blankly. It's Iron Man who redundantly explains that this visual device indicates mood: "It's gonna take more than color to bring people out of this grey mood," he says as he puts on the Iron Man costume (21.2). In 21.4, we see Iron Man urging people to "brighten up your lives with . . . these **delicious Hostess® Cup Cakes**!" Iron Man is tossing Hostess Cup Cakes down at the crowd, and if our eye is drawn downward by this action, we see beneath the blue-gray sky and the gray buildings, people in full comic book color, and the protesting outstretched arm of the Monotony Man. In the last panel, Iron Man claims that "you can't be bored, when you're eating **delicious Hostess Cup Cakes**." And now the Monotony Man, the last gray image in the panel, is running away in the distance. Color is an important element of the ads as well as the stories themselves, in this case rising to the level of a theme.

The idea of fun commodities permeates this version of *Uncle Scrooge*. Hostess will bring the reader "full-color" baseball cards; the Mickey Mouse club books are "NEW! FUN THINGS"; and the last three pages of this book are the visually dense ads for "Fun Tricks Free Things" from Gandalf Products. Even the social security plate–selling scheme promises that "everyone" will be "amazed and delighted" by the low price of their product. Satisfaction, as Gandalf Products puts it, is guaranteed. The only ad that does not quite promise fun or delight or for that matter boast of cheapness is the one for Whitman's *Starstream* line of science fiction comic books, which are instead "a bold new journey into science fiction adventure."

There is a theme to *Uncle Scrooge* #142 that was not present in *Four Color* #456. Iron Man's Hostess adventure seems to thematically underscore the importance of "fun" color in comic books, but rather than fun, "Back to the Klondike" has been described as a notable story for being "the only one to reveal a romantic side" to Scrooge (Andrae 200). The story plays with our expectations of Scrooge for suspense: in panel 6.4, Scrooge, having regained his memory of the Klondike, says: "I remember a girl! (sigh!)," to which Donald stands aghast and one of the nephews exclaims, "a **girl**!" In 6.6, Scrooge, looking wistfully off at the sunset, tells them that "Glittering Goldie" was "the only **live** one I ever knew!" In the next panel, the nephews and Donald are radiating lines of gleeful surprise. Even if we have somehow never realized that Scrooge is not usually a romantic, the other characters helpfully let us know that this is surprising, so even within the story he is not usually a romantic. In other words, this story has an unexpected focus on something other than colorful "fun," underlined by the recurring appearance of advertisements urging readers to pursue fun at all costs.

But on the next page, a six-panel sequence subverts this subversion of Scrooge's presumed character. In 7.1, the nephews ask if Goldie was Scrooge's "sweet-heart," to which he says "Bah!" In 7.2, Donald asks Scrooge why, then, does he get a "faraway" look in his eyes whenever he thinks about Goldie, in a panel that includes a gobsmacked-looking Scrooge with a *particularly* faraway look in his eyes. In 7.3, a scowling Scrooge explains that Goldie owes him a thousand dollars, or rather, as he continues in 7.4, compounded *interest* of fifty years on a thousand dollars, or one billion dollars, culminating in 7.5, where a deeply satanic-looking Scrooge with dollar signs flying off his brow cackles that he would be glad to see Goldie again. In the next panel, Donald walks away noting that "for just a minute, there, I thought Uncle Scrooge was **human**!"

It would seem that this is a straightforward example of Scrooge's emotions being transferred from "ordinary" pursuits to his insatiable quest for money, complete with the rank injustice of his desire to find an old (romantic) acquaintance after fifty years in order to charge her a billion dollars. So far, these sequences play out the same in 1953 and 1966 and 1977, and as they will in 2012, although the coloring has changed each time. For the next several pages Scrooge acts as a reader would expect, forcing Donald to carry him piggyback across the Chilcoot Pass to Whitehorse rather than take a plane, only to be berated by Donald when it turns out that Scrooge actually owns the airline that could have flown them for free. On page 11, Scrooge and the nephews enter the old Blackjack Ballroom still standing in Dawson City. Reminiscing in 11.6, a wistful Scrooge bears more or less the same expression as in 6.6, leading us to suspect that the inevitable pattern will repeat itself. In 11.6, Scrooge is recalling Goldie: "She was singing 'After the Ball' in a voice as pretty as the crackle of new bills!," and in 11.7, the bottom right-hand panel of this page, a grasping Scrooge has reversed to proclaim "Ha! One thousand dollars at compound interest! . . . Wait till I get my hands on that old gal!"

Yet the reverses continue: on page 27, the nephews, who have discovered that the elderly Glittering Goldie has been squatting on Scrooge's old gold claim for fifty years, and that she lives an impoverished life, tell Scrooge these things. In 27.5, Scrooge (with the same wistful look as in 6.6 and 11.6), says "Goldie! . . . After all these years" and, paralleling the movement between 11.6 and 11.7, reverses into 27.6 to say "Haaa! That makes it just **perfect**!" In 27.8, he claims he'll get everything "that old chiseler owns," but in 27.9 (again, the bottom right-hand corner of the page), Donald questions why Scrooge thinks he needs to comb his whiskers to collect on an IOU. The next several pages contain many of these reverses, from a ruthless Scrooge in 28.5 becoming deferential when he first sees Goldie in 28.6, to being bashful in 28.7 and enraged in 28.8. On the next page, Goldie reveals that she has very little indeed, having given her wealth to children left orphaned by mining disasters, then leaves to go "to the **poorhouse**—naturally!" (29.5). Scrooge rushes after her to suggest a deal on the bottom of that quarto page, but when we turn the page we find Scrooge proposing that he and Goldie race digging gold. The deal gets worse, as Scrooge tells the nephews to dig on a desolate knoll that they all know has no gold, and the nephews call him an "old **viper**!" (30.4). Goldie finds the most gold because she has found Scrooge's lost cache of gold nuggets, in what would seem to be an ironic reversal and comeuppance for Scrooge's heartless greed. But in the last panels of the story, Donald explains to the nephews that despite Scrooge carrying on about how he's forgotten where he buried the nuggets, Scrooge *has* been taking his memory medication, and that "he **rigged** that race so Goldie would find his cache!" (30.7). As Scrooge walks off in the distance, feigning (?) upset, the nephews regard him and speak the message of the story: "Well, whaddaya know! Good old Unca Scrooge!" (30.8). The story's interest in the nature of Scrooge's soul resolves with him having done a good turn despite losing his profit, but emphasizes the need for the character to save face as a thoroughly unromantic miser.

The nephews are more or less in the audience's position, as we find out alongside them that Scrooge can be a romantic but that he would rather not be seen as such. He is, as Donald put it earlier, human. While this is true of both versions so far, this reprinting is doing different things, because it is a different thing. The 1977 "Back to the Klondike" circulated as only one fictional story, interspersed with ads that proclaim the joy of getting free baseball cards with cupcakes, of making money in one's free time and using that money to buy Disney products like these. While *Uncle Scrooge* #142 is not *more* of a product than *Four Color* #456, it contains a different message about products and postulates some facts about the audience's activities and priorities in life. The message that even Scrooge has a romantic side is altered by the suggestion that it is of a piece with the fun on sale "at your favorite store"—fun to consume to stave off the Monotony Man. Since the story emphasizes that there are priorities for Scrooge that go beyond his greed, the fact that one iteration of this story is filled with artwork and text that attempts to get the reader to buy things suggests a gap between Scrooge's life and the reader's. If Scrooge stands for acquisitive thriftiness so astonishing that only romance with one duck woman has ever transcended it, the paratext is discouraging the reader from adopting this view, instead pushing fun deals.

The presence of these ads is important to understanding what "Back to the Klondike" is doing, but also of interest is how the ads flow. In *Uncle Scrooge* #142, ads take up pages 12, 16, 17, 21, and 32, in addition to the inside front and back covers and the back cover (which is identical to the novelty catalog ad on page 32). Each ad takes up a full page, with the exception of 12, in which two half-page ads appear on the same page. Pages 16 and 17 are two advertising pages facing each other and are also the central two pages of the issue—the only place in the pamphlet where a quarto sheet faces itself and the staples are visible. Pages 12 and 21 are also two parts of the same sheet of paper. They would face each other if the central two sheets were detached from the staples. Despite the asymmetry of the front and back matter (one advertising page on the inside front cover is mirrored by three consecutive pages of advertising at the end and the back cover), the effect created is one of regularity. Unlike *Four Color* #456, *Uncle Scrooge* #142 only reprints one Uncle Scrooge adventure. In its presentation of a single episode in Scrooge's life, punctuated by regular breaks for advertising, the "flow" of *Uncle Scrooge* #142 strongly resembles that of a commercial American television episode—in this case, re-presenting a story that was not designed to have ads at all. The closing, where a page of advertising is followed by an inside and outside back cover, resembles nothing so much as an extended repetitious television commercial. *Very* repetitious in this case, because all three ending pages advertise the wares of Gandalf Products, and two of the ads are identical though printed on different-quality paper. The ads in the 1977 re-presentation also alter the story through altering the "flow" of the pamphlet.

This has consequences when reading the book for the plot. Advertising pages appear in the following places in "Back to the Klondike" the story: first, after the cover but before the title page. Second, on page 12, the verso page after 11—on the page following the recto page in which Scrooge's sentiment is interrupted by his greed for the second time. Third, on both the verso and recto pages following 15, a page that ends on the lower right-hand corner with Goldie's voice calling Blackjack the bear off his pursuit of Donald and Scrooge. At this point in the story, we haven't met Goldie yet. Her voice comes from off-panel and is unidentifiable, so it could be argued in the style of Michael Millington that the advertising serves the purpose of suspense. One ad and two panels later, in 18.2, we find out that Scrooge can see "**a little old lady** walking away with the bear!" The fourth ad takes up page 21, on a recto page after Scrooge and Donald have successfully captured Blackjack and Scrooge is having honey uncomfortably licked off of him. This is the Iron Man adventure, which—along with the Hostess ad—is the only advertisement in the book labeled "ADVERTISEMENT" at the top. The fifth advertising sequence is on the verso page 32, after the conclusion of the story, with two ads facing each other across page 32 and the inside back cover.

Of these five advertising sequences, one (pages 16–17) serves to increase suspense, by enhancing the delay of the reader's progress. The fourth example is less clear because it ends with the characters having achieved their short-term goal of capturing the bear—when we come back to them postadvertisement, Scrooge is saying "now let's plan our next move" sometime later (22.1). This is a kind of suspense if not particularly dramatic, since we don't know what the ducks will do once they've neutralized the bear, but we also have no reason to think they'll do anything other than continue what they were doing before being interrupted by the bear, in this case digging for gold quietly at night. The second example might qualify as a kind of suspense as well, but since we have previously seen Scrooge reverse between sentiment and greed in much the same manner, we can accurately predict what we will see next. Of the five ad breaks in "Back to the Klondike" in 1977, then, maybe two out of five enhance any suspenseful quality in the original story. It is the second ad sequence that is most interesting. This is the area of greatest divergence between printings of "Back to the Klondike," as is particularly clear in the next mass market reprinting.

ANOTHER RAINBOW, 1984

Once his identity was publicly known, and after his retirement from writing and drawing comic books, Carl Barks was an active participant in his own legacy. Aside from creating and selling oil paintings of his former comics subjects and codifying titles for many of his untitled works, Barks corresponded with fans and editors, and re-created "missing" segments of his stories. For the 1981 Celestial Arts collection *Uncle Scrooge McDuck: His Life and Times*, Barks redrew four panels of "Back to the Klondike" to replace a deleted portion of the story. The resulting panels are, unlike the rest of the story, pencils that are visibly not inked, and perhaps the reason why a marginal explanation is necessary (Barks, *The Carl Barks Library* 84). The project, and particularly the use of black-and-white art that emphasizes Barks's work free from coloring by other hands, was continued and extended by Another Rainbow in their 1980s project the Carl Barks Library.

Between 1983 and 1990, Another Rainbow, a press founded by fans for the purpose of curating the definitive works of Carl Barks, released the Carl Barks Library (CBL) as thirty hardcover volumes in ten sets. From the Barks paintings to the essays, to the editing of the text itself, to the physical slipcases used to hold three volumes, these objects testify textually and materially to Barks's status as an auteur. The endpapers of each volume reprint Barks's later oil paintings, and in volume 1 of set III (which contains "Back to the Klondike"), the verso side of the flypaper reprints a photograph of Barks at age eighteen months. Although Barks's name is surprisingly minimized on the covers of these books, which turn his name into a CBL logo but preserve Walt Disney's name prominently, the spine of the slipcase unmistakably says: the Carl Barks Library of Walt Disney's Uncle Scrooge.

As part of this curation, this printing of "Back to the Klondike" restores several pages deleted from the 1953 printing. On what is page 12 of both *Four Color* #456 and *Uncle Scrooge* #142, Scrooge's sentiment is interrupted by greed for the second time. As noted above, in 1953 and 1966, turning the page showed Donald entering the room with plot-advancing information; in 1977, turning the page showed an ad for science fiction comics and a way for the reader to make money in their spare time selling social security plate holders. In 1984, turning the page begins a four-page flashback to Scrooge's origins. A younger Scrooge brings a giant gold nugget to the ballroom, only to have a younger Goldie leap for it. Goldie tries to manipulate Scrooge through flattery into revealing his claim's location. Goldie then drugs Scrooge and steals his gold, after which Scrooge returns to the ballroom and in a very large fight panel (82.1) defeats every man in the place. Goldie throws the nugget at Scrooge, which is when Scrooge makes her write an IOU for a thousand dollars ("at **compound interest**," specifies Scrooge, consistent with his earlier musings in 79.7). Then Scrooge abducts Goldie, forcing her to work on his diggings for a month so that she can "learn how hard a miner works for his gold" (83.4). The bedraggled Goldie, when Scrooge pays her fifty cents a day for her labor, "threw the money in [his] face and stomped off" (83.8).

This version of the story, in addition to showing Scrooge engaged in some reprehensible behavior toward Goldie, also makes *her* a more reprehensible figure by revealing her shady tactics. It also links Scrooge's punishing of Goldie to his treatment of his own relatives; in the present-day section of the narrative, Scrooge comments that he may "raise your wages to **twenty-two** cents an hour" (89.5). The nephews subsequently refuse to try to capture a bear for such a paltry sum, as in 91.5 Donald refuses to lure Goldie out of her cabin for twenty-two cents an hour. Despite the harmony of Scrooge's insulting wages, this flashback section shows us a Scrooge who primarily contrasts with the Scrooge of the present. While the present-day Scrooge first appears atop ninety-nine cubic feet of currency, the Scrooge of the Klondike Gold Rush wears patched clothes (confusingly it seems to be the same coat he is wearing in the present, but inexplicably in worse condition). He wears a fur cap rather than a top hat. In this context, his greed seems to take on a different tone: compare his proclamation in 81.6 that "nobody can take gold from Scrooge McDuck!" after his drugging and robbery to his vow in 96.7 to "get **everything** that old chiseler owns!"

Geoffrey Blum's introduction to Another Rainbow's set III foregrounds part of Scrooge's appeal as capturing "both the myth of the western frontier and a uniquely American attitude toward money which prevails to this day" (Barks, *The Carl Barks Library* 7) while noting the complexity of Barks's work. The essay following "Back to the Klondike" by Blum and Thomas Andrae transitions from the perhaps mythological Scrooge memory of a barroom brawl to Barks's inspirations in real history—most notably Ethel Anderson Becker's 1949 book *Klondike '98*. Blum and Andrae suggest that Barks uses the historical backdrop to contrast Scrooge's hard-work ethos with the rise of an end-of-the-nineteenth-century get-rich-quick paradigm. They read "Back to the Klondike" in terms of themes across Barks's work, both in terms of his portrayal of Scrooge as increasingly out of step with "new" money and in the ambivalent portrayals of gold rushes through the corpus. Other essays in Another Rainbow's volume develop Barks's attitudes toward censorship or reprint Barks's own writing about his life and work. The central figure of Barks is key, epitomized by an offhand note in a discussion about the role of collecting in Scrooge stories: Barks himself was uninterested in collecting, but after his editor Chase Craig suggested a story in which Scrooge attempts to turn a particular quarter into a valuable collectible, the subject became important to Barks's writing of the character. The paratext of Another Rainbow's edition is not interested in Craig or his editing except inasmuch as it sheds light on Barks's artistry, the appropriate focus of this library.

GLADSTONE PUBLISHING, 1987

Gladstone's 1987 printing of "Back to the Klondike" identifies itself as an "album" invoking European practices of reprinting comics, though it is only an inch larger in height and width than previous pamphlets; significantly more booklike than the previous periodical editions (for example, it includes a title page and a preface), this book is perfect bound and thus has a spine. The cover is heavier cardstock (and the volume comes with a small collectors' card summarizing the story). The introductory essay links the story to Barks's psychology. The new half-page from the 1981 printing appears again but has been inked by Dutch cartoonist Daan Jippes in a pastiche of Barks's style, and the explanatory note is gone. In a version of *Four Color*'s original chaotic bibliography, this is labeled as volume 4 in a series reprinting Disney works, not all of which are by Barks or feature the same characters.

Once again, Barks's work has been recolored, further emphasizing the way that editors have centered on the figure of Barks and recovering his artistry, so there is no need to preserve the work of the anonymous original colorist(s). Unlike the preceding color publications, the registration has been fixed; the paper used appears to be acid free, as the uninked white parts of the page are still white decades later. This is, in other words, a cheaper incarnation of the "high-value" version of Barks that was reprinted in the 1980s—maintaining many indicators of Barks's artistic value, even as the story preserves a Scrooge who pays starvation wages, in a book that retails at $5.95.

GLADSTONE PUBLISHING, 1996

Gladstone, by this stage the official publisher of Disney comics in North America, printed "Back to the Klondike" again as issue 26 in their newsstand series *Uncle Scrooge Adventures*, and two years later included it in another album printing, volume 2 of *Walt Disney's Uncle Scrooge Adventures in Color*, which also gives a cover title of *Uncle Scrooge McDuck by Carl Barks*. The inside cover is a catalog of the Carl Barks Library in Color; the inside back cover gives information about subscribing to this series. There is a reprint of a map of this adventure, taken from the 1984 Another Rainbow printing. In other words, this edition invokes many different kinds of reading: books, albums, and periodicals.

Four Color #456 cost 10¢; *The Best of Uncle Scrooge and Donald Duck* #1, thirteen years later and more than twice as long, cost 25¢. In 1977, *Uncle Scrooge* #142 cost 30¢. In the next decade, the Carl Barks Library cost $100 for each slipcase volume. The 1987 volume cost $5.95; the 1996 printing $8.95. In addition to outpacing inflation, it is also clear that the relative value of each printing is increasing: Gladstone's 1994 *Uncle Scrooge Adventures* #26, the "cheaper" version of the story in line with 1977, had a cover price of $2.95. The rise of the direct-market distribution system in the 1980s is part of the explanation: *Uncle Scrooge Adventures* was still sold through the newsstand distribution system, while it appears that *Uncle Scrooge Adventures in Color* circulated only through specialty stores and by direct order from the publisher. Since both 1990s editions reprint the same story with comparable production, it's clear that the added value is in the peritext attached as well as the physical materials used for the 1996 version.

This time, the story has been recolored with credit given to Susan Daigle-Leach, who has noticeably made use of digital gradients unavailable in previous printings. This gives Daigle-Leach the ability to create new divisions of meaning absent in Barks's pencil work: she frequently uses an "editorial" gradient that gives a character a halo or highlights a character against a background. Again, since Barks originally had no say at all in coloring, and evidently never expressed an interest in making it part of his work, the coloring of his work remains a field for the artistry of others (and Daigle-Leach was nominated for an Eisner Award for her work in this series).

Gemstone, the inheritors of Gladstone's Disney license, reprinted the story twice in periodical form, in 2003 and 2006, each time maintaining Jippes's inking and Daigle-Leach's coloring. Appropriately, given Barks's death in the year 2000, the 1990s printings indicate the achievement of a textual stability that, at least in North America, would appear more frequently than any other version of the story.

FANTAGRAPHICS, 2012

Fantagraphics Books began printing the Complete Carl Barks Disney Library in 2012. Fantagraphics was founded in 1976 by underground comics fans Gary Groth and Mike Catron in order to publish the *Comics Journal*, a periodical of comics criticism. Fantagraphics was highly influential in the art comics of the 1980s and indie comics of the 1990s (Wolk 46). The publisher is associated with the less commercial and more experimental version of comics promoted by creators such as Art Spiegelman and other publishers such as Drawn and Quarterly (Jenkins, "Should We Discipline?" 4). Bearing the motto "Publisher of the World's Greatest Cartoonists," Fantagraphics often reprints as elevated art the work of the "greatest" cartoonists of the less mainstream comics tradition, even when that tradition was enormously commercially successful in the past. The Barks series imitates (and follows almost exactly) other comparable Fantagraphics projects such as the Complete Peanuts, the Complete Crumb Comics, and the George Herriman Library. These reprints indicate a particularly material investment in the idea of cartoonist-as-auteur and an incarnation of fan connoisseurship.

In 2012, Fantagraphics published *Only a Poor Old Man* as the second volume in their Complete Carl Barks Disney Library. Physically this object isn't a comic book, because it is a hardcover approximately an inch thick. Not only is the idea of re-presenting the complete oeuvre of an artist based in the objective value of that artist and the consistent worth of all their work, but the books themselves make clear what is valuable. They are palpably more expensive, for one thing, and present *only* the work of Barks (though they include his collaborative works in which he wrote *or* drew works by other creators), whether stories of any length or covers, and they also include notes about each story. Fantagraphics doesn't seek to circulate a facsimile of the original but rather a product as close to Barks's mind as feasible. This edition thus bears the traces of fan history as well as the scholarly approach driven by auteurism.

Another relevant feature is the circulation of Barks's name and story. Aside from his name on the front cover (approximately the same size as that of Walt Disney), a photograph of Barks appears on the back of each cover. Some version of his biography circulates in each volume of the library. One of the classic examples of Gérard Genette's idea of paratext, the author's biography has long been understood to give meanings to the attached text. The story of Barks contains many pieces of information that could change how we read the story: he was a Westerner, for example, which perhaps changes how we think of his frequent invocation of Western American landscapes and tropes (Barks, *Only a Poor Old Man* 237). The most significant work done by Barks's biography is the idea that he toiled in obscurity for many years (238). The idea of "the Good Duck Artist" raises the notion that this object is salvage, a recovery from the shipwrecks of pop junk, and valuable because it tries to do justice to "the superiority of his work" (238).

Given Barks's tremendous importance, it is perhaps surprising to discover that every page of *Only a Poor Old Man* has been recolored. Artist Rich Tommaso's recoloring of Barks's work in *Only a Poor Old Man* is deliberately immaculate compared to the anonymous industrial labor of whoever did *Four Color* #456. The logic, though, is not quite that Fantagraphics is trying to reproduce the object exactly as it was when Barks stopped working on it. While Tommaso's recoloring is presumably justified on the grounds that Barks never did his own coloring, Barks's 1970s accounts of his work reveal that his labor stopped earlier than one might think: Barks's wife, Garé Barks, inked and lettered much of his work (Ault 67). In fact, they met when Garé first sought to become his letterer (68). This is apparently intimate enough to suit the project of making Barks the central figure, removing the obscuring effect of Western's anonymous coloring. Tommaso's recoloring is good precisely because it remains within the lines drawn by Barks (whether Carl or Garé), and because it is consistent, so it adheres to the goal of invisibility.

It also adheres to the goal of pastiche. Rather than being naturalistic (or even as editorial as Daigle-Leach's), Tommaso's coloring is an imitation of midcentury funny animal colors. Somewhat less garish than the original, presumably because he wasn't using a simple four-color system, Tommaso's coloring overall still looks like what one might expect from a 1950s comic book, with some particular reference to the original "Back to the Klondike." For example, Scrooge's coat is back to being green, but the face of the bear is now two-toned and suggests an entirely different animal. Tommaso's recoloring is not naturalistic for the exact reason that it is supposed to be invisible, and this also explains the changes to the bear's face. The overall effect is reminiscent of the continuity (or "invisible") editing style in film, whose use requires "minimal mental effort on the part of viewers" and which became the dominant style in mainstream American film because it is a system to "tell stories efficiently" and deemphasize the construction of the product (Corrigan and White 149). In "eliminating" color moving over the lines, the Fantagraphics version of *Four Color* #456 has minimized the traces of industrial production from the storyline itself, suggesting that the Barks work now is seen largely as the carrier of the Good Duck stories and only second as a mass commodity.

There is also the matter of how far backward it is possible to go. According to Barks, the industrial process for making his comics involved him sending the inked and lettered pages off to the publisher, who would photograph them and then destroy the originals, next creating lithographs that were then shipped to Poughkeepsie, and so on. While publisher IDW has begun to release a series of Artist's Editions of famous comic books, which reproduce the pages at the stage of the artist's pencil drawings, this is not an option for Barks, since these objects were destroyed as redundant once the photographs for lithography were taken (Ault 90). While Barks sketches exist, very few of them are versions of published images, and so Barks is excepted from the Artist's Editions line, where he would otherwise seem to be an obvious subject for IDW's physical demonstration of auteurist-cartoonist thinking. As if to confirm the insatiable fan desire to glimpse the Barks work on his drawing board, fan publisher Kim Weston released a 2023 "Original Art Edition" that pastiches IDW's line by reprinting life-size images from 1940s photo negatives of Barks's (non-Duck) art.

Elements of *Four Color* #456 are present in *Only a Poor Old Man* in various ways. There is the green coat, but also the context of the story. The flow of *Four Color* #456 is reproduced to the extent of sequencing the five stories. The priority is to reproduce the original context of work by Barks. This is also suggested by the fact that Fantagraphics is republishing all of Barks's Duck work in chronological volumes; these are themselves being published *out* of sequence, so eventually a reader will be able to put the complete works in complete order, but only at the end of the project.

In *Only a Poor Old Man*, the three one-page stories appear immediately before and after the two longer stories that made up the rest of *Four Color* #456, "Back to the Klondike" and "Something Fishy Here." These "one-pagers" have also been colored by Fantagraphics in their reprinting. This would seem to complicate the assertion that Fantagraphics, being primarily interested in Barks, is most interested in the art that can be undoubtedly ascribed to Barks (or incidentally to his wife, treated as an invisible transmitter). If the black-and-white lines of these Uncle Scrooge stories are what Barks sent in to Western, before Western subjected them to a somewhat sloppy coloring process, why did Fantagraphics recolor these stories, *especially* since they originally appeared in black and white? The answer lies in the overall idea of the Carl Barks Library: the demands of consistency placed on these stories by the idea of a library suggest that even stories that Western never colored should be colored *so that they match Barks's other work* as presented. This is a distinct stand of Fantagraphics, as Another Rainbow printed his work in black and white, perhaps hewing even closer to the idea that Barks's work had value totally distinct from how it originally appeared on newsstands.

Like *Four Color* #456, *Only a Poor Old Man* contains no advertisements. Very much unlike *Four Color* #456, *Only a Poor Old Man* is not a cheap product, retailing for $29.99—nearly three hundred times as much as *Four Color* #456 cost at the newsstand. The paper is higher quality than newsprint and seems to have been deacidified. The traces of industrial printing processes are quite visible in *Four Color* #456 and minimized in *Only a Poor Old Man*. Where *Four Color* has visible staples holding the sheets together, *Only a Poor Old Man* has a woven binding concealed by a hardcover spine. At the bottom of every sheet of *Four Color* #456, four visible perforation marks indicate that some machine handled the sheets; no such marks appear in *Only a Poor Old Man*.

So *Four Color* #456 gives us a sentimental Scrooge who pretends to be a viper, and *Uncle Scrooge* #142 gives us a Scrooge whose concerns are a world away from our own, but Fantagraphics provides a romantic antihero Scrooge. By showing him young and ruthless, and both he and Goldie in their heyday, when she was seductive and he kidnapped her, the character is remarkably different. Because it is a quasischolarly art book, the editorial decisions of Fantagraphics are more visible in the final product than those of Dell or Gold Key. An explanation for the discrepancies between stories is at hand in *Only a Poor Old Man*: in the notes to "Back to the Klondike" (218–21), writer and comics historian R. Fiore notes that "the entire flashback sequence... was deleted from the first publication" (219). Again, the focus on Barks's original intention is significant: these pages are figured as "missing" despite the coherence of the original story as published, and despite Barks's possession of replacement art. Who was it missing *from*? Obviously, from anyone who read the authorized printings between 1953 and 1981—the same time fans were circulating copies of the censored sequence—namely, more casual readers.

In fact, the sequence removed by Dell Publishing in 1953 was deleted precisely for its depiction of "adventure," both in the sense of violence and sexuality, and particularly because of their combination, when Scrooge kidnaps Glittering Goldie. This certainly indicates a discrepancy between how Barks understood his audience and who Dell believed their audience was. Barks describes the ensuing editorial letter from Western as saying that "[he] had violated a lot of their taboos and should have had sense enough to know it wouldn't work" (quoted in Ault 76). This was so far outside the norm of Scrooge's portrayals that Dell did not allow it to be printed, and it didn't appear until fandom's interest in Barks overwhelmed the publisher's prudence.

Fantagraphics has constructed "Back to the Klondike" as a work of art whose quality is primarily in the story being told, as envisioned by Carl Barks on his drawing board. Several things about the 1953 "Back to the Klondike"— the lack of ads, the black-and-white inside cover stories, even the invisibly deleted sequence, but most of all the discrepancy in quality between the story and the process of its circulation—allow for this kind of recuperative, quasi-scholarly, fannish reading. This possibility is altered, but not foreclosed, in the 1977 *Uncle Scrooge* #142, which contains an explanation of fun and consumerism that likens "Back to the Klondike" to a cheap cupcake. It's worth considering the tension with Scrooge's own spending habits: a one-page strip from *Uncle Scrooge* #6 (June–August 1954) features the duck refusing to spend five cents to read a newspaper article about a business success of his, instead waiting for the public library's free reading room to open (Barks, *Only a Poor Old Man* 203). A strip from *Four Color* #386 (March 1952) shows Scrooge buying a beggar a cup of coffee for ten cents, or rather giving the beggar his free second cup with his own purchase (*Only a Poor Old Man* 34). It is difficult to imagine Scrooge paying for cupcakes or comics; a box of Hostess Twinkies cost roughly $1.50 in 1977. In this version of the story, a distance between Scrooge and the reader is emphasized by the advertising paratext.

Finally, comparing these versions of the story demonstrates that the unspoken editor of the Carl Barks Disney Library is fandom itself, specifically the fandom that is interested in the idiosyncrasies of Carl Barks's particular vision of Scrooge, the coherence of that image, and the completeness of his work. *Only a Poor Old Man* is an attempt at creating an object out of what had been an abstraction: freeing the comic "Back to the Klondike" from its bounds in the cage of *Four Color* #456.

In the twenty-first century, there are few remains of that cage, only some details and endnotes; the actual book remains in private and rare books collections. *Only a Poor Old Man*, like all the volumes of the Fantagraphics library, is not cheap, not fragile, and not intended to appear alongside the work of the bad Duck Artists. The differences between these printings of "Back to the Klondike" (which are not even the *only* printings of the story, not even in English) should serve as an illustration of the material circulation of comic books. While different attitudes toward Barks's art have motivated these presentations, the result is that "Back to the Klondike" has appeared as different objects throughout its history. It would be too simple to say that Fantagraphics' 2012 version is the "best" because it presents the most material from Barks, but it would also be too simple to say that the 1953 version is the "real" story. Scholars who address Barks generally concern themselves with analyzing his individual vision and its appearance in his works. From this standpoint, it is primarily important that Barks can be considered an auteur "in the pure sense" (Ault 1), and the history of his publications is irrelevant. Other Barks scholars similarly focus on Barks's personality: Thomas Andrae posits that "understanding the origins of Barks's stories requires looking at the details of his life" (21); and Michael Barrier remarks that the distinctive key to Barks's "best work" is "that he shaped his stories in accordance with a view of life that was essentially pessimistic" and that "in story after story,

Barks revealed his understanding of how people's minds and hearts really work" (113). For an example of Barks analysis in which publication history and context could be important but go unmentioned, consider Geoffrey Moses's analysis of Barks's themes of modernity: Barks's stories often circulated juxtaposed with the literal products of modernity in the form of advertisements.

If this is what the analysis means for comic books, what does it mean for Uncle Scrooge, the concept that the comics seem to incarnate? The material context of a reader's encounter leaves the reader's relationship to Scrooge unclear and muddles any one author's idea of what Uncle Scrooge values. Many of the ideas in Andrae's monograph on Carl Barks are about the meaning of Uncle Scrooge as a figure with a heightened relationship to value, and take on an interesting light when considering non-Barks stories, the works of the other Duck Artists. To take an example, not by Carl Barks, from *between* instances of "Back to the Klondike," "The Fuddleduck Diggins" (in *Donald Duck* #125, May 1969) portrays some of the issues that are of frequent interest to Uncle Scrooge scholars such as Ault, Andrae, Barrier, and Moses: primarily, the relationship between Scrooge's thirst for wealth and moral values. In this story, Scrooge's cousin Rufus Fuddleduck, clad in the traditional outfit of the Western prospector, comes to Scrooge to make him a partner in his diggings. "**Wow!**" exclaims Scrooge, leaping into the air while looking at a sample nugget roughly the size of the one in "Back to the Klondike," "**What a nugget!**" Rufus Fuddleduck, like Scrooge in the earlier story, is afraid of claim jumpers and wants to bring his cousin into the business to outsmart them. Taking a helicopter (as opposed to "Back to the Klondike" in which Scrooge refuses to even consider flying), they arrive in the American West, only to be robbed by two bandits. Scrooge does not trust that his partners can get the job done, but this largely takes the form of him resolving plot dilemmas, as when he explains that he showed up in time because he's been following the other characters on radar through their whole adventure. The bandits block a hole at the diggings with a boulder, flooding the desert. "Before anybody else finds out," says Scrooge, "we'll buy up that whole desert for peanuts and turn it into a million-acre garden!" (10.4). This, it turns out, is what Rufus Fuddleduck always wanted to do anyway. When he announces this, Scrooge has a face reminiscent of his sinister visage in "Back to the Klondike" 7.5, but this comes at the *end* of the story rather than the beginning, as Scrooge devises a frankly beneficial scheme and pronounces the archetypal power to turn a desert into a garden. This forms a strange contrast to Barks's contemporary stories of Scrooge, in which the character becomes a source of ecological dangers (Andrae 272). Unlike in "Back to the Klondike," in this story we never doubt that Scrooge is a basically good person, with his greed portrayed as analogous to that of the amiable Rufus Fuddleduck—and the motive for the plot is a request for familiar help. This story is completely disinterested in Scrooge's past.

Donald Duck #125 is a different object again from *Uncle Scrooge* #142 and from *Four Color* #456, just as they are all different from *Only a Poor Old Man*. "The Fuddleduck Diggins" is followed by a five-page story about Goofy trying to operate a tow truck and instead foiling a bank robbery, a one-page Donald Duck story reprinting a newspaper comic strip, a one-page text story about the Disney version of the Three Little Pigs, and a story about a disguised burglar trying to steal a gem from Scrooge while Donald and the nephews are staying at Scrooge's home. These are interspersed with ads, primarily for other Gold Key products and subscriptions, and other issues; drawings of inventions sent in by readers; jokes *also* sent in by readers; and a brief "educational" page about prehistoric paintings, to say nothing of a comic strip ad for Lee brand jeans, and another for Sea-Monkeys. While it is possible to imagine a reprint of Duck comics that included "The Fuddleduck Diggins" in addition to "Back to the Klondike," elevating the former to the status of art, it is very difficult to imagine a facsimile that reproduces these other parts of the comic books.

Examining "Back to the Klondike" this minutely provides a case study in considering comic books as material objects. When we consider what "Uncle Scrooge" represents, it is important to pay attention to what, exactly, we are looking at. In Dell's *Four Color* #456, he is a flinty but ultimately sentimental children's hero. Two years later, in 1955, as comic book publishers faced government pressure to ensure that "the comic books placed so temptingly before our Nation's children at every corner newsstand are clean, decent, and fit to be read by children" (US Congress 27), Dell would refuse to join the Comics Magazine Association of America (CMAA) on the grounds that their clean image would provide an umbrella for unsavory publishers (Nyberg 116–17), just as Dell had refused to join the 1948 Association of Comics Magazine Publishers (US Congress 30). Instead, Dell would use their March 1955 comics to proclaim an "IMPORTANT . . . pledge to parents." The full-page pledge reprinted an award given to Dell president George Delacorte by the American Legion for "establishing and maintaining . . . clean and wholesome juvenile entertainment." "The Dell Trademark," explains the pledge to parents, "is, and always has been, a positive guarantee that the comic magazine bearing it contains only clean and wholesome juvenile entertainment." In a season of moral panic over comics, the Dell code "eliminates entirely, rather than regulates, objectionable material" (Barks, *Uncle Scrooge* #22, n.p.), outdoing the Comics Code established by the CMAA. While the 1953 Scrooge is part of an effort to provide unobjectionable entertainment, the Scrooge in Fantagraphics' 2012 *Only a Poor Old Man* is the protagonist of a work of art, a rough but romantic hero created by the genius of Carl Barks, from which we should not be distracted by the shoddy original context—nor, Another Rainbow and Fantagraphics posit, in a world after the demise of the Comics Code, should we be swayed by the fears of 1950s editors into suppressing any of Barks's art.

It has been traditional to consider Carl Barks's work despite its context. "Barks' stories were so popular, and so good, because he took pains where most writers and cartoonists for 'funny animal' comic books did not" (Barrier and Williams 198). As Bart Beaty has explained, fans saw Barks's work as having "a distinctly recognizable personal style [that] evinced a high level of craft within the aesthetic constraints of children's humour and adventure comic books and the factory-like working conditions of the Disney empire" (*Comics versus Art* 82). In this, he stands for the subject of comics studies in general: it has transcended and been refined. Less commonly observed is that in the process of making things like *Four Color* #456 into things like *Only a Poor Old Man*, a new object with a new valuation has been created. The history of "Back to the Klondike" is a history of appreciation in two senses: the immense labor and effort fans have expended on re-creating and recovering Carl Barks as an artist, and the increasing market value of his work. Given that "Back to the Klondike" is centrally concerned with Uncle Scrooge's efforts to collect on decades' worth of compound interest, we might follow fandom in trying to discern Barks's attitude to this salvage operation. If we did that, we might put a heavy emphasis on Scrooge's strange position at the end of the story, when the famous miser has surrendered a fortune but must pretend that he still values collecting over all else. If the story ends by confirming that Scrooge is a "good old" human as well as a ruthless tycoon, the Barks bibliography ends similarly, by observing that whatever its paratext, "Back to the Klondike" is a comic as well as a book.

The most recent physical form of "Back to the Klondike" is as a chapter in a mass market book. Although Barks's work strongly resists being seen as novelistic, the growing paradigm of the graphic novel is apparent in the material history of his recovery from the anonymous newsstand. While the 1984 and 2012 reprints of his work are both physically hardcovers, the 1980s book strongly resembles a set of comics, bound as signatures with ancillary material: the spine identifies the work as "Uncle Scrooge 1–20." By contrast, the 2012 volume has its own title, presents the reprinted periodical covers as an appendix, and identifies its volume and original printing numbers in front and back matter separated from the stories, which are arranged into one long flow of episodes. While Carl Barks is a paradigm of quality salvage recovered from the mass of commercial quality, representing shifts within the field of comics studies itself, we must look elsewhere for a book history that epitomizes the physical form of "graphic novels" coming to embody valuable comics in the first place.

Chapter 2

"I WILL GIVE YOU BODIES BEYOND YOUR WILDEST IMAGININGS"

Watchmen and the Editorial Construction of Value

The question "What is *Watchmen*?" is surprisingly difficult to answer. Most literary criticism of writer Alan Moore, illustrator Dave Gibbons, and colorist John Higgins's series *Watchmen*, originally published by DC Comics, contains both a summary of the complicated plot and some acknowledgment of the text's historical importance in the 1980s transition of comics from the status of "trash" to a new level of literary prestige in American culture. *Watchmen* is typically seen as a key text in this transition, along with Art Spiegelman's Pulitzer Prize–winning graphic novel *Maus* (serialized from 1980 until 1991) and Frank Miller's Batman miniseries *The Dark Knight Returns* (published in four parts in 1986). In Paul Williams's words, from this point onward the uncertain and chaotic first period of the graphic novel's history is over: "[M]oving into the second half of the 1980s, we have squarely entered the empire of the graphic novel" (190). The conception of *Watchmen* as a key graphic novel elides the fact that it was published from May 1986 until July 1987 as twelve individual comic books of the familiar North American size. Later reprints of *Watchmen* have physically manifested increasing prestige and value for the series, both emphasizing the value and importance of the series as well as converting *Watchmen*'s cultural capital into the literal kind. The changes in these reprints have constructed *Watchmen*'s significance as primarily relying on the text's psychological and historical realism and *Watchmen*'s importance to the history of the graphic novel. The small scale of textual changes has also reinforced the notion of *Watchmen* as an essentially perfect text. In this case, since the original author Alan Moore has had almost nothing to do with the text since its original publication, the methods of book history detail the long and complex life of the text under corporate control. These elements combine to make a book history case study of the materiality of a "classic" that stretches far beyond the actions of the original author and emphasize the role of DC Comics as a corporate producer of *Watchmen*, which has primarily taken place in materiality and through paratext. As Romain Becker has detailed in regard to another Alan Moore/DC comic, *Batman: The Killing Joke*, "editorial intent is an integral piece of how a comic is built, making editors co-creators rather than mere supporters" (para. 3).

Watchmen has been printed in the following major editions:

1. The original printing of twelve individual comic books from May 1986 to July 1987. These took the form of comic books of the standard North American size, but printed without advertising and on acid-free Baxter paper, a higher-quality alternative to both standard newsprint and midrange Mando paper.
2. A trade paperback, first released in late 1987, which became the standard edition. Significant paratextual revisions to this version occurred in 1995 and the early twenty-first century. By collecting nearly all the material in the original printings at approximately the same size, the trade paperback fundamentally changed the possible encounters of readers with the text.
3. The 1988 release of the series in France, in the form of six larger hardcover books invoking the European "album" format. In addition to translating the text, this release generated new cover artwork that reappeared in later editions and reorganized the story, facilitating yet another way to understand the text.
4. Also in 1988, the release of a limited edition hardcover, including significant paratextual materials about the conception and history of the series. This edition incarnates the idea of a prestigious reader invested in the text's background, and became the basis for later prestigious editions.
5. *Absolute Watchmen*, a physically larger and recolored 2005 version of the 1988 hardcover. Rather than a facsimile of the original, this edition makes the text "as intended" and focuses on the role of the original creators, most prominently colorist John Higgins, as most significant for the discerning reader.
6. An "International Edition" of 2008, which is a hardcover under a "new" cover based on old promotional art.
7. A "Deluxe Edition" of 2013, which presents a larger version of the standard paperback, incorporating the "bonus materials" of earlier prestige editions.

8. A 2014 "Artifact Edition," which reproduces original artwork for the series, incarnating a museal logic that looks back beyond the original publication.
9. A "Collector's Edition" in 2016, in which the series appears as twelve small hardcovers inside a slipcase. This edition transforms a nostalgic interest in the original serial publication into a remarkably expensive object at Can$163.
10. A "Noir" edition, also in 2016, in which the series is reprinted without coloring.
11. An annotated edition released in 2017, which licenses the reading of the series for its connections to extra textual information, as well as confirming the text's complexity.

Throughout this period, excerpts of *Watchmen* as well as prequels, sequels, and adaptations have appeared, always tied to marketing of the collected original series. Most of these printings have been part of a larger series of titles released by DC Comics, while others have been produced by other publishers. Reading *Watchmen* as book history reveals the investment of the corporate owners of the series in the prestige of an acclaimed graphic novel. Since 1986, DC Comics has defined *Watchmen* as a criterion of quality, and defined themselves as the publishers of valuable work like *Watchmen*.

The plot of *Watchmen*, structured around a group of retired superheroes investigating the death of a former colleague and gradually discovering a conspiracy to change the course of the Cold War, has been described as "convoluted" (Dietrich 121), and because of this quality of extreme complexity, scholars have found many incidents and characters worth remarking upon. However, a more relevant element in the circulation of *Watchmen* is its historical importance as a "revolutionary" text in the field of the American graphic novel. In discussions of American comics' "annus mirabilis" of 1986, *Watchmen* is an obligatory touchstone (Hoberek 8). Erin Keating and Jamie Hughes are among the few critics who cast *Watchmen* in terms of continuity with other traditions rather than as breaking with those traditions in American comics. While Keating's subject is specifically the treatment of the female characters in the series, she also cautions more generally that this commonplace understanding of *Watchmen* as revolutionary has other deleterious effects:

> To read the text's displacement and revisionary aspects alone is to miss half of the story.... It is imperative to recognize the many levels that are working in a comic book, not merely the ones that seem the most different and revolutionary. (1286)

Keating's perceptive comment implies that one major gap in academic treatment of *Watchmen* is to consider the book as a book, and to read it by discussing the differences between editions. In the case of *Watchmen*, where physicality and reading protocols have come to be overtly modeled on the novel through the "graphic novel," comics materiality is much the same as in other print media.

Comic books like *Watchmen* bear the history of the labor of employees of a corporation, DC Comics. Although *Watchmen* was the product not just of credited authors and editors but also of anonymous laborers, my focus is not on the number of hands but on the actions of this group of employees. I refer to DC Comics throughout this chapter as a single entity, but it is a corporate author in the sense that the hands that built *Watchmen* are all employed by the same entity. Jason S. Polley usefully distinguishes between *Watchmen* and "the Watchmen Industry," the panoply of products that have followed *Watchmen* and that are unified by their corporate owner, DC Comics, Inc. The many reprints of *Watchmen* are a key part of the Watchmen Industry, and therefore the method of descriptive bibliography traces the actions of DC Comics as they engaged in strategies to position *Watchmen*, Alan Moore, and themselves in the cultural field.

1986 TO 1988: DC DIVIDES *WATCHMEN* INTO TIERS OF PRESTIGE

Watchmen was originally published in the form of twelve individual issues of the mainstream mid-1980s size, each at a cover price of $1.50. These issues each consist of thirty-two pages of Baxter paper wrapped in a cover printed on glossier stock: seven quarto sheets and the cover, held together with two staples. Each cover shares the same layout: the title WATCHMEN is present in all caps in a vertical column taking up one-quarter of the page, and in smaller letters at the top left. Each cover was designed by Dave Gibbons to be an image in sequence immediately before the first panel of each issue, and a more detailed version of each first panel. *Watchmen*'s very distinctive cover would later become a trademark of parodies and homages but would also provide a blueprint for future iterations of the series itself.

Scholars Matthew Wolf-Meyer, Jamie Hughes, Jason Dittmer, and Erin Keating have separately argued that *Watchmen*'s subject matter is in continuity with some contemporary series. However, to take one specific example nominated by Dittmer, Marvel's 1985–1986 series *Squadron Supreme*, the physical differences are notable. Unlike *Watchmen*, *Squadron Supreme* contains advertisements and is printed on obviously poorer newsprint-quality paper—bleed-through and registration issues abound, and years later acidification has taken hold. Thus, the idea of relative "prestige" is a factor even in the original publication of *Watchmen*. The absence of ads removes the possibility of friction or resonance between the diegesis and the extradiegetic material. Wolf-Meyer calls this resonance "accidental media," and its absence from a series like *Watchmen* not only contributes to the series' positioning as important and valuable but also centralizes more editorial control over the paratext. Comic book publishing has various degrees of prestige signaled by paratextual moves as much as by the actual plot of the text.

Later editions bear the legal disclaimer that the material within was originally published in "magazine form" as *Watchmen* #1–12. The conception of *Watchmen* #1–12 as "magazine form" belongs to later forms from which it can be distinguished, and the phrase is present nowhere in the original publication. In *Watchmen*'s case, this retronymizing of the "original printing" happened extraordinarily quickly.

Late in 1987, a few months after the magazine publication of *Watchmen* had finished, the series was collected as a trade paperback (Harris-Fain 622). This trade paperback is the same height and width as the limited series, but three-fourths of an inch thick. Dave Gibbons did not see this collection as an inevitable consequence when work began on the series:

> In 1987, once a comic book series had run its course, that was pretty much the end of it. There might be sporadic foreign editions or reprints in the back of other titles, but even series conceived as self-contained stories, such as DC's *Camelot 3000*, were thereafter unavailable except in the back-issue bins. The notion of collecting just-published material and re-marketing it in book form was virtually unknown. The term "graphic novel" was shiny new and, frankly, considered a little pretentious by industry insiders. (Gibbons et al. 237)

Alan Moore came to see "graphic novel" as simply "a marketing term" (Moore and Gibbons, *Watchmen* #1, 2000). The speed with which *Watchmen* was collected is noteworthy: published between 1982 and 1984, *Camelot 3000* was not collected as a paperback until 1988, four years after it was published.

As Gibbons's mention of pretension would suggest, collecting through reprinting is a move of cultural prestige. Andrew Hoberek recounts that *Watchmen* was made possible by structural changes in the comic book industry (the rise of the direct market and specialty shops), but it also contributed to a later shift (toward the graphic novel). Hoberek notes, "On the one hand the label . . . confers a new, more privileged aesthetic status on the narrative in question.... [A]t the same time the advent of the graphic novel also constitutes an economic transformation" (14). Appearing at the "moment of transformation" gives *Watchmen* a particular interest, as Hoberek says; but *Watchmen* and the existence of *Watchmen*-like works were also the pretext for this status and economic change. Discussing this moment of transformation, Robert Hutton points out several resonant anomalies, most notably that although *Maus* is commonly credited with pioneering the "graphic novel" format, it was originally serialized (38). Even more importantly, Hutton notes that Pierre Bourdieu's concept of "negotiations within the cultural field" (Hutton 43) reconfigures how we understand whatever happened to comics in the late 1980s. In Hutton's conception, the corporations deliberately encouraged a shift to a mode of production centered on individual artistic expression (40–41) such as that of Alan Moore (or, for that matter, Carl Barks).

The "graphic novel" as a bound collection has reading protocols different from those of the individual issues. Aside from the cultural prestige of being a book rather than twelve pamphlets, *Watchmen* encourages a reading of the series in serial order, as well as a complete reading of the series. An object that collects all twelve issues, and particularly its labeling as a graphic novel, encourages the reader to adopt novel-reading protocols and read all twelve chapters in order from 1 through 12—by contrast, Carl Barks's *Only a Poor Old Man* rearranges the order of several publications, and the stories have neither a proscribed reading order nor a serial continuity. By making *Watchmen* a single book, DC Comics promotes some ways of reading the text and discourages others.

The trade paperback edition of *Watchmen* adds an epigraph after the body of the work. The quotation "Quis custodiet ipsos custodes?" appears in black print on the white endpapers of the volume, a quotation from the Roman poet Juvenal's sixth *Satire*. The quotation, the original of the phrase "Who watches the watchmen?," which appears in fragments at several points in the comic, might seem obviously relevant, especially as it is divorced from context: in Juvenal's poem, it is a racy joke about a narrator who wants to prevent other men from seducing his wife. However, In *Watchmen*'s collected edition, the quotation is also noted as the epigraph to the Tower Commission Report of 1987. A US government inquiry into the Iran-Contra arms-for-hostages scandal, the Tower Commission released its report in February 1987, while *Watchmen* was still being published. The quotation's role in the Tower Commission Report is clearly an indictment of law enforcement, since the report concluded that a US intelligence agency had been negligent in fulfilling its legal requirement to be overseen by lawmakers. The quotation's appearance in *Watchmen* and its connection to this real-life source is curious on the surface: because *Watchmen* takes place in an alternate universe, there is no Iran-Contra scandal and no Tower Commission in the text. This quotation concludes *Watchmen* by gesturing out at the reader's world. Paul Youngquist argues that, like the Tower Commission Report, *Watchmen* also identifies "the source of national security under such circumstances with a band of vigilantes." In this reading, *Watchmen* becomes prominently "about" American sovereignty and national security, but this is a reading that is licensed only by the trade paperback and not by *Watchmen*'s original appearance, where there is no epigraph. In the trade paperback, the Juvenal quotation positions the real 1987 and the fictional 1986 as reflections of each other. At the same time, it suggests that the skeptical position of *Watchmen* also applies to the real world. This citation places *Watchmen* in conversation with the world around it in an unusually direct manner, part of the trade paperback's agenda of positioning *Watchmen* as a weighty graphic novel with something to say about "real life" using the debased genre of superheroes.

Furthermore, presenting the series in linear order of publication emphasizes the "appropriate" narrative sequence to the exclusion of serendipitous nonlinear encounters. Given the story's investment in nonlinear storytelling, several intriguing possibilities come to mind, such as a reader becoming aware of one of the story's twists (for example, those concerning the identities of a murderer and a biological father) and then returning to earlier stages where almost no character is aware of this information, promoting an irony otherwise only present in rereadings. There are 479,001,600 permutations of *Watchmen*'s twelve issues, all of which save one are only possible by going against the "graphic novel" reading order.

Since 1987, the value of different versions of *Watchmen* are no longer fixed to the original issues but to the paperback. Like the "original printing," every other edition of *Watchmen* comes with a modifier (Deluxe, Essential, Annotated, Absolute) designated by DC Comics.

In 1988, *Watchmen* was reprinted in translation in France, and physically converted into the European album format, by Éditions Zenda. *Les Gardiens* was released in six hardcover volumes. Issues 5 and 6, for example, which had become chapters V and VI in the American paperback, became tome 3, titled "Rorschach" on the spine and cover. Éditions Zenda focused each of the six albums on a specific character. To enhance this decision to break up and rearrange the text, Dave Gibbons drew new covers for each album, with that tome's character at the center. The original covers appear as interior pages, curiously with the original (now inaccurate) monthly indication on each cover.

Because the French album size is significantly larger than the American comic book, the images in *Les Gardiens* are noticeably larger than the original printings. The seventy-six-page volumes (three-eighths of an inch thick) measure about 12⅝ inches high by 9 inches wide, significantly larger than the American comics (which are 10⅛ inches high by 6⅞ inches wide) and their collection. It appears that Éditions Zenda was blowing up photographs of the published American edition, resulting in pages such as 5.27, where all the original art but none of the new lettering is out of focus. As is emphasized by literally being photographs of the original comic book, this text is a representation of an original, inaugurating a trend that would loom large in later printings.

The end of each tome bears a mark of serialization that reminds the reader both of *Watchmen*'s completeness and its in-progress nature: an advertisement for all six tomes. The current and prior volumes are summarized with the same material that appears on the back cover, but the "future" volumes have question marks instead of summaries. They do, however, feature the cover artwork for subsequent installments, which necessarily indicates the "focus" characters of each tome.

The translation by Jean-Patrick Manchette required replacing Dave Gibbons's original lettering with new lettering by an unknown hand. While all text is still in capitals and the size and shape of balloons appear to be the same, the French lettering is distinctly different. Alice Ray's article on French translations of *Watchmen* points out that the Manchette translation was enormously esteemed (49), while a later translation (by a "traducteur fantôme" who remains anonymous) in editions published by Panini in 2007 has not been as fulsomely praised. From Ray's examples, one notable visible difference is the 2007 translation making a distinction that the 1988 version does not: for the handwritten journal of the character Rorschach, the lettering is distinctly different from the "default" letters. This decision is closer to the American original than the 1988 translation, though the 2007 version uses a significantly more difficult font that imitates handwriting. Ray has capably cataloged the at-times startling differences between French editions, emphasizing that all three versions simply look different. The decision to retain the original captions and bubbles while filling them with new French text also underlines the fact that the album is a translation. When *Watchmen* was translated into French, it was with the knowledge that the hypotext was an acclaimed American comic book, and the translation is an attempt to create the series again.

Watchmen was printed in hardcover in early 1988 by Graphitti Designs, a comics merchandise manufacturer located in Anaheim, California. This hardcover presents a completely black cover and black slipcase. The slipcase is blank except for the title in gold on the spine, while the black hardcover has the title and credits on the spine and the uncolored imprint of the smiley face with a splash of blood on the cover.

This edition includes a red ribbon bookmark sewn into the spine of the book. This object implies a different mode of reading than that of either the magazines or the trade paperback. Pausing during reading is possible with either, but, while the magazines and the trade paperback afford this reading practice, the red ribbon materially suggests it. The Graphitti Designs hardcover is more prestigious than any previous edition partially because it suggests an even slower and more considered reading, positioning the text as worthy of such a reading.

Graphitti Designs' second innovation in their hardcover is a collection of paratextual "bonus materials," including reproductions of script pages, sketches, advertisements, and notes by Moore and Gibbons. The Graphitti Designs edition focuses the reader's attention on the creation of the series. Bart Beaty locates the interest in "the truth behind the work" (*Comics versus Art* 112) in fanzine culture, and this publication of *Watchmen* is a publication for fans, presenting revelations about the text's foundations. A foreword by Alan Moore characterizes this paratext as "the first clumsy and faltering steps along the track" contrasted to "the steroid brute that eventually broke the ribbon on the finish line" (*Absolute Watchmen* 423). These materials describe elements of the story that were discarded or altered. Moore's pitch is reformatted into columns, and a later draft is interspersed with the first. Jaime Lee Kirtz points out that the appearance of these paratextual materials as a selling point speaks to fandom protocols of desiring an authentic understanding of authorship before the editing process (14). For the facsimile script pages, the surrounding text implies that what we're looking at is not just Moore's script but illustrator Dave Gibbons's personal copy of Moore's script, an artifact of the series' creation, messy with (implicitly Gibbons's) highlighting. Photographs of Gibbons's actual copy of the script, a significantly messier object than the facsimile, can be seen in his 2008 memoir/art book *Watching the Watchmen*. Graphitti Designs' revisions are a very early indication of a publisher's awareness that discerning readers would want access to this artifact as authentically but also as legibly as possible. The difference reveals that the purpose of the Graphitti Designs archive is to approximate archival materials.

The Graphitti Designs hardcover elevates *Watchmen* to an even more prestigious level, but it also transforms the text by attaching information about its creation. These two moves imply that learning about the creation of *Watchmen* is a part of appreciating and understanding the text. In much more detail than the trade paperback's back-cover biographies, Graphitti

Designs' material links *Watchmen* to the personalities and choices of the creators very strongly. By doing so, the publisher suggests meanings of *Watchmen*. For another possibility, the equivalent edition of 1984–1985's series *Crisis on Infinite Earths* includes memos between DC Comics' editorial staff and creators, providing very different paratexts for understanding a text. While such an approach positions the significant facts about the creation of the series in the editorial realm, Graphitti Designs' edition emphasizes the author and artist as creators whose particular choices are important for understanding the text.

The added material of the Graphitti Designs edition, later incorporated into DC Comics editions, marks the beginning of the *Watchmen* historiography being made integral to the actual series. While the paperback bore the reminder that *Watchmen* had originally been published in magazine form, the 1988 hardcover associates prestige with the singular material objects reproduced and altered in the series. Associating these objects directly with a copy of *Watchmen* suggests that this information should be seen as a part of *Watchmen*, not as articles of history to be sought out but rather as integral to the most lavish edition. In a 2016 discussion of comic historiography's "museal" turn toward facsimile documents, Daniel Stein points out the continuity between such reprinting and earlier fan practices of collecting (285). The fact that a smaller specialty house, rather than DC Comics itself, produced this edition bundling *Watchmen* with items of museal interest in an expensive package, suggests that DC Comics did not fully anticipate the fans of *Watchmen*. The bonus materials of the Graphitti Designs edition are an early version of the trend Stein identifies, reproducing artifacts in mass quantities for devoted fans, implicitly expanding the category of devoted fans.

In a period when most series went uncollected in single volumes, *Watchmen* had within years of its release become a mass market trade paperback and a prestigious hardcover. By 1988, there were multiple tiers of *Watchmen*, and implicitly multiple kinds of readers, differentiated by cultural prestige but also by their level of archival interest in the text. Ironically, at this time Alan Moore became extremely disenchanted with DC's business practices (notably those related to the promotion of, and rights to, *Watchmen*) and would refuse to contribute to future editions—a potent severing of the book from the actual person of the author in what feels like a reverse of the canonization of Carl Barks.

1995 TO 2005: DC INCREASES THE VALUE OF *WATCHMEN*

In 1995, DC Comics changed the cover of American printings of the trade paperback. The eleventh printing (Grand Comics Database) and onward bear an extremely abstract image of an oval bisected by a vivid splash of red liquid. Taking a central image of the series, the new cover—the cover of the UK editions printed by Titan Books from 1987 onward—"zooms in" on the splash of blood over the smiley face (figure 2.1). If this is the central motif of the series, it seems more surprising that for almost ten years it was not the cover of the American collection.

Figure 2.1. *Watchmen*, original UK paperback cover.

Figure 2.2. *Watchmen*, original US paperback cover.

From 1987 to 1995, the American paperback cover showed a shattered window with shards of glass tainted with blood (figure 2.2). While several shards of glass are visibly suspended in the air beyond the broken window, the blood-spattered smiley face can also be seen in the lower right-hand corner, facing the reader. Unlike every other cover in the series, the older cover is not an image that is easily sequenced immediately before ensuing images in the storyline. Most closely resembling 1.3.7, a composition that reappears at 11.26.4, the older image apparently takes place a split second after this image from the series. DC's decision to use this cover means that in a key period in which *Watchmen*'s reputation began to assume its current shape, American readers did not encounter *Watchmen* with a strikingly abstract cover. While the ocular/visceral imagery recurs throughout the series, readers might instead encounter a version of *Watchmen* that wears a different face.

The "window" cover is a symbolic representation, not a moment that literally occurs in the text. Here, key signs (the Chrysler Building = New York, but the geodesic dome and the zeppelin = another possibly future history, and the blood on the glass = bodily violence) contextualize the spattered smiley face in a way unlike any composition in the actual book. This symbolic image is also thematically the opposite of the Titan Books cover of 1987 onward. While the Titan Books cover announces the overlay of the visceral atop the iconic abstraction of illustration, the original DC cover omits a beaten body entirely, leaving only traces of blood.

With our proleptic knowledge that nearly every subsequent edition of *Watchmen* will bear a variant of the eleventh edition paperback cover, it's easy to say that DC Comics was adjusting the packaging: *Watchmen*'s eleventh edition cover is not the *Watchmen* logo, but it presents an image so iconic that it already featured in merchandise such as pins. In some later editions, the title *Watchmen* would be removed from the cover entirely, leaving only the eye and the spatter. This removal completes the transformation from a cover that somewhat resembles the covers of other comic books into an iconic, simple image distinct from ordinary comic book style. As David Barnes suggests, *Watchmen*'s migration from comic book series in a comic book store to book on the shelves at bookstores has involved *Watchmen* and Moore himself becoming "commoditized brands for the hip, cool, cynical and armchair revolutionary" (54) against Moore's will. The replacement of a more realistic, symbolic image with a simple abstract one for the very product that appears in bookstores was a key part of that commoditization.

In March 2000, DC Comics reprinted the first issue of *Watchmen*. In their "Millennium Edition" series of reprints, DC reprinted single issues of "the best and most vital examples of our art form," according to a note from

Paul Levitz, executive vice president and publisher at DC Comics, printed on the inside front cover. The cover of *Watchmen* is altered for this edition, with the front bearing an embossed gold Millennium Edition seal and the original cover framed by the DC logo and a brief editorial note. This note interestingly identifies this object as "the first issue of the classic maxiseries by Alan Moore and Dave Gibbons," despite the word "maxiseries" not being present in the original series (though it did exist at the time and is thus arguably not a retronym). An essay on the inside front and back covers by author and DC manager of editorial operations Robert Greenberger hails *Watchmen*'s achievements as an example of how "Comic Books Examine Themselves." The essay positions *Watchmen* as an unprecedented achievement that "helped signal to the mainstream media that comics were growing up." The Millennium Edition paratext positions *Watchmen* #1 as an important milestone in the history of comic books, and also as an advertisement for DC's trade paperback, which Greenberger mentions "remains in print today."

On the back cover of the Millennium Edition is an advertisement for the PlayStation video game *Resident Evil 3: Nemesis*, the first advertisement to appear in any version of *Watchmen*. The discordance of this image is easy to overstate, but the largely CGI image is wildly out of tone with *Watchmen* #1. This contrast with the overtly commercial intrusion should draw our attention to the way that the Millennium Edition is proclaiming itself to be timeless, classic, and important.

DC Comics' Millennium Edition series consists of sixty-two comic books. The oldest—*Detective Comics* #1, March 1937, the ultimate source of the company's name—and the newest, *JLA* #1, January 1997, are thus made the first and last "best and most vital" comics in the history of DC. The Millennium Editions are a celebration, a chain of triumphs and milestones—and they focus on beginnings, whether the first appearance of characters or the beginning of different series. In the narrative of DC's larger history created by the Millennium Editions, *Watchmen* #1 is important not because it began *Watchmen* or because it was significant in Moore's and Gibbons's careers, but because *Watchmen* began a significant moment of comic book history, and *Watchmen* begins with *Watchmen* #1. The Millennium Edition thus positions *Watchmen* as an important DC Comics property. While the Millennium Edition and all the collected editions participate in the sense of *Watchmen* as an important, prestigious comic book, the Millennium Edition is unusually overt in telling the story of *Watchmen* in relation to the publisher.

In 2005, DC Comics produced the Absolute Edition of *Watchmen*. The slipcase of the Absolute Edition is 12¾ inches high by 8½ inches wide, roughly the height of the European album but about half an inch narrower—and 1¾ inches thick. The hardcover inside the slipcase is 12½ inches high by 8⅜ inches wide, while it's 1½ inches thick, significantly larger than the original issues. The hardcover reproduces many of the Graphitti Designs edition's claims to greatness and value as literature and as an object (for example, the red bookmark and the paratextual bonus materials), but at a more affordable price. The Absolute Edition is also the first printing to receive pagination that continues throughout the entire text, making the text a more seamless book.

DC imprint WildStorm's group editor Scott Dunbier developed the idea of the Absolute Edition format, inspired by European comics (Hedges 201). Candida Rifkind has suggested that the material awkwardness of similarly oversized books indicates in each case that "it is not a book designed for casual and impromptu reading" (229). As a line of reprintings, the Absolute Editions partake of the same reading protocols and inevitably suggest an elevation. The fact that they are all the same size makes the line primarily an incarnation of the idea of importance. Furthermore, because the material for the Absolute Editions is drawn from a larger mass of works, their exclusivity suggests a higher valuation of that material, a physical canon of comics not meant to be read casually.

The 2002 release of the Absolute Edition of *The Authority*, volume 1, established the trend of presenting works with a single writer, in this case Warren Ellis. In 2003, J. Scott Campbell's *Danger Girl*, Alan Moore's *The League of Extraordinary Gentlemen* (volume 1), and volume 2 of *The Authority* were all released. After halting production for a year, the Absolute Edition became a standard format in 2005 with seven releases, including *Watchmen*. While the list of titles—*Planetary, Crisis on Infinite Earths, The League of Extraordinary Gentlemen* (volume 2), *Batman: Hush*, and *Luthor/Joker*—are generally not as acclaimed as *Watchmen*, they do represent a group of "prestige" series with relatively untangled author and artist identifications, continuing the concept of comics auteurism.

Generally, Absolute Editions appear as the culmination of those series' publication histories. For example, *DC: The New Frontier*, written and drawn by Darwyn Cooke and released as a miniseries in 2004, was collected as a trade paperback in 2004 and 2005, and then as an Absolute Edition in 2006. Absolute Editions are apparently not for collecting previously uncollected series. Their purpose is not to make accessible what has previously been prohibitively expensive; indeed, quite the opposite. The purpose of Absolute Editions appears to be to create an expensive object and to incarnate the most prestigious edition available to a general audience. While their choice of titles ranges enormously in terms of the degree of critical acclaim, the Absolute printing confers an importance on the material reprinted. The explosion of the Absolute Edition line indicates that DC's marketing division perceives that an audience exists, an audience for whom copies of Geoff Johns's *Green Lantern: Rebirth*, for instance, are worth $100. In the introduction to *Absolute Green Lantern: Rebirth*, writer Brad Meltzer proclaims that the worth of the series is partially its relationship to fandom: "Written by a fan. Written for the fans. For us. I love it for that. . . . Instead of trying to be cool or meta or the oh-so-popular self aware" (Johns and Van Sciver n.p.). The Absolute Edition is the physical manifestation of popularity among fans, notably the kinds of fans who would spend a hundred dollars on an oversize edition of a comic book with a foreword proclaiming the comic book's lack of pretension. As Romain Becker remarks, it is the culture of fans as collectors/speculators that allows the continuing "compiling and/or altering of material" to make financial sense—the creation of "new products based on old comics" (para. 24).

The contents of the 2005 Absolute Edition of *Watchmen* are significantly different from the series that was printed in the 1980s. For the Absolute Edition, colorist John Higgins reworked his contribution to *Watchmen* and created what is now the standard appearance of the series. The indicia calls this the "(NEW EDITION)" after the title, an acknowledgment that all paperback and hardcover editions of *Watchmen* since 2005 are reprintings of Higgins's 2005 work. The most radical change in coloring for the 2005 and subsequent editions was Higgins's decision to use the new digital technology to, as Sara J. Van Ness puts it, simulate an older print culture. *Watchmen*'s comic-book-within-a-comic-book, the pirate story "Tales of the Black Freighter," appears in pre-2005 editions as roughly contiguous with the storyworld of *Watchmen*. As Van Ness indicates, in the Absolute Edition, every panel from "Tales of the Black Freighter" is redesigned to look like a specific kind of comic book, namely a more cheaply printed comic book than *Watchmen*: "[O]riginally, these panels were colored in much the same way as their 'real world' counterparts. . . . [T]he panels featuring scenes from *Tales* now include a classic comic-book texture; each of the colors in these panels consists of a visible dot-like pattern" (41). As Van Ness says, "the style mimics less-advanced printing technology" (41). This technique means that later versions of *Watchmen* include a starker contrast to "Tales of the Black Freighter." By adding a false "comic-booky" comic book within *Watchmen*, the Absolute Edition emphasizes that *Watchmen* is unlike those comics—the Barks Library, but with contrasting simulations of the Other Duck Artists included.

Strangely, a contemporary (2008) Deluxe Edition of a work by Moore—1988's *Batman: The Killing Joke*, drawn by Brian Bolland—also alters John Higgins's original coloring. Mervi Miettinen has gone into some detail about the textual consequences of the decision to replace Higgins's 1988 coloring with Bolland's 2008 coloring, but suffice to say that the key in Moore's absence is Bolland's claim that the 2008 edition more closely represents his original intention (Miettinen 11) while the reprinting of Moore's script once again invokes the writer as creator. Even more strangely, the 2018 Absolute Edition of *Batman: The Killing Joke* reprints *both* colorings, suggesting an appeal to connoisseurs who want to see three variants, each dominated by the work of a different cocreator. The logic of Absolute Editions is to convert subcultural capital into an actual purchase price with ostensibly authoritative products.

A later development within the Absolute Editions suggests yet another approach. *Absolute Batman Year One*, published in 2016, collects a four-issue storyline from Batman comics of 1986 and 1987. The Absolute Edition consists of two hardcovers in one slipcase, with the first reprinting remastered and recolored art from previous collections of the storyline. The second hardcover reprints the original publication, with ads removed but letters pages maintained, and printed on paper stock that closely replicates the original interiors and covers. Scanned from the published comic books as opposed to the original art, this second hardcover presents a strikingly different relation to comics nostalgia. *Year One* shows that even within the context of the oversize deluxe reprints of the Absolute Editions, the aim could be a re-creation of the original physical object. This possibility should indicate that the aim of *Absolute Watchmen* is very much to create a new, definitive edition of *Watchmen*. That such an edition was needed suggests the extent to which *Watchmen* plays a different role for DC than *Year One*: there has to be a best *Watchmen*.

Roy Cook and Aaron Meskin assert that as with art prints, comics are typically seen as "multiple artworks"—"that is, that they have multiple instances, where interaction with any appropriate instance is sufficient to count as a genuine interaction with the work itself" (57). Their conclusion for comics is that, "although the ordinary reprinting of comics does not produce new works of art, comics, at least under certain non-extraordinary circumstances, allow for distinct editions that are themselves distinct artworks. Nevertheless, editions of comics are not standardly works of art in their own right, and these insights are as a result somewhat limited" (58). Thanks to the recoloring and particularly Higgins's insistence on the superiority of his 2005 work, Cook and Meskin suggest that the Absolute Edition of *Watchmen* might be considered a distinct artwork, marking a key moment in the transition of the book *Watchmen* from comic book to graphic narrative and "art" book. At one point, Cook and Meskin consider the major criteria for an "art-instance" (an instance of an artwork that is itself a distinct artwork), concluding: "If multiple works that allow for art-instances must involve interpretation . . . then this would again throw at least some doubt on the claim that comics or prints could have art-instances, since in neither case do we naturally think of the production of instances as interpretive" (60). Historian Roger Chartier expands upon this reasoning by invoking the singular figure of the printer/publisher. Placing the Absolute Edition alongside other editions (which Cook and Meskin correctly identify as distinct for the purposes of collecting [62]) emphasizes that, although comics are not generally thought of as involving interpretation in editions (Cook and Meskin 63), most editions of *Watchmen* have involved interpretation by DC Comics.

The paratext is where most variation has taken place. Higgins's recoloring and some minor "corrections" by Gibbons are the only changes ever made to the main text of *Watchmen*. Setting aside translations and extratextual materials by other authors, *Watchmen* has remained an extremely stable text. The 2005 changes confirm, however, that the purpose of reprinting *Watchmen* is not to replicate the famous text from 1986–1987 but the one that readers believe should have existed at the time. The small scale of these changes over time reinforces the notion, key to DC's construction of the graphic novel, of *Watchmen* as an essentially perfect text.

In a 2009 piece for *Booklist*, a magazine for public librarians, Gordon Flagg points out the existence of "an oversized, slip-cased hardcover" (the Absolute Edition), but recommends the trade paperback as the one to stock to meet customer demand (34). The materiality of the Absolute Edition, as well as the work done by Higgins and Gibbons on the text, combine to suggest two unavoidable facts about the Absolute Edition: it is attempting to be the finest copy of the text, both for consumers and in terms of representing what the creator intended (though in fact the author of *Watchmen* did not intend for any of this to happen); and this edition is not the one that should circulate most easily. By making the future cheaper editions contain the emendations of the Absolute Edition, DC uses that edition as an exemplar. However, the existence of a separate Absolute Edition reveals a publishing strategy that includes very expensive versions of existing comic books. The notion of a market of fans for prestige editions would continue to dominate later *Watchmen* history.

2008 TO 2017: *WATCHMEN* BECOMES "ESSENTIAL" TO DC'S CONVERGENCE REGIME

In 2008, about three months before the release date of the *Watchmen* film adaptation, DC reprinted *Watchmen* #1. This edition of #1 presents *Watchmen* as "THE GROUNDBREAKING SERIES" on the cover. The cover is an image of Rorschach leaving an alleyway, having just beaten a graffiti artist who has sprayed the phrase "WHO WATCHES THE WATCHMEN?" on a wall. The cover image closely resembles 6.15.6 but is a 1986 advertisement drawn by Dave Gibbons (Gibbons, *The Watchmen Portfolio* n.p.). The black-and-white original has been colored in black and yellow, and a brief epigraph from Rorschach has been removed. The original ad mimicked the cover design of the series, so this printing simply replaces the advertising words "A 12 ISSUE DELUXE SERIES BY ALAN MOORE AND DAVE GIBBONS" with the quotation above. As this pedigree suggests, this image is symbolic of the character and the tone of the series, a vignette that does not exactly take place in the series. By literally placing an advertisement on the cover, this edition of *Watchmen* #1 presents itself as an even less subtle advertisement. The timing suggests that the 2009 Warner Bros. film adaptation is the product being advertised.

The International Edition of the trade paperback, also available in North America, was released on September 10, 2008. The contents appear to be the same as the (apparently American) paperback, but with a new cover drawn by Dave Gibbons. This image presents the main cast of the series in superhero garb, standing in front of a large, yellow clock. The cover is based on an illustration originally published in DC's character guide *Who's Who Update '87* #5, published in late 1987, though it has been recolored. The International Edition has a cover that strongly resembles promotional art, assembling the characters in a symbolic scene in which they are formally posed.

This cover strongly resembles the cover of the hardcover edition, first released on November 5, 2008. The hardcover is a standard-size reprinting of the 2005 Absolute Edition. The cover of this hardcover edition is based on advertising art drawn by Gibbons for *DC Spotlight* #1, a 1985 free publication advertising upcoming DC titles. As with the International Edition, the cover presents the cast in front of a yellow clock.

This sudden proliferation of minute variants is related to the production of the Warner Bros. film, released in the United States in March 2009: the inside front dust jacket of the hardcover edition mentions the upcoming movie. This strategy worked: a *Publishers Weekly* report from March 16, 2009, notes that while *Watchmen* has "quietly sold well" for years, the release of the movie has propelled it to the top of the paperback bestsellers list (Donahue 19). While the hardcover edition is presumably not a direct part of this chart, this immediately prefilm activity testifies to DC's and Warner Bros.' use of media convergence and cross-promotion.

Published serially on iTunes, the twelve parts of *Watchmen: The Complete Motion Comic* were released one episode every two weeks between October 2008 and March 2009, except that the first episode was released in July 2008. *Watchmen: The Motion Comic* is the only serial publication of *Watchmen* after 1987. Directed by Jake S. Hughes, this digital comic's creation involved photographing the original Gibbons art (C. Smith 362) and even enlisting Gibbons to draw expansions so that full images that never appeared in their entirety in the original series could be panned across by the camera. Considering *The Motion Comic* as a version as well as an adaptation forces us to consider how many elements can be altered from the hypotext. As Craig Smith points out (365), the presence of Dave Gibbons complicates matters.

The format of the motion comic has been described separately by Smith and Drew Morton. The process involves replacing the distinctive form of the comics gutter with "in-between art" (C. Smith 364) to make each panel an animated scene. Some motion comics make use of a multipanel frame and thus approach the page grid of print comics (C. Smith 367). The *Watchmen* motion comic does not, so the viewer never sees more than one image at a time. Brandy Ball Blake has pointed out that perceiving multiple images simultaneously has particular thematic resonance for *Watchmen*'s print edition, which makes use of the fact that the reader can see "past" and "future" panels (7). Blake's reading of *Watchmen* hinges on a readerly perception that is not possible with the motion comic because, in Morton's words, the form of the motion comic replaces spatial sequence with temporal sequence (134).

While dialogue appears onscreen in the form of Gibbons's original captions, actor Tom Stechschulte performs as every speaking character. Stechschulte acts as these characters by assuming different voices, but it is quite obvious that every piece of dialogue is being spoken by the same person, unavoidably suggesting that this version of *Watchmen* is being read to us. As Morton points out, the story moving at a "cinematic" pace means that dialogue and narration are being read over different images (373), changing the "under-language" (Moore's phrase) of the text, the juxtaposition between words and images. *Watchmen: The Motion Comic* also removes the appendices to each chapter, subtracting significant information.

The physical release of the *Watchmen* film also engages with the material history of the comic book. The five-disc Ultimate Cut release of the film contains, in addition to the lengthiest cut of the film and a digital copy, the complete *Motion Comic*, which itself contains within its case an ad for the paperback, Absolute, and hardcover editions of the comic book as well as the video game. These editions should be understood in the context of media convergence. As Henry Jenkins ("The Cultural Logic") points out, one side of convergence involves corporations participating increasingly efficiently across media, making the official appearance of *Watchmen* in different media also a symptom of DC Comics' role in a larger media conglomerate. The books, movie, DVDs, iTunes releases, and video games of 2008–2009 all appear to have advertised for each other.

Published on May 29, 2013, the Deluxe Edition is a hardcover slightly larger than the International and hardcover editions of 2008. The Deluxe Edition publishes *Watchmen* in a physical format developed by DC Comics previously for other series. The bonus materials focus on Dave Gibbons's role in the series, presenting "Conceptual Sketches, Process, and Development" (n.p.), and a foreword by Gibbons is touted as new material added to this edition, according to DC's online catalog. No material from the Absolute Edition is reproduced. Gibbons's introduction centers on the idea of the "glimpse," an imperfect and partial sight to explain both *Watchmen*'s development as well as the series' artistic success: rather than the aggregate of all human experience, "it is for the storyteller to offer the tantalizing glimpse and for the audience to supply the closure which it suggests" (n.p.). Gibbons also proclaims that *Watchmen* "is finite, as closed and complete as a varnished oil painting or, perhaps, a delicate clock mechanism" (n.p.), implying that the "bonus material" in this edition is a viable addition to the series while expansions are not. Gibbons's sanctioning role as a creator is important enough that his implicit limiting of the meaning of *Watchmen* must be allowed by DC because it also authorizes such innovations as the Deluxe Edition.

DC's Deluxe Editions provide a physically larger product than the original publications in terms of trim size and include bonus materials such as sketches and commentary. David Pearson uses the term "de luxe" to refer to the early modern practice of printing editions of the same text on larger paper: "The result was the same book, textually and typographically, but more generously spaced out with wider margins. This appealed to discerning and affluent book buyers and was a common habit particularly towards the end of the hand press period, in the eighteenth century" (89). The printing practice produced a book that contained the same text but was rarer and more expensive, and encouraged annotation of distinct hand copies. The contrast suggested by this use of "de luxe" highlights DC's positioning of an expensive edition for discerning readers as one that provides more information about the creation of the series. Deluxe Editions typically focus on the artist (*Batman Unwrapped*, Deluxe Edition, by Andy Kubert), or the writer (*The DC Universe*, Deluxe Edition, by Neil Gaiman), or a team. Some engage in multiple categories. *Batman Noir: Eduardo Risso* collects several stories for the purpose of organizing them by artist but also creates the stories in black-and-white versions. Notably, Deluxe Editions are not specifically intended for the expansion of existing material: they can also be for material that has never been collected before. They are always originally hardcovers, but there are also softcover versions of Deluxe Editions. The general purpose of the Deluxe Edition is to produce an edition of distinction, and the use of bonus material and larger paper is part of the same strategy. Although these Deluxe Editions imitate the luxurious Graphitti Designs editions, they appear instead as part of a line that emphasizes prestige and access to materials such as sketches, color guides, and proposals.

On December 4, 2013, DC published *Watchmen* #1 as part of their "Essentials" line in which single issues were reprinted and priced at one dollar. None of the twenty-two issues printed as DC Essentials in 2013 tell a complete story, and therefore their low price seems like an obvious effort to sell copies of the rest of the narrative. At the same time the Deluxe Edition appeared, DC was also releasing the cheapest version of *Watchmen* ever produced, positioning it as "essential," a frequently used term that requires some contextualizing. The term is reminiscent of both Marvel's line of (cheaper) Essential reprint collections and DC's own Essential Vertigo reprints of the 1990s, but the font and timing suggest that the 2013 printings are connected instead to DC's ongoing marketing of certain series as Essential in their annual free physical catalogs.

On the cover of *DC Essential Graphic Novels 2016*, Batman and Superman are seen atop a pile of defeated supervillains, reading *Watchmen* and *The Dark Knight Returns*, respectively. On the cover of *DC Essential Graphic Novels 2018*, the Justice League appears, with Batman again reading *Watchmen*. A brief comic sequence in *2016* shows Batman explaining to his sidekick Robin that this catalog is designed "to help guide new readers to DC's reading collection, starting with the essential 25 most culturally relevant graphic novels." Batman mentions that this catalog is also useful for existing readers. Robin asks if *Watchmen* is covered; it is listed first. The 2016 corporate canon of the twenty-five most culturally relevant graphic novels unsurprisingly begins with *Watchmen*, since it is identified as "the greatest graphic novel of all time" and as such could hardly be anywhere else. The claim and the positioning reinforce each other, as does consistency: *Watchmen* appears in the same place and with the same claim in the catalogs for 2014, 2015, and 2017. In a revealing mixed metaphor, the ad copy posits that the "seminal story is the benchmark against which all other graphic novels and comic books are judged" (*DC Essential Graphic Novels 2016*, 6). While the catalogs advertise DC products and suggest reading orders for bibliographically bewildering superhero collections, their clearest function is indicated by the use of the term "essential": distinguishing a canon within the company's products.

The catalogs use varied approaches to what we might think of as "essentiality." In the 2015 catalog's section devoted to the work of writer Neil Gaiman, we are informed that his 1989–1996 *The Sandman* is "one of the most popular and critically acclaimed graphic novel series of all time" (102), recognizably the same criteria being applied to *Watchmen*. Another section gathers graphic novels that connect to movies and TV shows. *Superman Chronicles*, volume 1, contains "the first adventures of the Man of Steel" (46), while other historical claims involve creative teams working together for the first time or a bold new direction for a character or concept. We are told that Fábio Moon and Gabriel Bá's *Daytripper* is "one of the most unique and compelling graphic novels of the past decade" (21), *Essential Graphic Novels 2015* making an appeal to the reader's response and the work's specificity rather than, as with *Sandman*, a mention of its critical reception. *Watchmen*'s role in this catalog is to be the benchmark.

The Essential Edition of *Watchmen* #1 is a cheap way to purchase the first chapter of the essential collection of *Watchmen*. Given the belief that comic books' move toward the graphic novel has brought them success and acclaim, reviving the comic book to sell the graphic novel seems to be a curious strategy, but it can be explained by the continued existence of specialty stores and audiences. By pricing the Essential issues at one dollar, DC nominates their canon as a starting point, implying that the reader should start with these cheap reprints before purchasing the significantly more expensive collections. Essentiality is clearly marketing rhetoric.

Watchmen and *The Dark Knight Returns*, both from the mid-1980s, are the oldest works among the Essential issues. Only six of twenty-four Essential reprints are from the twentieth century. While it is unlikely that DC meant to suggest that nothing they printed for decades prior to 2000 aside from these six titles is really worthwhile, the significance of this chronology is that the more recent series are likely to still be ongoing or have direct descendants. While canon formation often skews in the other direction, the Essentials are tilted toward the present for commercial reasons.

After the 2009 film, DC reprinted a series of non-*Watchmen* issues that they gave away for free with the framing "After Watchmen . . . What's Next?," characterizing an audience that did not read comic books before seeing the film (or before reading *Watchmen*). The series of reprints eventually dropped the *Watchmen* connection and simply became "What's Next?," but the structure lived on in marketing, as the unifying concept shifted from *Watchmen* to DC. The other meaning of "essential"—an essence—points unmistakably to the publisher as the organizer of meaning. DC's use of the word "essential" beginning around 2013 and their use of *Watchmen* to define and be defined by the marketing concept reveals the extent of the relationship between the publisher and the series.

Later editions of the standard trade paperback exhibited changes. DC Comics changed their logo to retain consistency with corporate redesigns. The paperback edition came to lose the distinctive *Watchmen* title on the front cover, producing an object closer to Gibbons's original 1987 book design, with an even more abstract cover. The changing *back* covers of the trade paperback are more striking.

The back cover biographies of Moore and Gibbons have changed, and blurbs have appeared above those biographies. In the 2014 edition, we are informed that this object is "one of *Time* magazine's 100 best English-language novels since 1923" with "over 2 million copies in print," an "Eisner Award winner," and a "Hugo Award winner" (Moore and Gibbons, *Watchmen* [2014] cover copy). *Time* pronounces it "a work of ruthless psychological realism, it's a landmark in the graphic novel medium" (Grossman), while the *New York Times Book Review* proclaims it "remarkable . . . The would-be heroes of *Watchmen* have staggeringly complex psychological profiles" (Itzkoff, review excerpt). Both quotations interpret and draw the reader's attention to the psychological aspect of *Watchmen*. *Entertainment Weekly* says that *Watchmen* is "a masterwork representing the apex of artistry," quoting screenwriter Damon Lindelof: "the greatest piece of popular fiction ever produced" (Jensen, review excerpt). The *Entertainment Weekly* quotations are taken from a 2005 piece in that magazine by Jeff Jensen titled "*Watchmen*: An Oral History." *Time* magazine's ranked list, also from 2005, is the source of the quotation from that magazine (Lacayo and Grossman). The *New York Times Book Review* quotation is from a 2005 Dave Itzkoff review of *Absolute Watchmen* ("Behind the Mask"). These quotations are precisely intended to justify attention being given to a graphic novel, which is not the typical subject of a *New York Times* book review, an oral history in *Entertainment Weekly*, or a list of best novels. Lindelof's quotation stands out as hyperbolic: claims of "landmark" status and "remarkable" alongside "masterwork" (the omitted qualifier "in its respective medium" changes the idea of "apex of artistry" in excerpting Jensen's quotation) seem debatable alongside the colossal claim that *Watchmen* is better than every other piece of popular fiction ever produced (Jensen, review excerpt). These quotations proclaim that *Watchmen* is popular, and very good, and point toward the work's psychological realism. Perhaps most interesting is that only two of these four blurbs explicitly reference the idea of a graphic novel at all.

Claims about the 2014 paperback edition appear in a paragraph between the blurbs and the biographies:

> This edition of WATCHMEN, the groundbreaking series from Alan Moore, the award-winning writer of V FOR VENDETTA and BATMAN: THE KILLING JOKE, and Dave Gibbons, the artist of GREEN LANTERN, features the high-quality, recolored pages found in WATCHMEN: THE ABSOLUTE EDITION with sketches, never-before-seen extra bonus material and a new introduction by Dave Gibbons. (Moore and Gibbons, *Watchmen* [2014] cover copy)

The 2014 printing is a normal-size reprint of the 2013 Deluxe Edition. The shift of features from the larger, higher-priced Deluxe Edition to the standard paperback indicates their apparent importance. Because of the same impulse that leads to overstated claims of *Watchmen*'s importance, even the standard *Watchmen* now includes behind-the-scenes material. *Watchmen* itself is now Deluxe.

2014 TO 2017: PLACING THE FOUNDATIONS OF *WATCHMEN* IN MUSEUMS

The Artifact Edition of *Watchmen*, published in April 2014 by IDW Publishing, is just over 12¼ inches wide, 17½ inches high, and seven-eighths of an inch thick—by far the largest printing of *Watchmen* yet in terms of trim size, and intended by IDW to simulate the original art: "Each page is printed the same size as drawn, and the paper selected is as close as possible to the original art board" (IDW Publishing). It arrives inside a plain cardboard case (not for shipping purposes, as it carries the bar code and pricing information). On the front cover, a scan of Gibbons's art portraying a photograph lying in the desert sand is a replica of the original artwork for the cover of issue #4, but it also alludes to the concept of the artifact. The photograph of pre-accident Jon Osterman and his ex-girlfriend Janey Slater was intended to memorialize the deceased Osterman after his terrible accident and becomes the subject of issue #4's lengthy nostalgic reverie. The photograph's partial burying in the sand, along with the partial footprints, may allude to Percy Shelley's sonnet "Ozymandias," a frequent *Watchmen* allusion in which "two vast and trunkless legs of stone / Stand in the desert" while "the lone and level sands stretch far away," but in context the photograph is connected more strongly to nostalgia than to hubris. On the back cover is a replica of Dave Gibbons's signature, in glossy embossing over the cover's matte finish. As Gibbons explains in a 1987 letter, he would sign his original artwork to verify its authenticity for sales purposes (Gibbons, *Watchmen: Artifact Edition* 151)—a striking inversion of the planned destruction of Carl Barks's anonymous original art. The signature's appearance on the back of the Artifact Edition itself is performing the same function of certifying that this is all authentic. But, while the interior pages are photographs of Gibbons's signed work, the signature on the back cover is actually a replica of a replica of this authenticating mark.

In an interview with IDW editor in chief and chief creative officer Chris Ryall, scholar Jeffery Klaehn inquired about IDW's related Artist's Edition line. According to Ryall, the line is successful because "those books are the closest most people can ever come to owning a page of original art from the stories included in the books. Seeing these amazing artists' process at the exact size as it was drawn, with all the pencil marks, white-out, scribbles, notes and other such things that make original art so appealing, is something comic fans really enjoy" (Klaehn 92). As Klaehn notes, and Ryall agrees, this project is resonant with the goals of the San Diego Comic Art Gallery, opened by IDW in 2015. The fact that art gallery goals are seen by publishers as connected to the aims of archival and reprint lines suggests a convergence of publishing practices and the museal turn in comic book collecting. According to Klaehn, the Artist's Editions "were pioneered and are superbly run by Special Projects Editor Scott Dunbier" (92), the same person who conceived the Absolute Editions for DC. Dunbier had been an art dealer and then worked at WildStorm when it was a publisher separate from DC (Hedges 198), and his appreciation for the value of original artwork has clearly influenced his editorial work at IDW. The Artifact Edition is an approximation of original comic artwork, and similar ideas of canonicity and prestige are at work in the Absolute and Artifact Editions.

If the layout of a museum exhibit is significant, then the structure of this volume, which divides the series' interior artwork from all covers, coloring material, and promotional artwork, is worth considering. After Gibbons's foreword, we see a table of contents for "Watchmen interiors" and the next 105 pages (covering a selection of Gibbons's original art). After these pages, a second table of contents explains the "Additional Materials": the covers, including the paperback covers, advertisements and the French folio, art from the Mayfair Games role-playing game, color guides by Higgins, and early concept art. Included under the rubric of "Early Watchmen concept art" are four pages from the ledger of Gibbons's art dealer, Paul Hudson, showing sales of the art earlier in the edition. Also appearing are a 1987 letter from Gibbons certifying the art, an advertisement taken out by Hudson to sell the art, and a later sketch from Gibbons to Hudson in which the character Rorschach whispers an offer of artwork for sale. The insistence on the material history of the artwork reproduced makes this volume a museum not of *Watchmen* but of *Watchmen*'s art, concluding with a focus on epitextual events taking place parallel to the publication of the series.

By presenting this information as an edition of *Watchmen*, the Artifact Edition carries out the goal of circulating this artwork but also makes a strong claim that the materiality of *Watchmen* is an important feature of the series. As comic books continue to position themselves as worthy of museal treatment, the use of museummania to create further physical commodities should not be overlooked. Publishers and owners of intellectual property have a special interest in physical, museal permutations of comic books, as they are products that also promote other products. While museal logic leads to the Artifact Edition, the Artifact Edition's existence promotes the cultural value of the cheapest paperback edition of *Watchmen*.

In 2016, two distinct editions of *Watchmen* were released. The first, the *Watchmen Collector's Edition*, re-represents the story in twelve hardcovers sold inside a slipcase; the second, *Watchmen Noir*, re-presents the story without coloring. The slipcase of the *Watchmen Collector's Edition* harks back to the Absolute Edition and the Graphitti Designs edition, but the individual "chapters" becoming independent objects is one of the few times that an edition of *Watchmen* has physically invoked the original publication. It is the only time other than 1987 when all twelve issues were printed as twelve physical objects. Each hardcover says NOT FOR RESALE on the back cover, suggesting that this expensive (manufacturer's suggested retail price [MSRP] $125) object is presenting a deluxe, collected version of the original *Watchmen* experience. The Collector's Edition is also a unique treatment of *Watchmen*, the only title so far to receive this treatment from DC. The edition's content is little different from the now-standard paperback, though the paratext has been changed significantly. Pull quotes are confined to a small piece of paper attached with glue onto the hardcover spines, suggesting its superfluity even though this piece of paper is the only description of the purpose of the Collector's Edition. Aside from the usual collection of blurbs, the small piece of paper's only descriptive sentence is the claim that "[f]rom ALAN MOORE, the award-winning writer of V FOR VENDETTA and BATMAN: THE KILLING JOKE, and DAVE GIBBONS, the artist of GREEN LANTERN, the WATCHMEN COLLECTOR'S EDITION is DC Comics' first-ever slipcase collection featuring the entire 12-issue series reproduced as oversized, single-issue hardcovers, utilizing the recolored pages found in WATCHMEN: THE ABSOLUTE EDITION." The phrase "single-issue hardcovers" blends eclectic terms. Even in French hardcover albums, it was necessary to pair issues to create a book-length document. Positioning *Watchmen* as continuing to pioneer new comics forms thirty years after initial publication, the paratext of the Collector's Edition mainly participates in another reconfiguration of the series' iconography and the affirming of its status as an important and valuable item.

The slipcase forgoes the most common icon of the bloody smiley face in favor of other images drawn from earlier publications. The bottom of the slipcase is a Rorschach blot on a white background, while the top is red, awash in abstract blood that can be seen "dripping down" the spines of the individual hardcovers. The spines of the hardcovers form the image of two human skeletons embracing while being annihilated. The image originally appears in chapter 7, at 16.2 and then 17.6. Around the slipcase are the images of the characters from the covers of the French editions, the first time that these images have been on the covers of the North American *Watchmen*. This edition is a pastiche, combining physical elements of the 1986 Graphitti Designs edition (the slipcase), the 2005 Absolute Edition (the coloring), the original magazines (the disarticulation of "chapters" into "issues"), and the French albums (the images on the slipcase).

Material changes have consequences for the text. In *Watchmen*, the spread at the center of chapter 5, in which the panel layouts are symmetrical throughout the chapter, undergoes changes in different editions. In the original issue #5, the spread is at the staples holding the issue together, making it extremely easy to open the object to show these two pages. In the Collector's Edition, the stiffness of the hardcovers combined with their small size render this spread almost impossible to perceive, since it is very difficult to flatten the issue. The physical construction of the Collector's Edition means that the spine would have to be broken to view the entirety of more than one page at a time, encouraging readers to hold each hardcover partially open in the manner of an old, rare book. Because each hardcover consists of two signatures, chapter 5's center is now only the center of the issue in terms of page count. In the case of *Watchmen*'s Collector's Edition, the comic becomes something glimpsed imperfectly, leaving us to focus primarily on the elaborate housing.

Reluctance to create new iconography of *Watchmen* features prominently in the other 2016 release, *Watchmen Noir*. According to the indicia, *Watchmen Noir* was first printed on October 21, 2016, roughly a month after the

Collector's Edition (printed on September 2, 2016). Where the Collector's Edition uses recoloring as a selling point, the Noir edition, like the Artifact Edition, strips away John Higgins's work. An approximation of the work immediately after Dave Gibbons inked it, *Watchmen Noir* presents a counterfactual version of *Watchmen* as though Higgins had never worked on it at all. In this way, the Noir edition contributes to the creation of multiple tiers of *Watchmen* the physical product. By the 2020s, it is possible for a bookstore to stock a great many versions of *Watchmen* in a variety of price ranges from the cheapest paperback (MSRP Can$25.99), to a hardcover version of that same paperback (MSRP Can$53.99), to an annotated hardcover (MSRP Can$65.99), to an oversize hardcover (MSRP Can$112.00), to a box set of individual hardcovers (MSRP Can$163.00), to an enormous volume of reproduced sketches and original artwork (MSRP US$125)—and the spectrum can be extended even further to include the digital version, motion comic, companion volumes, and supplemental material. This is the Watchmen Industry.

Finally, the latest notable edition of the series to date, *Watchmen Annotated*—which refers to itself as *Watchmen: The Annotated Edition* inside the volume—was released in December 2017. A square volume of 12 by 12 inches, *Watchmen Annotated* presents the original series in black and white. Beside the artwork, space has been added for writer Leslie Klinger's annotations. The style follows William S. Baring-Gould's 1967 *The Annotated Sherlock Holmes*, which presents Arthur Conan Doyle's original texts alongside notes about historical context, allusions, internal logic, and chronology; and probably more directly, the online annotations of writer Jess Nevins, epitomized in his work on Moore's *League of Extraordinary Gentlemen* series.

While the text reproduces *Watchmen*, it also presents Klinger's interpretation of *Watchmen*, and DC Comics' interpretation of Klinger's *Watchmen Annotated*. Interpretation is the precise issue around which Klinger explains his authorship: "The aim of this volume is not to criticize or analyze or dissect *Watchmen*. Like all great works of art, it speaks in its own voice, and each reader will walk away with his or her own interpretation of the story. Rather, this volume aims to enrich the experience of the reader" (8). On the back cover, DC Comics, by contrast, emphasizes the revelatory nature of the annotations and situates this quality in Klinger: DC Comics is "proud to present an all-new retrospective edition of this legendary work," which "reveals the hidden foundations of this milestone in modern storytelling" because "Klinger provides the reader with a unique and comprehensive view of *Watchmen* as both a singular artistic achievement and a transformative event in the history of comics as a medium" (Klinger, cover copy). While part of Klinger's foreword seems to reassure the reader that his purpose is not malign (not to "criticize" or "dissect" the book), it's difficult to see a way in which "hidden foundations" could be revealed without analyzing the original.

Metaphors of autopsy and excavation give little indication of Klinger's focus. His focus on *Watchmen*'s verisimilitude, and particularly its historical references, raises the question of why this particular marginalia would be officially sanctioned. By attaching historical information to *Watchmen*, which only contains ostentatiously fictional treatments of history, *Watchmen Annotated* suggests that history is a necessary part of the text. As the headline of one news article about the volume forecast, "Watchmen Will Be Annotated—And Remind You about Vietnam" (Johnston). *Watchmen Annotated*, which is not intended to become a standard version of the text, is a manifestation of an understanding of the value of *Watchmen*: *Watchmen* can be annotated with information about its historical allusions, adding value to the text. John Anderson and Bradley Katz suggest that the similarly annotated *Maus* CD-ROM highlights *Maus*'s relationship to the events it portrays. Although *Watchmen* is unlike *Maus* in its relationship to history, the act of historical annotation performs the same work of emphasizing that element of the text. The decision to focus on one level or another, on some details and not others, on one set of references and not another, is an interpretation, making it particularly important that *Watchmen Annotated*'s focus on creation, chronology, and history is DC Comics' most sustained sanctioned interpretation.

Watchmen Annotated follows in the vein of the supplemental materials of the Graphitti Arts edition and the Artifact Edition, as well as materials like fan annotations and Dave Gibbons's art book/memoir *Watching the Watchmen*, in constructing *Watchmen* as being valuable because it can be studied in detail. Other comics have been annotated; other comics have their original art circulating in facsimile. Other comics have even been released as "de-collected" volumes in a box set, most prominently Kodansha's anniversary collection of Katsuhiro Otomo's *Akira*. But the specific pattern of how DC Comics has treated *Watchmen* is, by design, unique to *Watchmen*. For thirty years, *Watchmen* has occupied a unique place in comic books, as a critically acclaimed comic book portraying a detailed version of the real world, which nonetheless belongs to the genre of superhero comic books. With its author absent on principle, *Watchmen* is a text interpreted by its publisher and presented in the form of a physical object, as a graphic novel that signifies quality because it is more detailed and more structurally complex than most superhero narratives.

At the beginning of the 2020s, *Watchmen* was available digitally as a motion comic, as twelve digital issues, as a digital collection, as a digital version of the Deluxe Edition, as a digital version of the Noir edition, and as a digital version of the Annotated Edition. Amazon classifies the Deluxe and Annotated Editions as "collected" editions but the noir and "standard" editions as graphic novels, and groups all of these versions as iterations of the same "series," *Watchmen*. A straightforward division between material and digital is simply inaccurate (Würth 133), and the same discourses of prestige in the Watchmen Industry take place in physical and digital versions.

On the other hand, the digital editions open the possibility of a different kind of reading. Since it can be read using a "guided view" option, whereby individual panels can be displayed in sequence, the digital *Watchmen* can be read in a fashion that would be almost impossible in any existing physical form, a fashion that makes "comic books more accessible to readers" (Resha 73). In 2005, novelist, fan, and comics writer Walter Mosley conceived of the Maximum Edition of *Fantastic Four* #1 for Marvel Comics. To recapture his youthful reading experience, in which "as a young person [he] could completely concentrate on each frame of the comic book" as opposed to his current practice in which "[he] look[s] at the whole page, read[s] far too quickly, and move[s] on," Mosley scanned the comic and created a system whereby each panel is a single image blown up to many times its original size, "as large as possible" on his computer screen (Mosley 82). The physical printing of *Maximum FF* is a curiosity, a physical version of a process that can now be approximated by anyone with an internet-connected screen; a similar project would not be attempted again until publisher Abrams ComicArts' "Panel by Panel" line in 2021 (which also began with *Fantastic Four* #1). But the reading Mosley describes is a major component of digital comics, particularly when viewed on screens significantly smaller than the original size of the comic book. This panel-by-panel viewing without glimpsing at an entire page or being aware of page breaks strongly resembles the style of motion comics. While it might be tempting to figure this kind of reading mainly in terms of defamiliarization, as is the case for Mosley, the digital *Watchmen* also raises the possibility of readers whose first interaction with *Watchmen* is seeing it panel by panel, with some enlarged or shrunk—and as Adrienne Resha points out, of readers who learn to read this way. In this reading, the unit of the page, as designed by the original creators, is irrelevant, as is the use of a page structure to convey meaning—significant in the case of *Watchmen*'s distinctive recurring page layout of nine panels and the equally significant variations from the same. Lukas R. A. Wilde notes that even the phrase "digital comics" seems to betray the same kind of anxiety as "graphic novel" in cultural positioning through its identification as a variation of a familiar form (8). Garyn Roberts argues that, "though experiencing an upturn in popularity and profit due to the enormous success of blockbuster movies based on their content, standard format comic books have become the old legends to which contemporary media pay tribute" (210). The association of comics with materiality continues to be defined by the existence of digital comics.

A revising of comics' material history has also been provoked by the rise in prestige of American comics. In the retrospective book *75 Years of DC Comics*, alongside former DC president Paul Levitz's text, a panel from *Watchmen* is reproduced. The panel (3.1.4) is the first scene of a young boy, Bernie, who throughout the series sits on the street beside a newsstand and slowly reads a single issue of a comic book. The Bernie panel is displayed in Levitz's book because it exemplifies the "heavy details" of Gibbons's art and features "two of the many everyman characters who illustrate the narrative's effect on common humanity" (598). These two characters appear throughout *Watchmen*, respectively commenting on current political events and attempting to understand the comic-book-within-a-comic-book that is included in the text. Levitz's text celebrates these characters as counterpoints to the more elaborate main plot of *Watchmen* and to represent the splash of "gritty realism" across the series. The changing context in which Bernie's material encounter with comics is found ensures experiences less and less like Bernie's. Levitz's retrospective is a typical book from German publisher Taschen, purveyors of fine, oversize coffee table art books. It presents a lavishly illustrated history of the American comics publisher in the form of an immense book (roughly the size of an Absolute Edition) with a retail price in 2017 of $200.

Since 1987, however, DC has made *Watchmen* less and less like the comic book being read in *Watchmen*, and made Bernie more and more into an artifact of the 1980s. *Watchmen* has come to exemplify a certain kind of prestige comic book, one that transcends its genre subject matter and context through the use of realism and becomes timeless rather than remaining dated. Bernie, as a reader of cheap, physical newsstand comic books, is what DC's *Watchmen* has left behind even as it reproduces the panels of Bernie reading. Just as the coming of the digital made visible the peculiar body of print comics, the "graphic novel" body and name that *Watchmen* assumed constructed the newsstand as a past market. To draw a metaphor from *Crisis on Infinite Earths*, a series that in 1986 very closely resembled *Watchmen* materially, *Watchmen* was a harbinger not just of a changed future but of a changed past. Reading one of the epitomal "1986" graphic novels in terms of book history emphasizes the techniques and strategies, from physically larger editions to emphasis on historical referents, that *Watchmen*'s corporate owners, DC Comics, have used to create and shape the prestige of the series, and reveals the significant role of DC Comics in writing the graphic novel chapter of book history.

The history of *Watchmen* is unusually well documented because it epitomizes the "new" comics materiality of the post-1980s period, yet the history of the "old" comics materiality remains shadowy. To study *Watchmen* or Carl Barks's Uncle Scrooge as epitomizing comics materiality and to stop there is to overlook the value of a case study in their inverse: a comic book that was never salvaged and remains tied to the cheap newsstand pamphlet period.

Chapter 3

MONEY, MONEY, MONEY
Reading Richie Rich

If you find a comic book with Richie Rich on the cover, the odds are good that that comic book was printed in the 1970s. In that decade, publisher Harvey Comics printed large, and increasingly large, numbers of *Richie Rich* comics. Harvey Comics also replaced their other titles with *Richie Rich* publications and rebranded other titles to feature Richie Rich. While Casper the Friendly Ghost, the other most notable character published by Harvey Comics, is more prominent in marketing outside comics, Richie Rich holds the distinction of having appeared in a staggering number of comic books. As a published character, peak Richie Rich occurs sometime in that decade, in what fans have called the "Richie glut"—a period in which dozens of comic books featuring Richie Rich were published every month. Moreover, the entire history of the character takes place in a larger publishing context defined by the concepts of fad and glut. From the height of the glut in the 1970s through a period of several decades to the present day in which Richie Rich has not been consistently published, the history of Richie Rich is a history of expansion and collapse. The story of the character and the values associated with him reveals the importance of the concept of branding in comic book history, and the way that the branding of comics changes based on the context of material circulation. In Richie Rich's afterlife following the collapse of his publishing line in 1994, the character has been remade into a satirical figure at odds with his original stories—and a material focus on the circulation of his comics, as seen through distant reading, explains why.

THE HARVEY BRAND, 1940–1960

Alfred Harvey Publications was founded in New York City in 1940 by Alfred Harvey, former managing editor for comic book publishers the Fox Feature

Syndicate (A. Harvey). Confusion persists as to the year of Harvey's founding, probably due to the company's later acquisition of *Speed Comics* and *Champ Comics*, which had been published by Brookwood Publications since 1939, and to the fact that Harvey's first two titles, *Pocket Comics* and *Fun Parade*, were not published until the spring of 1941 (A. Harvey). Alfred Harvey's background with Victor Fox, founder of the Fox Feature Syndicate, is worth noting. Fox had left National Allied Publications after their 1938 success with *Superman*, forming a company with the intent of imitating the Superman character. In the ensuing lawsuit, it was determined that Fox's character Wonder Man was a legally liable imitation of the enormously popular Superman (Quattro 20). In a larger sense, the comic book industry as a whole, as with the comic strip, newspaper, and pulp industries from which comic books arose, was defined by an idea of imitating trendy properties, however indirectly. Superman is the most prominent character to create such a fad, but characters such as Dick Tracy (Goulart, *The Adventurous Decade* 75–76) received the same treatment in comic strips and books. Indeed, what many believe to be the earliest nonreprint comic book, 1933's *Detective Dan: Secret Operative no. 48*, is a transparent imitation of Dick Tracy. While not necessarily predominant, the comic book industry at midcentury was characterized by fads—multiple publishers imitating perceived trends in "a long procession of replacement genres" (Kidman 27).

The other relevant strategy of comic book publishing is the "glut." The glut strategy seems to have originated in the magazine industry, as traced in the career of publisher and prominent practitioner Martin Goodman. Blake Bell and Michael Vassallo have argued that the publishing practices of Goodman's magazine empire are key to understanding the decisions he made for the company that became Marvel Comics (8), most notably his exploitation of a trend with a great number of titles. In a 1974 interview, Goodman's editor Stan Lee described the resulting editorial environment:

> We'd be very big in Westerns and suddenly the Western field dried up and we had to find a new trend, and we'd be doing a lot of super-heroes and then there was a lack of interest in super-heroes so we had to find a new trend . . . and we'd do romances or mysteries or funny animals . . . Whatever. (Lee 37)

Unlike Goodman's firm, Harvey Comics was not a previously established publisher, nor did it have publications other than comic books. Nonetheless, the strategies of publishers like Victor Fox and Martin Goodman shed light on Harvey Comics' creation and treatment of characters. Richie Rich would emerge as part of a turn to children's humor in Harvey Comics, a trend that redefined the publisher's brand. Both aspects of Richie Rich—part of a trend and the subject of a glut—were part of the cultivation of Harvey Comics' publishing brand.

Harvey Comics existed for some time before a stable brand emerged, and the permutations of Harvey show how the eventually dominant trend came to prominence. According to Alfred's son Alan, the family records are unclear on the precise order of events, and "there were at least a dozen 'Harvey' corporations and partnerships coexisting at different times in Harvey history" (A. Harvey). This multiplicity of companies was common practice: according to Bell and Vassallo, Martin Goodman used eighty-one different companies over time (35). By 1948, however, the cover of most of their comic books bore the brand Harvey Comics, and the brand had a consistent appearance.

The recurring brand is significant because by the late 1940s Harvey Comics also had a coherent, recurring concept behind most of their titles: licensing successful characters from other media. A representative 1941 title was *Green Hornet Comics*, based on the radio and film character. Further licensed characters included comic strips *Blondie*, *Dick Tracy*, *Terry and the Pirates*, and *Joe Palooka*, all of whom also appeared in film and other media. Some titles were reprints of newspaper comic strips: as Harvey artist Ernie Colón later recalled, his first job at Harvey was as a "paste-up guy . . . cutting up stats of *Dick Tracy* and *Terry and the Pirates* and pasting them up into comics format" (Arnold, *The Best of the Harveyville Fun Times!* 331). Another element of Harvey's editorial strategy, which would later become extremely relevant for the character of Richie Rich, was Harvey's creation of multiple titles featuring each property—combining miniature character-focused gluts with license exploitation. *Blondie* spun off into *Dagwood* as well as *Daisy and Her Pups*, and *Joe Palooka* led to both *Humphrey* and *Little Max*. *Sad Sack*, created by Sergeant George Baker for the wartime US Army magazine *Yank*, became the most significant of Harvey's licensed successes, with a comic book running from 1949 to 1982. As a successful series, *Sad Sack* was accompanied by a host of other, shorter-lived spin-offs and variations such as *Sad Sack's Funny Friends* and *Sad Sack and the Sarge*. As Harvey Comics became a coherent publishing brand, it also cohered a set of industry-wide business practices in a particular combination.

The most significant group of Harvey's licensed characters came from theatrical cartoons made by Famous Studios. Formerly Fleischer Studios, the animation company was renamed Famous when it was purchased by the film studio Paramount. Casper the Friendly Ghost, Harvey's most prominent character outside the realm of comic books, first appeared in a series of

Famous Studios cartoons in the 1940s and 1950s. Casper was a very successful theatrical and later television cartoon character, starring in fifty-five theatrical cartoons, a number comparable to contemporary comic strip/cartoon character Popeye the Sailor Man. The comic book license for the character of Casper the Friendly Ghost, originally acquired by St. John Publications in 1949, was purchased by Harvey in 1952 along with other Famous Studios characters such as Baby Huey, Wendy, Spooky, Herman and Katnip, and Little Audrey. At least the last two of these are widely regarded as imitations of more successful characters: Little Audrey seems to have been created to avoid paying cartoonist Marge Buell for the rights to Little Lulu (Kremer 61), while Herman and Katnip appear to be obvious imitations of Tom and Jerry (Jacobson, "Sid's Kids" 48). In 1958, Harvey Comics bought all the Famous Studios characters outright rather than licensing them (Jerry Beck, quoted in Arnold, *The Harvey Comics Companion* 320). While Casper's 1950s comics have a banner reading "Paramount Pictures famous star," in the 1960s the cartoons would be packaged for television as Harveytoons, inverting the transmedia relationship between brands in a convergence regime. While the structure of Harvey's publishing strategy involved licensing successful characters from other media, that strategy also used a particular kind of content, imitative of larger animation trends. As a result, Harvey became deeply associated with the "big-foot" style, so called because of the prominent physical features of stereotypical children's animated cartoon characters (Jacobson, "Sid's Kids" 44).

The editorial strategy of late 1940s Harvey Comics involved Harvey imitating inoffensive publishers such as Dell (with its Disney licenses) by publishing existing family-friendly characters who had been developed by other companies. Fan historian Mark Arnold has suggested that St. John Publications' poor financial condition presented a licensing opportunity that would have been a natural fit for Dell, but that Harvey outbid them (*The Harvey Comics Companion* 32). This kind of purchasing was also not exceptional: at the same time, Charlton Comics was purchasing licenses from publisher Fawcett as the latter shut down their comics production (Schenk 82). While the particular choices about what licenses were pursued in Harvey's strategy should be understood in the contemporary context of growing moral panic about comic book genres in the late 1940s, this should not be seen as an uninterrupted trajectory toward this kind of "big-foot" content. Richie Rich was an alternative to controversial content but was not necessarily created as a reaction to the same.

Harvey Comics participated in the three most significant comic book fads of the mid-twentieth century: the genres of romance, horror, and war.

In 1949, Harvey launched a line of romance comics that would last until the following year. During the industry-wide "Love Glut" inaugurated by the enormously popular *Young Romance* published by Prize Comics in September 1947, Harvey launched seven romance titles (Nolan 74), none of which reached ten issues. "About nine months after EC started up their horror titles" (Benson 5), Harvey launched a line of horror comics with *Witches Tales* #1 (January 1951). In June 1951, Harvey Comics attempted to turn an existing title (*Blondie*) into *Chamber of Chills*. In August, superhero title *Black Cat Comics* became *Black Cat Mystery Comics* with the eponymous superheroine having become hostess of a horror anthology; perhaps Harvey was inspired by the October 1949 change of Timely Comics' *Captain America* into *Captain America's Weird Tales*. By June 1952, the fourth Harvey horror title, *Tomb of Terror*, had been added. Intriguingly, with the exception of some issues of *Black Cat Mystery*, the horror titles were not branded as Harvey on the cover. In the inside indicia, *Tomb of Terror* and *Black Cat Mystery* are listed as being published by Harvey Publications, Inc., while *Witches Tales* and *Chamber of Chills* are listed as being published by Witches Tales, Inc., located at the same New York City address. In the letters page of rival EC Comics' *The Haunt of Fear* #15 (October 1952), that title's host the Old Witch issues a warning:

> There has been a magazine on the stands for some time . . . published by a rival company . . . called WITCHES TALES. . . . This rival organization also publishes CHAMBER OF CHILLS and TOMB OF TERROR. In no way should these magazines be construed as products of E.C. They are not . . . I repeat, NOT . . . E.C. Magazines! (EC Comics 98)

The Harvey titles were indeed imitations: as Harvey Comics editor Sid Jacobson remarked later, "no one else [in the industry] knew anything, except [EC Comics]. And I said, 'Why don't we strive to do this?'" ("You Could Get Away with Murder!" 28). All four of these titles ended after the December 1954 issues, dissolving into other genres. *Tomb of Terror* became the science fiction *Thrills of Tomorrow*; *Chamber of Chills* became mystery series *Chamber of Clues*; *Black Cat* went back to superhero reprints; and, most curiously of all, *Witches Tales* became *Witches Western Tales* and shortly thereafter *Western Tales*. During this period, Harvey also published war comics, apparently to tie into the Korean conflict as well as in further imitation of EC Comics. With four titles, Harvey's war line was as large as their horror series but lasted nowhere near as long, although *Warfront* was published until 1958. In the early 1950s, Harvey Comics were not yet fully invested in any one particular kind of content, nor with one audience. However, the omission of the Harvey brand from the covers of horror titles suggests that that genre in particular was viewed as exceptional for the Harvey concept.

Harvey's imitation and expansion of these trends occurred even as these genres were coming under scrutiny from official bodies. An explosion of anxiety around horror and crime comics in the early 1950s took form as the Senate Subcommittee on Juvenile Delinquency's inquiries into the industry triggered the formation of the Comics Magazine Association of America, whose Comics Code successfully suppressed the crime and horror genres in American comics. After the congressional hearings on comic books in April and June 1954, the CMAA was formed in September. The increased moral panic around comic books should not be overlooked as a context for Harvey's line of kid's titles: characters like Richie Rich functioned *as an alternative* to controversial comics.

Harvey's *Black Cat Mystery* and *Chamber of Chills* were cited in psychiatrist Fredric Wertham's influential 1954 anticomics book *Seduction of the Innocent*. Perhaps concern over reception is why Harvey Comics' horror titles lack the brand on the cover, and two are published by a differently named corporation with the same address, meaning that nothing but the address existed to tie together *Witches Tales* and the contemporary *Little Dot*. The congressional report refers to just such a situation when it mentions that only a small group of people owned all these companies: "[T]hese corporations, through such devices as common-stock holders and officer and family ties, are in actual fact owned and controlled by a relatively small group of men and women" (US Congress 4). The appendix to the Interim Report indicates that the government was fully aware that the Harvey Comics Group included Witches Tales, Inc., so this structuring must have been for the perception of consumers. In the early 1950s, a distinction existed between the Harvey Comics brand of more family-friendly titles and their controversial horror comics, despite a shared creative and editorial team. This distinction was not unambiguous: one anomalous example would be the famous *Harvey Comics Library* #1 (April 1952), which was sensationally packaged as *Teen-Age Dope Slaves* but is in fact a licensed reprint of *Rex Morgan, M.D.* newspaper strips (Goulart, *Comic Book Encyclopedia* 330). Harvey Comics pursued a business strategy of packaging relatively innocuous content alongside more sensational, controversial material. The absence of the Harvey logo on the provocative cover of *Teen-Age Dope Slaves* seems to indicate a conscious effort to associate the company with particular values and thus brand their products in a particular way. To Joe Sutliff Sanders, this period is the last stage in a transition of comics from a wide and mixed audience in newspapers to an audience of children in comic books: disavowals of crime and horror were part of a lengthy attempt by American comics publishers to prove themselves "squeaky-clean" and able to police themselves, with a resulting overt association with children (25–26).

This is the publishing context in which Richie Rich was created, and it sheds important light on how Richie became so important as a brand and to the larger Harvey Comics brand. He first appeared in *Little Dot* #1, cover-dated September 1953—during the horror comics controversy but one year before the institution of the Comics Code and months before the congressional hearings. It's not clear how much awareness there was of the hearings before they actually began, but the turn toward family-friendly comics must have been obvious as an exploitable trend. The Comics Code essentially forbids the hallmarks of crime and horror comics in particular, although Part B's injunction that "[s]cenes dealing with, or instruments associated with the walking dead . . . are prohibited" seems not to have troubled Casper; nor did infant devil Hot Stuff or witch girl Wendy evidently present evil alluringly despite their accoutrements. The treatment of Casper's morbid elements is suggestive of a turn in the general environment: artist Ernie Colón claims that later he and his colleagues "made a conscious effort not to refer to death in any way" (19), though the original 1940s Casper cartoons had him emerge from his grave. The turn toward a child-friendly style and genre informed even characters who, like Richie Rich, predated the Code.

Richie Rich first appeared as a "backup" character in the pages of *Little Dot*, meaning that he did not appear on the cover and his stories were physically secondary. Kremer explains:

> [I]n order to get second-class entry [mail] in the comic, you couldn't have a comic book with all one character, you had to mix it up with a couple of characters and you had to put in like a two page text. . . . If we had *Little Dot*, we had to get a character in the back; that became Richie. Richie was not a big character in the beginning; he was a little five-pager that padded the book for *Little Dot*. (48)

This was a common practice: Little Dot herself first appeared in 1949 as a backup in *Sad Sack* #1 (Arnold, "A Family Affair" 29).

The example of Hot Stuff, another Harvey character of the 1950s, is instructive to understand the choices made with Richie Rich. Hot Stuff was apparently created incidentally, as a childish devil in an unrelated comic (Jacobson, "Sid's Kids" 44, 47), but the design seemed promising and so was developed into a series, beginning in *Hot Stuff* #1 (October 1957). The fact that

Hot Stuff launched in his own title without any time as a backup character indicates that Harvey was capable of giving a new character their own title. Presumably they felt that the market would make a Hot Stuff title profitable. The fact that Hot Stuff received this treatment despite concerns about the irreverent concept, while Richie Rich did not receive his own title until seven years after his debut, suggests that Richie was not originally seen as a character with as much potential as Hot Stuff. For Harvey at the time, "potential" was most likely licensing potential: Casper the Friendly Ghost was then seen as the company's most successful character for his appearances on television cartoons and his growing use in advertisements. Richie Rich eventually proved popular enough to receive his own title, *Richie Rich*, the first issue of which is cover-dated November 1960.

THE RICHIE RICH BRAND, 1953–1971

The appellation "The Poor Little Rich Boy" appears on the front cover of every issue of *Richie Rich* as a regular part of the logo. It also appears in the title panel of almost every story starring Richie Rich, and at some point in 1962 it became a part of the registered trademark *Richie Rich*. As Colón states, the phrase began as an appropriate description but was also a limitation that needed to be transcended: "With Richie, the character was first called 'The Poor Little Rich Boy,' and he was lonely within his mansion. But that wasn't enough. . . . [I]f all you keep talking about is money, money, money, it gets repetitive" (Cabarga 11). In the first appearance of Richie Rich, "The Dancing Lessons" backup story in *Little Dot* #1, Richie wants to go play baseball but his "mater" insists that he practice dancing, because "it will be very **useful to you**" (Cabarga 13.3). Richie sneaks out to play baseball with his friends, and when a bully steals their equipment, Richie uses his dancing skills to outfight the bully. Other early stories feature Richie's wealth as a problem for him because it compels him to behave in ways antithetical to middle-class masculinity.

At times, Richie's wealth tempts him to behave unethically. In "The Big Race" in *Little Dot* #3, Richie is set up to win a scholarship in a soapbox derby thanks to his (purchased) superior vehicle: the ethical dilemma is that Richie doesn't "need a scholarship, but [unwealthy competitor] Johnny **really** does!" (Cabarga 19.4). The stories often resolve this problem by explaining that while Richie's wealth, which is impressed upon him by his wealthy parents, puts him in ethical (and often gendered) dilemmas, these problems are ultimately resolvable for the benefit of all. Although his "pater" says "I know you'll do your **best**!" in the race (Cabarga 19.3), Richie sabotages himself, and when his father discovers why he is losing despite having "the *best* car that money could buy" (21.6), Rich Senior congratulates his son for not profiting on this venture: "I'm prouder of you than if you had **won!**" (22.8).

In early stories, dramatic tension comes directly from the gap between Richie's wealth-enabled privilege and his morality. In later stories, the immoral temptations of wealth are displaced onto other characters. His mean cousin Reginald Van Dough (first appearance in *Little Dot* #7, September 1954) uses his wealth to belittle and taunt Richie's friends, suggesting that the major difference between them is their attitude toward the less wealthy. In Reggie's first appearance, Richie and his friends are enjoying Richie's gigantic pool when Reggie arrives and indulges in a series of harmful pranks abetted by his suffering chauffeur Harkins and other trappings of the Van Dough wealth. When Richie and friends are enjoying inflatable pool animals, Reggie hatches a violent plan to destroy them, shouting "Harkins! Get my **air rifle** out of the limousine!" (Cabarga 31.2). When Harkins protests, Reggie threatens to "have father fire you!" In Reggie Van Dough stories, Richie becomes the protector of his less fortunate friends against a version of himself. In "The Boy Miser" (*Richie Rich* #32), Richie's father has a nightmare that Richie is "like his **selfish** cousin **Reggie!**" (340.4) and refuses the charity that is his responsibility. The nightmarish Richie even out-Scrooges Scrooge McDuck in refusing to pay two million dollars to build a vault in which to store the piles of money he refuses to spend. The role of charity and kindness in Richie Rich stories clearly posits a proper role for money: to enhance the lives of those without money, for no gain except gratitude. The peril for Richie in these stories is that there are temptations and pressures to enhance his own life, and that there are other people who seek to misuse money. Despite stressing the importance of altruism, the stories suggest that money is also a reward for such righteous behavior, since they are insistent that Richie has considerably *more* money than Reggie.

Richie's love interest, Gloria Glad, presents dramatic tension through her active distaste for money. While many stories present Gloria as a willing beneficiary of Richie's monetary wooing, the stories focused on their romance are quite clear that Gloria is a middle-class girl who finds Richie's ostentation distasteful. In one story, "The Money Touch" (*Richie Rich* #32), Richie and Gloria are walking in "the really **wild** part" of the Rich estate, where there is "not a sign of civilization or the rich things you have in your mansion" (Cabarga 335.1). Unfortunately, nearly every innocuous interaction Gloria tries to have with the "wilderness" unveils hidden riches: a safe descends from a tree when Gloria picks a switch concealed as a daisy; an old shack turns out to activate another safe hidden under a false boulder; even an unmoving cloud turns out to be filled with money (so that Richie's mother can cause it to rain on needy children). "That **does** it!" declares Gloria, "I'm **sick** of all this **money stuff!**" (338.6). In the end, when Gloria retreats to her home to simply have ice cream, it turns out that even that is the site of a secret Rich vault, to which revelation Gloria rolls her eyes in disbelief. In a different Gloria story from the same period, Richie sees a psychiatrist at her request to stop himself from "throwing money around like confetti" (345.4), "after **all** the times I've asked you **not** to spend a lot of money on gifts for me!" (345.1). The story ends by suggesting that the transference of wealth is contagious, as Richie's psychiatrist, now wealthy from the fees charged for curing Richie's spendthrift ways, is running amok in a restaurant, tossing money into the air and "suffering" from Richie's "spending disease!" (349.7). Gloria's presence serves to tell the audience that even well-intentioned spending can be disapproved of by the less fortunate, particularly when associated with emotional relationships. If the challenge in Reggie stories is for Richie to be virtuously wealthy as opposed to malevolent, the challenge in Gloria stories is for him to not spend money on inappropriate "goods." Both stories derive from the original concept of the "poor little rich boy," in which Richie's yearning to be an ordinary boy is at odds with the temptations and affordances of his colossal wealth.

In one recurring theme that plays on the "poor little rich boy" idea, Richie is frustrated by his inability to not turn a profit. The story "It's a Gift" (*Little Dot* #64) turns on the (unknown) writer's deconstruction of this idea. Richie wants to buy something for Gloria for her birthday, and she suggests "something **inexpensive**" (Cabarga 194.2), a watch advertised as on sale for $5. Richie has $25 on hand, but it turns out that the watch actually costs $500. Richie tries to decide if it would be right to borrow money from his own savings to pay for it, or to ask his father for money, ruling both out but curiously not considering Gloria's pronounced dislike of expensive presents. While pondering this dilemma, Richie is struck on the head by a falling flowerpot and loses the memory of his own identity. Despite this, various passersby know who he is, and so his confused attempt to buy a nearby painting becomes profitable when a passing wealthy woman repurchases the painting from him, on the assumption that "no member of the Rich family ever buys anything that won't make a **profit!**" (196.7). Several other characters operate on the same assumption, as the bewildered Richie is taken advantage of by a series of people who try to defraud him but in fact inflate his cash on hand to $2,250. This amount of money is heaped around him when he hits his head again and remembers who he is.

A related variety of Richie Rich stories treats Richie's uncanny profitability (reminiscent of Scrooge's money-delivering pigeon) as a curse that forever sunders him from leading a normal boy's life. In "Gets Away from It All" (*Richie Rich* #6), Richie has saved money to go on an archaeological vacation, which his father thwarts by impressing a staff into service and purchasing the South American land where Richie wants to explore. Remarks Richie: "**Gee!** I can't get away from Dad's money even for **two weeks**!" (Cabarga 267.1). Richie's breaking point comes when an earthquake reveals that his land is rich with oil. With oil surrounding Richie and his archaeologist friend, Richie angrily yells "**Oil?! That's it! I've had it! I've just got to get away from it all!**" (268.6). Ultimately this is impossible, as Richie's escape to a desolate hurricane-struck bungalow in the Florida Keys ends with him discovering a chest full of jewels. Other stories also conclude with frustrated dreams of not making money: the wordless tale "Any Luck?" (*Little Dot* #40) has Richie on an absurdly profitable fishing expedition, ending with him angrily tossing his fishing pole aside. It strikes oil, and in the concluding panel we are informed that the oil lease has been rewarded to a furious Richie. This is also how Richie's attempt to take his friends on a Florida vacation goes in "Oil's Well" (*Little Dot* #15): "We hunt for two years and you boys find oil in **one day**!" says Mr. Rich (80.7). The boys, terrified by their encounters with alligators and a wild boar, simply want to leave the Everglades. The sudden eruption of oil is a recurring device to turn Richie's innocuous activities on their head, but far from being the only method of ruining Richie's profitless fun, oil is simply the most intrusive form of sudden profit.

From 1960, Richie Rich also existed as a brand for a line of comic books that was increasingly important to Harvey Comics in terms of circulation. By 1966, all of Harvey Comics' titles based on licensed newspaper comic strips had been canceled. The remaining "big-foot" style humor comics were published under the Harvey World cover brand. At the end of 1971, Harvey Comics saw a three-month line-wide publishing gap during which a series of spin-offs were canceled. "During this period of major restructuring, it was recognized that *Richie Rich* was turning out to be the line's bestseller, and so a new title was ordered—the first new Harvey World spin-off in seven years, Ri¢hie Ri¢h Fortunes ('71–82)" (Arnold, *The Best of the Harveyville Fun Times!* 33).

As Colón states, the basic Richie plots produce very repetitive stories. Inspired by the Belgian *Tintin* series of *bandes-dessinées* written and drawn by Hergé from 1929 to 1976, Colón injected the genre of adventure into Richie stories. The adventure storylines became more prominent in 1970s Richie, taking elements of the Richie plots and combining them with ideas from noncomedic genres, most prominently adventure, science fiction, horror, and superheroes. A new element of danger becomes predominant in these stories. Thieves in earlier Richie stories appear as a necessary consequence of the fabulous Rich fortune, but they are comically inept, and—much like Carl Barks's Beagle Boys—their criminality is often represented by a uniform: the striped shirt and bandit eye-mask. Later thieves are both more sinister and more deceptive. In 1969's "Mutiny on the Oceanic" (*Richie Rich Success Stories* #23), a would-be pirate called Manta masquerades as the captain of Richie's new yacht. Criminals are also now armed with more frightening weapons than the cartoon coshes of the past. "My gosh," says Gloria, "they've got **guns**!" (Cabarga 231.1), and indeed, the gang constantly threatens to use them. Richie and Gloria of course outwit the villains, but the stakes do seem closer to *Tintin*'s international intrigue than to the idea that Reggie Van Dough might wreck a pool party.

In other stories, antagonists very close to supervillains appear. These include a physicist named Paul Diable who, under the influence of "a **bad dose** of that **radio-active material**," dons red tights and begins calling himself Devil in *Richie Rich* #57. There is also Dr. N. R. Gee, a man with a red lightbulb for a head who menaces Richie throughout the 1970s; Dr. Disguise; the Onion; and other gimmicky criminals. Supernatural characters begin to appear in this period as well, culminating in the *Richie Rich and Casper* series where the two constantly battle weird beings and mad scientists. In this landscape, the money is, as Colón planned, only a device to involve the characters in adventure plots. While comedic tales of Richie's profits are all about his desire to not always be making wealth, the adventure stories focus on attempts to steal or wreck existing wealth. This trend reaches an important stage in 1968's "Richie Rich and the Missing Crown" (*Richie Rich* #71), in which a race to locate the lost crown of Richard the Lionheart doesn't rely on Richie being wealthy at all.

THE RICHIE RICH GLUT AND CRASHES, 1971–1994

Over the course of the 1970s, Richie Rich became Harvey's primary character in terms of comic book production. In the 1970s "Richie glut," other Harvey titles such as *Little Dot* were canceled and replaced with Richie Rich–centric spin-off titles, to a degree that made Richie Rich the "star" of an unprecedented number of comic books. By 1980, Richie was featuring in a shockingly wide variety of comic books. Colón would later comment, "We had something like thirty-three titles all under the Richie Rich banner, all in one month!" (Cabarga 11). Aside from *Richie Rich*, other Richie titles included *Richie Rich Million$* (beginning in 1961); *Richie Rich Dollar$ and Cent$* (1963);

Richie Rich $ucce$$ Stories (1964); *Richie Rich Fortune$* (1971); *Richie Rich Bank Book* (1972); *Richie Rich Diamond$* (1972); *Richie Rich Ja¢kpot$* (1972); *Richie Rich Money World* (1972); *Richie Rich Ri¢he$* (1972); *Richie Rich & Jackie Jokers* (1973); *Richie Rich & Casper* (1974); *Richie Rich & Dot* (1974); *Richie Rich Billion$* (1974); *Richie Rich ¢a$h* (1974); *Richie Rich Gem$* (1974); *Richie Rich Profit$* (1974); *Richie Rich Vault* (later, *Vault$*) *of Mystery* (1974); *Richie Rich Gold and $ilver* (1975); *$upeRi¢hie* (1976); *Ri¢hie Ri¢h Zillionz* (1976); *Ri¢hie Ri¢h & Cadbury* (1977); *Ri¢hie Ri¢h & Dollar the Dog* (1977); *Ri¢hie Ri¢h & Gloria* (1977); *Ri¢hie Ri¢h Invention$* (1977); *Ri¢hie Ri¢h & His Girl Friends* (1979); and *Ri¢hie Ri¢h and His Mean Cousin Reggie* (1979). Even this lengthy list does not include the titles of digests and one-shots. Colón's statement is, astoundingly, barely hyperbolic: in October 1977, thirty titles were printed under the *Ri¢hie Ri¢h* banner. The company's belief in Richie Rich as a profitable brand can also be seen from the fact that in 1976, the Harvey World titles headlined by female characters—*Little Lotta*, *Little Dot*, and *Little Audrey*[1]—were canceled, with the characters revived in 1979 as the costars of *Ri¢hie Ri¢h & His Girl Friends*. The history of Richie Rich is appropriately a history of bibliographical excess.

According to Richie artist Warren Kremer, the character was financially successful despite a lack of promotion:

> [T]hat character sold on the top of the line. The sales were phenomenal. And we never did any promotion on it, never spent money, we never pushed it, never took ads out on it, never did *anything* on it. Everything "Richie Rich" became, it became on its own merit, story content, art content, cover, coloring, whatever. Because, now that I'm working at Marvel, I see the money that's spent on ads, promotions, everything to push their product. If Harvey had ever done that, *Richie Rich* would have maybe sold *twice* as much, I don't know. (55)

Harvey tried persistently to imitate Richie Rich with a series of monomaniacal characters. Kid comedian Jackie Jokers became the last major Harvey character to headline his own series in 1973, until after four issues it was changed to *Richie Rich & Jackie Jokers*. Komix Kid—created by Alfred Harvey's son Alan Harvey—as well as Adam Awards, created by Alfred's son Adam, seemingly never appeared outside of advertisements. Billy Bellhops, created by Alfred's son Russell, appeared in a 1977 one-shot that features Richie Rich on the cover, while time-traveling space kid Timmy Time, created by Colón, only appears in a one-shot from the same year in which the character meets and introduces himself to Richie Rich. Harvey Comics was unable to replicate the Richie Rich formula.

Despite the glut strategy, or perhaps because of it, "by the early 80s, revenues had almost totally dried up" (Krieger 10). Alan Harvey maintains that Harvey's problems were unrelated to sales: he describes the company as having been "devastated by lawsuits, period." The lawsuits could be referring to *Sad Sack* artist Fred Rhoads's long-running lawsuit against the company (Arnold, "A Family Affair" 35), or a pay dispute that led Colón to exit the company, or a lawsuit from the family of then-deceased Robert Harvey (Arnold, "A Family Affair" 33). Health problems for Alfred Harvey led him to be ousted by the board of directors and replaced with editor Sid Jacobson (Jacobson, "Sid's Kids" 51). Additionally, the larger context of comic books was not favorable for a publisher like Harvey:

> Another big strike against Harvey was the advent of the direct market. During the '70s, fewer and fewer [newsstand] outlets took on comic books into their inventory, considering it a money-losing proposition. The comic industry staved off a debacle by filling their pages with advertising, switching to cheaper paper, using horrible new printing processes, running more reprints, and raising their prices virtually every single year. (Arnold, "A Family Affair" 35)

Colón claimed that sales of Richie Rich in particular were fine: "Casper did well in marketing but not so good in actual comic sales. Richie was the opposite" (78). Whatever the cause, Harvey Comics ceased all publication in 1982.

Harvey Comics resolved their legal issues and returned with comics cover-dated October 1986. In each, a brief letter from "The Harveys" on the inside front cover explained that the company had been reorganizing, and that "[w]e at Harvey are today very happy to once again be doing what we do best, publishing comic books, and from your letters we know that the reappearance of our comics will make you a little happier, and this is the real reason for our happiness" (*Richie Rich* #219). In 1989, appropriately youthful American entrepreneur Jeff Montgomery bought Harvey Comics. He endeavored to revive the company and expand their holdings (back) into other media ("Richie Rich Finds a Friend"). Montgomery's strategy reemphasized adaptations, both comic books adapted from other media and other media based on Harvey's comic books. This can be seen as a return to emphasizing Harvey Comics' pre–"Richie glut" techniques, though it was also likely imitating the children's-license-heavy editorial direction of Marvel's

1980s Star Comics imprint. Maintaining the family-friendly orientation of the Harvey brand, Montgomery-era Harvey also published Nemesis Comics, with licensed titles oriented toward adults: superhero *Ultraman* and TV adaptation *SeaQuest*. Montgomery's deals resulted in the live-action films *Casper* and *Richie Rich*, and he also sought to once again pollinate Harvey Comics with existing licenses, from musical group New Kids on the Block to sitcom *Saved by the Bell* to *Back to the Future*, specifically the Saturday morning cartoon series. New Kids on the Block received a treatment similar to that of glut-era Richie Rich, featuring in seven titles from 1990 to 1992, including one-shots and the *Richie Rich and New Kids on the Block* and *Wendy and New Kids on the Block* series.

Montgomery's orientation toward Hollywood would produce ironic results. The live-action *Richie Rich* movie, directed by Donald Petrie and released in theaters in 1994, is extremely faithful to the earliest Richie Rich stories and distills the ideology of the Reggie Van Dough stories into an anxiety over downsizing and loss of unionized American manufacturing jobs. Despite the film's faithfulness, Montgomery did not succeed in all his aims due to the deal with film studio MCA, which directed profits from the film to that studio (Carvell 48): the Harvey Entertainment Group did not see profits from either *Richie Rich* or the successful follow-up, *Casper* (1995) (Eichenwald). The last Richie Rich comic books published by Harvey in North America, *Richie Rich Million Dollar Digest* #34 and *Richie Rich* #28, have the same cover date of November 1994. Harvey's final distribution deal, with Marvel Comics, ended in 1997.

AFTERLIFE WITH RICHIE RICH, 1994–PRESENT

As a business, "Richie Rich" stands for excessive expansion and a crash, followed by three decades of near invisibility. While Richie stories were frequently reprinted in digest form up until 1994, since then the only reprintings have been during an unsuccessful 2011–2012 revival, and the second volume in Dark Horse Comics' Harvey Classics trade paperback series in 2007 (the source of Leslie Cabarga's remark above about stories "rescued" from their original printing). People are not, as a general rule, reading Richie Rich stories, nor have they been in significant numbers since at least the 1980s. The character's transmedia presence seems to prove the rule through exception: a two-season Netflix sitcom beginning in 2015 rearranges the Richie Rich stories to the point where this Richie is a self-made trillionaire for his invention of an environmental energy source, and his interactions with his nonrich father and jealous sister (the comics Richie has no siblings) form major sources of tension. Instead of the wealth-averse Gloria Glad, Richie's best female friend is Jenna Ortega's Darcy, characterized by her improvident spending. Whatever the quality of the series, its divergence from major themes of the comics should underscore that people are not really reading Richie Rich at all, even as they continue to talk about him. It is my contention that this allows for the character's strange afterlife since the mid-1990s.

Scholar Ian Gordon has remarked that in relationship to the culture of consumption in which they were created, "any number of issues of *Richie Rich* . . . could be used to demonstrate a variety of points, such as the dangers of conspicuous consumption, the inappropriateness of using things to gain affection, and the duty of *noblesse oblige* that the very wealthy owe the less well off" ("Culture of Consumption" 160). Gordon explains three possible messages, without discussing any specific Richie Rich story. He notes that the subtitle, "The Poor Little Rich Boy," indicates the theme of conspicuous consumption as being dangerous, but that "on another level, this comic . . . offered a notion of limits in an age of mass consumption, in that the solutions to Richie's problems lay not in material wealth, but in other qualities," and finally that the comic's insistence that material wealth "does not cripple the soul if one has a moral base" is a version of American exceptionalism (160). While Gordon's general remarks are valid readings of *Richie Rich*, and in some ways my reading above demonstrates that all three of his messages (and more) are at play in Richie Rich stories, in practice very little discourse about Richie Rich is interested in Richie for his own sake, preferring to use the fixed (and seemingly stable) idea of Richie to discuss other people and other matters, most prominently former US president Donald Trump.

There is no direct connection between the two—aside from the curious fact that the Trump International Hotel and Tower at 1 Central Park West in New York City is a retrofit of the Gulf+Western Building, which housed Harvey Comics' editorial, advertising, and marketing offices during the 1970s boom. The use of Richie Rich in reference to Donald Trump has very little to do with Trump's career and more with a converging perception of his character and that of Richie Rich. Trump's political career seems to have reversed the exigence of the juxtaposition, turning a useful tool with which to parody Trump and other wealthy Americans into an inability to discuss Richie Rich without invoking Trump. Richie Rich is, after all, not the most well-known wealthy fictional character, nor even the most well-known wealthy cartoon character. Nor is he the harshest portrayal of an exaggeratedly wealthy person, cartoon or otherwise.

A parody of Richie Rich hints at why characters such as Scrooge McDuck or Jay Gatsby are comparatively rarely brought up when Trump is the subject. In the 2000 *Simpsons* episode "Behind the Laughter," the titular cartoon family is the subject of a different reality TV parody. The conceit is that the characters have been playing themselves, and at one point behind-the-scenes events lead to the removal of Bart Simpson from the role of "Bart Simpson." He is replaced by "his good friend" Richie Rich, who is seen pronouncing (a version of) Bart's catchphrase "Don't have a cow, Mother" while effetely dabbing crumbs from his lips using paper money (Groening, "Behind the Laughter" 0.14.11–17). The joke in this entire episode is the idea that the Simpsons have been, unbeknown to us, wrestling with lucrative success, and the tension between remunerative fame and their apparently precarious blue-collar existence is the same one that charges Richie's appearance. *The Simpsons* is consistent in its rare references to Richie, as seen in a 1991 episode in which siblings Bart and Lisa Simpson discuss two Harvey characters:

> BART: I think Casper's the ghost of Richie Rich.
> LISA: Hey . . . they do look alike.
> BART: I wonder how Richie died.
> LISA: Perhaps he realized how hollow the pursuit of money really is and took his own life. (Groening, "Three Men" 0.01.37–46)

The hostility in *The Simpsons* jokes about Richie Rich indicate the prevalence of a hostile reading of Richie Rich. In a tone different from *The Simpsons* jokes, Tim Hensley's 2010 graphic novel (originally serialized in *Mome*) *Wally Gropiu$* primarily spoofs teen comics of the 1960s. The title character, with the appellation "the Umpteen Millionaire," is a pubescent petrochemical magnate who supposedly solves crimes and has adventures, and Hensley parodies the trappings of Richie Rich as part of a surreal and at times horrifying critique of subjects ranging from Archie Comics to Abu Ghraib, the Iraqi prison and site of human rights violations by US Army personnel. In Dan Parent and Fernando Ruiz's comic book series *Die Kitty Die*, a parody of show business by way of parodying Archie's *Sabrina the Teenage Witch* and most of the Harvey roster, Richie Rich is represented by Maxi Millions, a child billionaire with a dollar-sign-shaped cowlick who is simultaneously the actual character and the subject of comic-books-within-the-comic book. In the 2017 graphic novel *Die Kitty Die: Hollywood or Bust*, Maxi Millions is revealed not only to have murdered his parents to gain their inheritance but to actually be an aged child star who was forced to "settle for a career as a third rate comic book character" (83.5). "Millions" is ultimately torn to pieces by the revenant Sammy Showbiz, a version of Richie's pal Jackie Jokers, accompanied by the reanimated corpses of real-life actress Zsa Zsa Gabor and nonfictional comedian Paul Lynde. The hostile reading of Richie Rich seen in these jokes, which position the character as offensively wealthy, surreally entitled, and despicable, underlies the character's use in critiques of Donald Trump.

A lengthier parody in the December 1991 issue of *National Lampoon* suggests a reason why. The story occupies a midway point between a hostile critique of the stereotypically wealthy and a parody of Richie Rich specifically. The issue uses pop culture to spoof class in America: the opening table of contents illustration, using comic characters to suggest a class war, features the dirty Pigpen of Charles Schulz's comic strip *Peanuts* hoisting Richie Rich's head (bearing an unfamiliar sneer) on a stick. The extremely profane parody of *Richie Rich* in the middle of the issue is written by humorist Larry Doyle and drawn by Harvey artist Angelo DeCesare as an exact imitation of the Harvey comics. In a storyline that loosely resembles Tom Wolfe's 1987 novel *The Bonfire of the Vanities*, a sociopathic "Richie Riche" kills a woman of color and her child while driving his car and is arrested for the subsequent killing of a police officer. Richie is sentenced to death "by spanking." Shortly before the sentence is to be carried out by a ludicrous Riche-brand gadget, Richie, who is sobbing that he is "just a poor little rich kid" (page 50, panel 2), is pardoned by the governor, who we discover immediately afterward has been bribed, a situation never to be revealed since Richie's family also owns the media. In the ensuing Letters Page, Richie responds to "reader letters" and displays a total lack of sympathy, in one case insisting that in a previous (nonexistent) story he was right to pursue a thief who had stolen a loaf of bread to feed his starving baby daughter (51), an obvious reference to Victor Hugo's novel *Les Misérables*. The cover of this issue pointedly puts the slogan "HE'S RICH AND YOU'RE NOT" above the logo. This parody demonstrates that as a character consistently portrayed as enormously wealthy, an exaggeration or subversion of the character is a simple way to satirize actual social situations. Unlike Wolfe's *Bonfire of the Vanities*, in which fictional bond trader Sherman McCoy must be established as a figure of privilege before he becomes involved in a racially charged vehicular crime, Richie Rich begins as an easy caricature for a similar concept. Because he is already a caricature of extreme wealth, Richie Rich lends himself to a satirical mobilization of that exaggeration.

Invocations of Richie Rich as a critique of wealth are simply not references to a *narrative* about Richie Rich. Richie's comic adventures do not really license the idea that calling someone "Richie Rich" is a damning insult.

There is a pronounced hostile reading of Richie Rich the character, but this hostile reading of *Richie Rich* is not ultimately a *reading*. It does not engage with the fictional narratives surrounding Richie. The tension in the field of Richie Rich is precisely the gap between the content of Richie Rich narratives and their afterlife as very specific invective. I contend that the majority of people invoking the name of Richie Rich are, counterintuitively, not referring to the character as he appeared in fictional stories, whether the film or the extremely large number of comic books. As this history shows, the various plots of *Richie Rich* involve a complicated relationship to wealth and the appropriate role of the same. There are wealthy malefactors like Reggie; there are people who find ostentatious wealth distasteful like Gloria; there are drawbacks to the relentless pursuit of wealth; there are things more important than money; and there are, as Colón would have it, plots more interesting than inventories of Richie's wealth.

Russell Belk, in his study of different American comics involving "themes of extreme wealth" (26), points out that Richie Rich "might well be known as the world's nicest little boy. Far from being selfish, he uses his wealth to help others" (36); and that the major theme of the *Richie Rich* series is not making wealth, but having it. In Belk's quantitative analysis, Richie was tagged with more positive qualities than the other wealthy characters (Scrooge McDuck, Archie's Veronica Lodge, and the Fox from DC's *The Fox and the Crow*). This, at least, is the impression a human would get if they read a lot of Richie Rich stories. Yet even Belk's quantitative method, drawn from consumer research, is unable to avoid the fact that humans also read something else in Richie Rich: "Despite Richie's prosocial characteristics, coders informally reported less liking for him than for other major comic characters examined" (37). If they're not reading Richie Rich, what are people seeing?

ON NOT READING RICHIE RICH

My methodology in arriving at the above conclusion was to read a large number of Richie Rich stories, much as Bart Beaty does with Archie in his *Twelve-Cent Archie*. Particularly, because they were easiest to find, I consulted Leslie Cabarga's Harvey Classics collection published by Dark Horse Comics in 2007. Since Richie Rich has been out of print for twenty years, this is by far the easiest way to legally read any Richie Rich stories. Circulation of old issues of *Richie Rich* in comic book stores and at conventions is irregular and unreliable. Furthermore, a Beaty-esque project of reading every issue of *Richie Rich* from some period of time would most likely simply conclude that even Richie Rich's adventures—positioned above as his "nonprivileged stories"—are fantasies of white Americans acquiring unclaimed natural resources. The imperial meaning of the character hardly qualifies as subtext: a "sample" story prepared by Ernie Colón to explain the pacing of Richie Rich stories features the character using an American flag to "claim" Bolivia, the story's conflict arising from a Bolivian taking exception with a machete (printed in Arnold, *The Harvey Comics Companion* 465–70). Ultimately, Richie Rich stories are close enough to Disney Duck stories that substantially the same criticisms can be leveled against them as are frequently, and most famously by Ariel Dorfman and Armand Mattelart, deployed to critique Uncle Scrooge. The major complicating distinction is that Uncle Scrooge is never as central a character as Richie Rich, and more importantly, he is rarely intended to be as sympathetic as Richie. Richie Rich is manifestly intended to capture our sympathy.

The Richie Rich problem is that despite the surface level of all his stories, Richie is the subject of considerably more hostility than Scrooge McDuck, who is enormously esteemed, even widely beloved. It is not so much that the critiques of Richie Rich found on Twitter do not approach the level of sophistication of Dorfman and Mattelart's Marxist analysis. The problem is that these critiques seem to be of an entirely different character. Dorfman and Mattelart rightly argue that a major feature of these kinds of comics is the way they disguise ideology as "non-ideological" children's stories, and this disguise is a subtext of the *National Lampoon* parody, in which Richie Rich proclaims that he is "just" a poor little rich kid as he's about to be executed for his crimes. However, to read social media discourse about Richie Rich, nobody has been fooled by this disguise. The hostile or ironic reading of Richie Rich is overwhelmingly the popular reading. It is, further, difficult to believe that most people have formulated a Marxist critique based on close readings of Richie Rich stories. Studying the Richie Rich problem in more detail suggests an entirely different method of reading.

The problem of these divergent readings is applicable to other texts. Paul Davis distinguishes between a narrative and its reappearances in later popular culture, coining the term "culture-text" to refer to texts that live far outside their narrative. As Davis suggests with the example of Charles Dickens's novel *A Christmas Carol*, texts can come to be "about" different things through adaptation:

> Each period re-creates the story in response to its own cultural needs. Each contributes to the evolving culture-text of the Carol by re-reading Dickens' words and imagining its own text for the Carol....

For the meaning of the Carol is not determined by the words of the author. Its meaning is created anew by each generation of readers. (13)

Pointing out that this is not unusual, Davis argues that the meaning of all literary works emerges from the interaction between "text and culture-text, from the versions of the story created by its readers" (13). Studying the culture-text clarifies the reading process that these readers are engaged in. This has a particular significance for comics studies, in that Western comics typically consist of enormous bodies of text that comparatively few readers have studied in any detail or completeness, meaning that characters and narratives frequently exist very far away from any original. Cumulative close reading, as Davis engages in, is one way to perceive a culture-text, but comic books have generally circulated not as a beloved classic adapted through the ages but rather as an enormous number of consumer items encountered in childhood. A more distant methodology, less focused on secret meanings and more on aggregated effects, is a new way to look at an enormous archive and perceive what cannot be seen in a collection of stories. Furthermore, the object of discussion here is slightly different from "the total of all Richie Rich stories." After all, those stories evince a suspicion and wariness that tallies quite closely to critiques of Richie Rich: while Richie Rich never becomes a drug addict in the comics, the idea that "money doesn't mean a happy life" is the explicit moral of a great number of Richie Rich stories. In the stories of Richie Rich, Richie is embedded in a variety of generic narratives. But no one, when calling Donald Trump Richie Rich, is implying that Trump has fought supervillains, or that he would rather be playing baseball, or that oil rains down upon him in the middle of vacations like a petrochemical Midas. Where is this other Richie Rich? In the stories we see Richie frustrated, perturbed, gleeful, triumphant over Reggie, embarrassed about Gloria, terrified at gunpoint. In parodies we see him sneer. But where exactly is Richie Rich smug?

While Paul Davis maintains that culture-texts can come to be "about" different matters than the original text, that explanation sheds no light on why Richie Rich, a text with few adaptations, has a culture-text radically opposed to the original text. While the uptake of Richie Rich is nothing like the elaborate, continuing life of *A Christmas Carol*, it consists of a development (the rejection of the text's ambiguities) suggestive less of later ironies and more of immediate repurposing. The landscape of parodies, jokes, and tweets that make up the hostile reading is an ongoing adaptation of Richie Rich, playing off an existing element of the stories by closing off one dimension of the relatively complex narrative. Unlike *A Christmas Carol*, what is adapted with Richie Rich is a set of recurring ideas rather than any one fixed narrative: in the hostile reading, references to specific Richie Rich narratives are far and few between. What is referenced when Richie Rich is invoked—in parodies, in casual conversation—is not the sum of the stories that a human could find through reading Richie Rich. In fact, since 1994 essentially no one has read new Richie Rich, and few read the stories for some time before that. When we do look at Richie Rich stories, the picture suggested is extremely different from the character's afterlife as a culture-text. Faced with the puzzle of Richie Rich's movement through popular culture with no actual narrative attached, distant reading of the *object* Richie Rich rather than the stories will reveal what we collectively know about Richie.

For the purposes of studying comic books like *Richie Rich*, a scholar is faced with a very large but complete corpus. There are 1,723 individual comic books published in the *Richie Rich* line from 1960 to 1994, and they all contain some consistent sites of visual meaning.

To perceive the variance of ideas being projected onto Richie Rich, one particular visual element of every Richie Rich cover, his face, appears most relevant. His face appears on all 1,723 Richie Rich–branded covers published from 1960 to 1994, as regular a part of his brand as his name. Isolating Richie's face, we can see that it conveniently consists of a very limited number of elements, altered and rearranged to produce different effects. Even though several artists drew Richie Rich in this period, the visual variations are in terms of line rather than basic approaches. This effect paradoxically enhances the minute differences even while the similarities are overwhelming. That paradox is probably the case for all recurring characters, but with Richie Rich the effect is enhanced by the consistency and simplicity of Harvey's house style. The 1990s run of Richie Rich covers often simply used art from covers from thirty years earlier, because the artistic style had changed so little.

The major elements of Richie Rich's face are his eyes, his mouth, his eyebrows, and his teeth. Richie's eyes being open, closed, or half-lidded, or the two eyes being different, would all produce different expressions and "count" as different faces regardless of the other elements. In terms of eyes, there are therefore three different eye expressions possible within the observed system of Richie's face. Including the possibility of eyes being different, there are five. If we were to include the distinction between left and right eyes as being significant, we would have seven.

Each element produces another exponential set of possible faces. His eyebrows can be curved downward, or upward, or in two different directions. Combined with the eyes, this indicates twenty-one possible faces. If we consider which eyebrow is curved upward or downward as significant, we have twenty-eight possible faces. If we include a lower diagonal, then we have another twenty-eight faces possible. Of course, these elements are based on the observed faces. In fact, it would be quite possible to draw Richie Rich with his eyebrows straight across, or with no eyebrows at all, or with four eyebrows for that matter.[2] One further piece of evidence for the small-*c* conservatism of Richie Rich's art style is that a great many possible faces never appeared on the cover of any issue. Overlooking the possibilities that were never used at all in the corpus of Richie Rich faces focuses the study on trends within Richie Rich and not Richie Rich's participation in or lack of participation in trends outside the series.

These four elements presented significant variation, but they were still tempered by the remarkably limited set of differences in the actual history of Richie Rich. In the Richie Rich cover corpus, there are twelve different ways to draw Richie's mouth, ranging from a horizontal line to a full circle, from a whistle created by portraying his lips to blowing on a horn, shown by the sudden appearance of his cheeks. Again, while there are a great many ways to represent a human mouth, only twelve of them ever appear on Richie Rich's face in this corpus. These mouths include Richie's occasional jowl, his chin (which appears in two mouths), and the varieties of his mouth that include his teeth.

By far, "positive" mouths outnumber "negative" varieties; or, mouths that are curved upward outnumber those that curve downward. Furthermore, the "tags" or categories of faces strongly emphasize the mouth as the site of variation. We have not yet seen what face predominates, nor have we seen the history of Richie's many faces, but there has already been interpretation. Finally, even only counting the limited elements in the observed features of Richie Rich, there are 480 possible faces. Only 43 different Richie faces, however, ever appeared on the cover of *Richie Rich* comic books.

In the interiors of issues, due partially to the exponentially larger sample size, one would expect more variation, and a casual look at any given issue, where we see perhaps 120 instances of Richie's face, suggests that this is true. On the covers, it would seem that there was a very distinct set of limitations on the artists. We could see this as a further testament to their artistic conservatism or desire to avoid experimentation and variety—to keep the brand as stable as possible. In other words, there is a consistency to Richie Rich's facial expression that begins to suggest what the character means to those who perhaps never read his stories but saw many of his covers.

This method turns Richie's face into a series of permutations. For example, a Richie Rich with his eyebrows curved up, his eyes wide open, his mouth a circle, and his teeth absent, would indicate an expression of surprise. If the first three elements were the same but his mouth was curved downward, it would indicate much the same emotion but with a slight edge of dismay because it would add a frown to the other elements. As it happens, the former of these was the eighth face encountered (appearing first in July 1964), while the latter is the twelfth (appearing first in October 1967).

Even these simple elements generated a possible 480 faces. Many of these never occurred in the corpus. Some of them are impossible: if Richie's mouth is absent, his teeth cannot also be shown. Yet there are many possible faces that do not appear: for example, there are no covers of Richie Rich where his face is drawn with his eyes closed and his mouth absent. There are covers where his eyes are closed and he is smiling (the first of these appears in July 1961). Already this analysis has determined that there are several Richie Rich faces that never appeared on the covers of his comic books, an absence that would be difficult to perceive or verify without distant reading.

Assigning a number to each face in the order in which it appeared on the covers creates a visualization of the covers. This transformed the covers of Richie Rich from a sequence of images into a sequence of numbers, each reflecting a different combination of Richie's facial elements. Because the numbers are in chronological order, ordinal and chronological order are heavily correlated. In figure 3.1, the first data point appears in the lower left-hand corner because Richie's face on *Richie Rich* #1 is also Face #1, although there is no particular reason that it should be so except that by doing this the graph becomes a history (again, only of covers, since Richie first appeared seven years previous to *Richie Rich* #1). While this reflects the fact that Richie Rich covers were released in a sequence, it does not have any meaning in hindsight, particularly now that the archive is no longer necessarily encountered in this order.

The other side of this decision is that the graph shows more exceptional faces at the top, because now the *x*-axis is time and the *y*-axis is not just the number of faces but also their order of appearance.

Several anomalies are fairly clear on this graph: the gap in data points around August 1984, for example, represents Harvey's publishing hiatus between 1982 and 1986. Faces 37 through 43 each only ever appear once. The greatest variation in faces occurs in the second half of the 1970s; two-thirds of all faces Richie Rich would ever evince appear between 1974 and 1981, the height of the glut. The significance of different shades of gray is that the data comes from different *Richie Rich* series, and this graph therefore also indicates no significant correlation between any given series and any set of faces, with some anomalies, such as Face #26, which only ever appeared in one series over a span of several years, or Face #12, which in the early 1990s

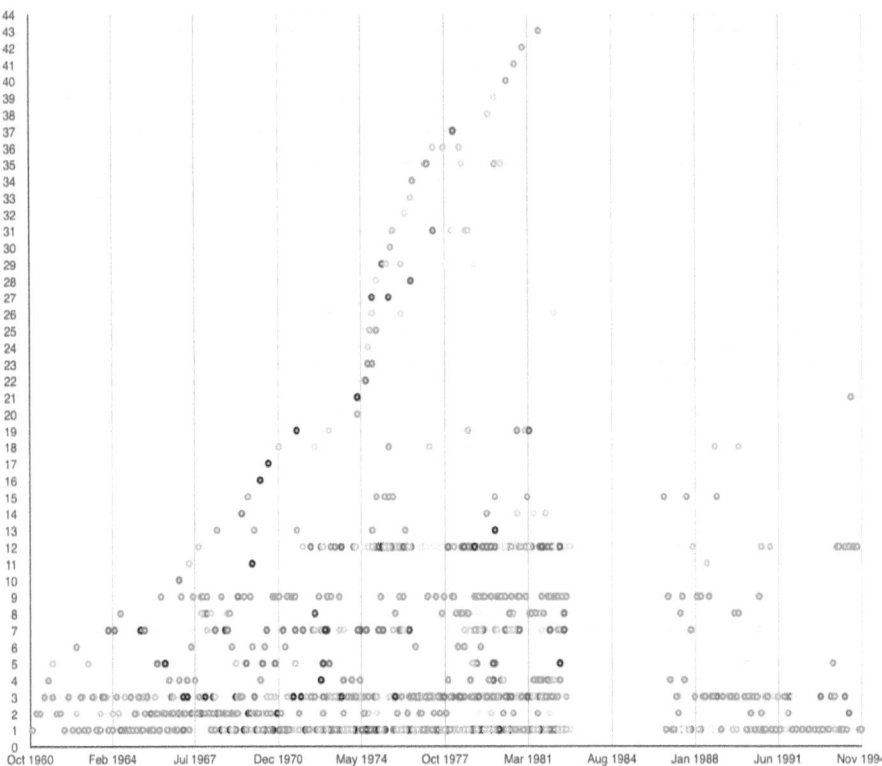

Figure 3.1. Richie Rich faces on comic book covers over time.

seems to have only appeared in one series. In practice, there is some correlation (nearly every cover of $upeRi¢hie, in which Richie is a superhero, has him scowling), but not a strong one (that face does appear elsewhere).

Probably the most significant anomaly is, in fact, the history of Face #12. Despite being the twelfth face ever in evidence on the cover of *Richie Rich*, not appearing until nearly seven years into the publishing history here, it becomes as densely common in the 1970s as the first three faces, with occurrences happening more than once every month. Within this line, we can also see a period ending in October 1977 in which only one series appears to be carrying Face #12s. This stands out as significant, in other words, even without knowing what emotion is displayed using Face #12.

Consulting the codebook, it turns out that Face #12 is eyebrows curved out, eyes wide open, no teeth, and the mouth open but curved downward—it is, in fact, fear. After first appearing in 1967, this expression became extremely prominent in several consecutive issues in the mid-1970s. Beginning in issues cover-dated May 1975, almost all the covers of the seventeen series Harvey was publishing under the *Richie Rich* name bear Face #12, lasting until September of that year. This Summer of Fear seems to be an extraordinary moment in the history of Richie Rich. It seems suggestive of a major creative and editorial course change, presumably related to Ernie Colón's epiphany about how to tell Richie Rich stories. This coincides, indeed, with the majority of Colón's work for Harvey: he was a freelancer with them from 1955 to 1980 but does not seem to have drawn stories until the early to mid-1960s. Whether the change to covers was meant to signal a change in the inside contents, or whether it reflected a change that had taken place sometime before, the Summer of Fear is interesting because it indicates the most significant generic shift in all of Richie Rich's covers. In total, 196 covers out of 1,723 carry Face #12, making it the third most common face in the Richie Rich cover corpus. Despite the fact that in fall 1975 these covers went away, they soon returned: the period in 1977 when Face #12 was only appearing in one series was due to the continued publication (beginning in November 1974) of *Richie Rich Vault$ of Mystery*, a thriller-themed series. Unlike the contemporary series *Richie Rich Gem$* (September 1974) and *Richie Rich Profit$* (October 1974), which also began with runs of Face #12, *Vault$ of Mystery* persisted even after the July through October 1976 period, when no Face #12 appeared anywhere in the now twenty *Richie Rich* series. By 1978 and 1979, Face #12 was again appearing intermittently across the line, though after the 1982–1986 hiatus, it was unusually slow to reappear. In the context of the rapidly expanding number of *Richie* series, usually pointed to as the reason for Harvey's financial troubles and suspension of all publications, the role of Face #12 suggests that generic experimentation, followed by a cautious retreat and a gradual resumption, was an aesthetic method to turn a profit, just as multiplying titles was a publishing method for the same purpose—this would appear to be, in fact, a graph of a linewide fad.

Two anomalous covers are worth noting. The covers of *Richie Rich $ucce$$ Stories* #43 (April 1972) and *Richie Rich Vault$ of Mystery* #11 (July 1976) both present an insoluble problem for this tagging system. On the covers of both, Richie Rich is represented by multiple faces because both covers portray a transformation by showing Richie's ordinary state, a transitional state, and then the ultimate result. On *Vault$ of Mystery* #11, Richie is transforming into an infant, going from an expression of shock to his standard smile. Each of these expressions is already accounted for in the tagging system, but it's unclear how to record this issue. On *$ucce$$ Stories* #43, a Richie who is happily drinking a milkshake is transformed into an immense Mister Hyde–like monster. While the "first" expression is standard, the expression of the monster—red circles in his eyes and a smile from which fangs protrude—is entirely without precedent in other covers.[3] Predictably enough given the split between covers and interior art, even the monstrous Richie on the cover of $ucce$$ Stories #43 is a good deal less grotesque than the character in the story.

The general import of these covers is clear: Richie is being menaced by some transformation. Both covers are part of the trend toward "adventure" in the 1970s series, and they are explicable with reference to the major shift epitomized by the region of Face #12, the Summer of Fear.

As significant as the anomalies of Face #12 and the "Jekyll and Hyde" cover are, the more valuable part of this graph for my original inquiry is instead the most common faces, clustered at the bottom of the graph and also appearing at the far left. These are the faces that appeared first and most often, and in the context of the *Richie Rich* line, those are the same thing. Quite aside from the general shape suggesting that the character was fully conceptualized in 1960 after his many appearances in *Little Dot*, and that while experiments like the Summer of Fear would occur but only as deviations from the still-dominant faces 1, 2, and 3, they also suggest the "average" Richie Rich face. Face #1, for example, appears on 898 covers—more than half, more than all other Richie Rich faces combined. Face #2 only appears 89 times but is still the fourth most common Richie Rich face, while Face #3, the second most common, appears 245 times. The vast majority of Richie Rich faces, in other words, are Faces #1 and #3, with #2 notably less.

The graph privileges two obvious features in addition to limiting itself to Richie's faces. It privileges a chronological sequence, and the most common face of Richie Rich. At the bottom of the graph we can see that these happily correspond. In other words, the first face that Richie Rich presented on the cover of *Richie Rich* #1 would become his most common face for the next thirty years of *Richie Rich* covers. Although the character Richie Rich predates his first cover appearance on *Richie Rich* #1 by seven years, and one would expect the brand to be correspondingly stable by its first cover appearance, this fact still underscores the simplicity and conservatism of the covers.

The art within issues of *Richie Rich* displayed considerably more variation, and it is entirely believable that even a flagship character like Richie could have been drawn with more variation. As the example of the monstrous Richie above implies, the standard Richie Rich style (or Harvey style, for it was consistent across the publisher's children's output) could even suggest what a "monster" version of Richie Rich would look like, while the monster in the actual comic bears only the faintest indications of being a version of Richie Rich. In other words, the covers are perhaps the most consistent and least experimental aspect of a generally standard style. This has more to do with consistency (across time and titles) in portrayals of Richie and his main cast than consistency across different characters within the stories.

Several primary sources indicate that visual consistency was implemented for ease of drawing. Artist Howie Post explained Richie's character design as a principle borrowed from animation, suggesting that Casper and Richie Rich don't so much look like each other as that they both look like a figure who is easy to draw repeatedly because they are interchangeable (81). Warren Kremer, the artist most associated with Richie Rich's standard style, admitted that he designed a formula to draw the character: a circular head with open eyes, onto which any expression could be created (Janocha 67). Kremer indicated that his own work was an imitation of his mentor Steve Muffatti, the earliest Richie artist, who had been an animator previously (Benson 47). Critic Ken Parille has observed that Harvey's house style is

> perhaps the longest-running "look" in the history of American comic books, lasting from the 1940s through the '80s . . . far more visually and thematically coherent than that of any other American comics publisher.

Later artists would retain Richie's design while varying their own style, depending on the genre. Within most Richie "adventure" stories (a category that includes stories in the horror and superhero traditions), there is a notable contrast between the style in which Richie and his main cast are drawn, and the style in which the other characters appear. Looking at a story like the Colón-drawn "Mutiny on the Oceanic," there is a striking difference between Richie (and Gloria) and other characters. Colón, in fact, seems to play up this difference, focusing on Manta's face in particular.

However, rather than look at exceptions, the graph in figure 3.1 should make clear the preponderance of the norm. The covers from the Summer of Fear change style dramatically and very noticeably in a very short span of time, drawing our attention away from Face #1. What this distant reading shows is instead the most common element of the corpus. In this case, it is Richie Rich, happy.

Over the course of his stories, Richie Rich is often fearful, neurotic, surprised, confused, worried, or sad. These emotions are rarely ever present on his covers. Setting aside the many theoretical faces that never appeared at all, sixteen of the forty-three observed faces only ever appeared once. Although the tag "the Poor Little Rich Boy" suggests that emotions like sorrow or envy are a basic part of the character, in fact feelings of joy and happiness overwhelmingly predominate. Yet the less common expressions on Richie Rich's face on his covers in fact exemplify the range of emotions that arise in the stories within. Within the narratives, a variety of things happen to Richie, and he expresses a range of emotions.

But Richie Rich on the covers of *Richie Rich* is essentially always happy. This is also significant because on essentially all covers, he is in the presence of wealth, while the stories often place him in ordinary settings or even deprivation. In other words, the Richie Rich of the covers luxuriates in a way that the Richie of the stories seldom does.

The ultimate significance of the Richie Rich covers is in the context of their material circulation. Between 1960 and 1994, the newsstand market for comic books in North America (a market understood to include venues such as supermarkets, grocery stores, gas stations, drugstores, and all establishments not primarily dedicated to selling comic books) collapsed, with comic books coming to be primarily distributed through the direct market. This was accompanied with a precipitous decline in readership, but also a redefinition of comic books from being a general medium associated with children toward one largely monopolized by older readers. While some comic books continue to be sold at the "newsstand" (now usually a supermarket or convenience store), the shift was disastrous for Richie Rich.

Richie Rich's decreased popularity in the 1980s can be seen as a consequence of Harvey's oversaturation of the market with the Richie Rich product, or later, more nebulous business decisions made in the 1990s. It can also be seen as evidence that the title was "left behind" in the older distribution system,[4] available to comics' more traditional audience, at a time when the medium in North America was undergoing significant structural shifts. As can be seen from these structural factors, the Richie Rich product was never marketed directly to Richie Rich fans as opposed to general audiences, and it was never primarily distributed in venues defined by a self-selecting interest in comic books.

In other words, from 1960 to 1994, Richie Rich was a product in the context of newsstands and grocery stores. This means that the cover of any given issue of *Richie Rich* was likely seen by large numbers of people, some of whom went on to buy and/or read the issue, and some of whom did not. Part of the "audience" of *Richie Rich* covers would be people whose engagement with comic books was limited to seeing them while shopping for unrelated items. What we see when we look at the covers of *Richie Rich* appears to be the covers of comic books, and they are that, but they are also the fronts of products intended for display in supermarkets. In the context of a bookstore, *Richie Rich* has covers; in the context of a supermarket, it has packaging. The element that distinguishes the two is properly considered the brand of Richie Rich.

The use of Richie Rich to criticize Donald Trump derives from a resemblance between the two characters. It is not the superficial similarities of their "narratives" (inherited wealth, distinctive hair) that has caused this, but rather the similarity in their brands. More pointedly, because they both have experienced the same brand of success, they are both vulnerable to the same negative brand, of appearing smug, spoiled, or out of touch. The claim that Donald Trump, as @ShaynessMac says, *is* Richie Rich fifty years later underlines the strength of the association. What affords this allusion is the brand of Richie Rich as distinct from his narrative, a brand that is itself allowed by the material context of Richie Rich's circulation as a physical product in historical context. Stories that are also products turn the characters into brands. Distant reading enables us to perceive the brand: what all those humans in all those grocery stores simultaneously know about Richie Rich. The materiality of Richie Rich as, ultimately, a product in a supermarket is revealed by this analysis, and the method of physical circulation and material context reveals a different aspect of the text.

In other words, the Richie Rich brand is simplistic and arguably toxic. The most stripped-down narrative of Richie's stories involves him showing a friend, and the reader, some variety of gadget or trick made possible by colossal wealth; this is more or less the only image that ever appears on the covers, unleavened by Hergé-style adventure. Puns about value are as constant as his cover companions as images of gold, currency, oil, paper, and general excess. Satires of the character, and satires using the character, make use of this side-effect of the character's material circulation—he is shorthand for a dislikable, privileged, and smug heir.

A short-lived revival of the character, by Ape Entertainment in 2011–2012, underscores this point by contrast. Emphasizing the adventure element, the covers of this series hardly present the character as wealthy at all. Although it did not succeed, this attempt takes the only approach that could possibly defeat the legacy of the Richie Rich brand, by representing the more easily acclaimed Colón-style content of the stories. Richie Rich, in a sense, is a casualty of the material conditions of midcentury American comic books. He is so inextricably associated with his own mass market packaging, with a wider audience than any of his comics, that it would take tremendous effort to rescue him from his position as the smuggest rich boy in the cultural trash heap. While stories about Richie Rich presented a varied and complex relationship to value, that complexity is almost always trumped by the very simple relationship to value present in Harvey's marketing.

In theory, the quality of Richie's stories, and particularly the work of auteurs-in-waiting like Ernie Colón (who, foreshadowing this move, is discussed frequently here despite the fact that most Richie Rich stories are uncredited), creator Warren Kremer, and even long-time editor Sid Jacobson, could be used to reposition the character in future printings. Perhaps if Harvey had used Hergé-style covers and the album format, rather than supermarket digests in which Richie bathes in pools of money, the poor little rich boy wouldn't still be a prisoner of comics' historical low place in American culture. However, even the potential of a Barks-style salvage operation (and continuing efforts at transmedia success) means that Richie Rich does not truly epitomize the long shadow of American comics' trashy materiality. For that, we need a comic where trash is part of the brand.

Chapter 4

TRASH CULTURE
Dubble Bubble Funnies and the Theory of Premium Comics

Dubble Bubble Funnies are a series of comics published on 2 by 2½ inch pieces of waxed paper attached to the inside of the wrapping of individual pieces of Dubble Bubble Gum; in the late 2010s they were priced at 10¢ each and manufactured by Concord Confections, a division of Tootsie Roll Industries. Since 1950, *Dubble Bubble Funnies*, formerly *Fleer Funnies*, have centered around the character of Pud, a boy in a striped shirt. Pud's narratives circulate in an unusual material form that strongly encourages the reader to consider them to be garbage: the comic serves as wrapper for the gum, and the reader will likely throw it away once they get the gum. Some comments about gum even indicate that the wrapper is to be used to wrap the gum after chewing, as shown by journalist Beatrice Trum Hunter's remark that "[d]isposal of chewing gum can be done easily in the original wrapper" (Hunter 22). The circulation of the comic as wrapper changes the meaning of the text. Furthermore, just as candy is a product that troubles the boundary between food and junk, comics' historical association with trash prompts an acknowledgment of the way trash, candy, and comics have been culturally bound together as categories of junk. The packaging of comics with candy makes obvious the shared status of these materials in consumer culture, and this association also demands a serious consideration of the conceptual category of "premium comics": comics that are circulated as marketing.

For Carl Barks's Uncle Scrooge stories, the physical changes from pamphlet to hardcover form signify a shift in the cultural capital of Barks's work; similarly, the publisher's construction of the value of Alan Moore and Dave Gibbons's *Watchmen* involves decades-long adjustments within the "bookness" of *Watchmen*'s materiality. Comics have also circulated in forms other than the comic book, forms where the absence of "codexité" is the defining feature. Comics offered as "premiums"—inducements to consumers to purchase items—are an undertheorized material form of comics, where the cultural values associated with the materiality of "the book" or "the magazine" are replaced by the visibility of consumer culture in such marketing schemes, and by the related concept of trash. In the only academic discussion of bubble gum comics to date, Ian Hague's analysis of the way that the comics are experienced by the senses acknowledges that some comics are associated with a particular food and taste, noting Topps Gum's character Bazooka Joe (141), and that the comic's identity includes the taste of the bubble gum. His remark that "the comic's edible content can be consumed fully without the entirety of the comic being destroyed" (138), to distinguish bubble gum comics from comics that can actually be physically consumed, suggests that one way to look at bubble gum comics is as a text and a food that are independent of each other and come to be associated through packaging, one of several ways that "comics come to be associated with particular food products" (143). Beyond observing that eating and reading of these two objects are associated with each other by the Topps corporation, Hague does not offer a reading of Bazooka Joe comics. The specific *way* that the gum (as an edible product) and comics (as wrapping for that product) are bound together creates a theoretical space that lets us read certain bubble gum comics themselves as ambivalent about consumer culture.

Because bubble gum comics are related to the way that candy, comics, and garbage function in consumer culture, it is necessary to first understand how these ambiguous, liminal categories work in such a culture. The categorization of comics as "junk"—whether food or culture or in the form of actual garbage—is not a tragic or undesirable flaw in the history of comics but instead an important part of comics materiality. Because *Dubble Bubble Funnies* circulate as part of the wrapping of bubble gum, their use of humor to portray the life of the main character Pud becomes a negotiation of the tension between a moralistic idea of gluttony, and the need for artifacts of consumer culture to sanction mass consumption. For my case study, the corpus is a one-kilogram bucket containing 175 pieces of 10¢ Dubble Bubble gum, purchased at a wholesale retailer in mid-2017.

It should be noted that the unusual physical form of bubble gum comics makes it enormously difficult to treat artifacts such as *Dubble Bubble Funnies* as texts. Rather than being "serialized" in the sense that episodes are periodically distributed through retailers, the comics that make up *Dubble Bubble Funnies* are distributed more or less randomly, whether purchased wholesale or individually.

GUMS AND PREMIUMS

The history of Pud, the Dubble Bubble gum of which he is the mascot, and the Fleer Corporation, which created and originally produced both, can be established from outside the text and provides a useful anthropology of gum. The practice of chewing plant products such as bark and resin can be found in many cultures since before recorded history (Mathews 36), but the industrial product of chewing gum is specifically based on indigenous Mesoamerican practices related to the natural latex exuded by the *chicozapote* or sapodilla tree of the Yucatán Peninsula (Mathews 5). Little information is available concerning the history of the local Maya culture's use of *itz*, the natural product, to create *cha*, a chewed substance (Mathews 6). More information is available about the cultural place of *tzictli* (and a natural bitumen-adulterated variety, *chapapote*) in the Nahua culture, because early Spanish chroniclers discuss the subject (as "chicle"), albeit from a recognizably European and moralistic perspective. One explains that "the chewing of chicle [is] the preference, the privilege of little girls, the small girls, the young women" who "chew chicle in order not to be detested" because it scents the mouth, and also notes "the addicts termed 'Effeminates' . . . and the men who publicly chew chicle achieve the status of sodomites; they equal the effeminates" (quoted in Mathews 8). The cultural place of gum is linked to religious practice: Jennifer Mathews notes that in visual portrayals of the feminine goddess Tlazōlteōtl, in her aspect as a purifier, she is "frequently portrayed with bitumen on her face and around her mouth, further emphasizing gum in general as a feminine symbol" (10). One epithet of this broom-wielding goddess, "Tlalquanai," refers to her eating filth to cleanse a person, just as the name "Tlazōlteōtl" literally means something like "filth goddess" (DiCesare 118). In Nahua cosmology, anthropologist Catherine R. DiCesare argues, the same "numinous, ambivalent" force stood for (among other things) filth, sex, sin, purity, cleansing, and the eating of gum (110). Scholars have also suggested that the other gum-chewing culture of Mesoamerica, the Mayan, inspired the figure of Tlazōlteōtl with the thinly reported goddess Ix Hun Ahau, who may also "eat" sickness and filth (Knowlton 326). From an anthropological perspective, the physical fact that chicle (and its later synthetic imitators) is a substance "used up" in chewing links it to liminal ideas of food and waste; it is not surprising that more than one culture would treat gum this way. This purifying waste was mediated by Tlazōlteōtl/Tlalquanai and her earthly followers, who included prostitutes. Because the American practice of chewing gum (and later bubble gum) is directly descended from the Mexican practice, it is worth noting that the link between gum and cycles of "filth" and "cleaning" predates the industrial production of gum in the United States. The later American adoption of this substance replaces Tlazōlteōtl/Tlalquanai with the also ambivalent force of consumerism to negotiate the treatment of this physical substance.

Despite originating in Mexico and Central America, in the twentieth century chewing gum became inextricably associated with the United States. In Donna Gabaccia's history of turn-of-the-twentieth-century struggles over what foods "became" American, she points out the curious fact that "[w]hat makes foods American—at least to outsiders—is how they are produced, packaged, and served, not who manufactures or eats them or how they taste" (175). Gabaccia's research points to xenophobia as an underrated determinant in what foods became quintessentially American, but she locates this xenophobia on the personal level; that is, it is directed at the actual owners of food production businesses. Despite the fact that the practice of chicle chewing is Mexican—and moreover, apparently introduced to Americans by General Antonio López de Santa Anna, a significant and infamous figure in American culture (Redclift 25)—and that almost all chicle was obtained from Mexico until the 1950s, gum managed to instead become associated with American rather than Mexican culture. The case could be made that because gum was popular *in* America, it was associated with Americans. This would shed light on practices such as the inclusion of gum in World War II army rations (the "Assault Lunch" described by Redclift, 133), presumably motivated by gum's popularity in the United States but also becoming a self-fulfilling prophecy by putting gum into the hands of Americans sent overseas to represent their country (Redclift 146). According to candy historian David Carr, during the Second World War, the National Confectioners Association of America "poured $1 million into a 1944 campaign to promote the link between candy and those brave American GIs" (67). Chewing gum as a specific kind of food now had a particular cultural association with American identity.

The product with which *Dubble Bubble Funnies* is associated, bubble gum, has a further cultural specificity as a subset of gum. Strangely, the concept of bubble gum seems to have preceded its technological attainment, possibly tracing back to the concept of preincluding the "wet" quality of chewed chewing gum (Stewart 113). Bubble gum was successfully concocted in 1928 by Walter Diemer, an accountant for the Fleer Corporation of Philadelphia. Diemer's gum was softer and stretchier than regular gum, and, as intended, made it possible to blow bubbles. Sold under the name Dubble Bubble and manufactured in Fleer's Philadelphia plant from 1930 to 1995 ("Fleer Closes Philadelphia Plant"), the gum (and just as importantly, Diemer's failure to patent his formula) inspired the entire "bubble gum" category of candy

(Jamieson 50). Gum in general is widely seen as exemplary of nineteenth-century American culture's fixations on regularity and gratification. As Michael Redclift puts it, "Chewing gum celebrates a bodily function in an immediately pleasing way, unlike many other forms of consumption that are more indirect but are no less necessary" (34). Marketing is extremely important in the history of bubble gum as a variety of chewing gum: "There were so few intrinsic qualities to gum that developing extrinsic ones became a competitive industry: in fact, chewing gum demonstrated anything the consumer wanted it to demonstrate" (Redclift 124). While chewing bubble gum, the consumer can blow bubbles, which does not change the taste but produces a frivolous experience. Bubble gum, in contrast to most food products and even chewing gum, affords the possibility of unproductive play; it is inherently associated in American culture with the activities of children. The product around which *Dubble Bubble Funnies* are wrapped is therefore understood to be an unusually frivolous and childish subset of a particularly American product.

Being a particular kind of gum, bubble gum is also a particular kind of candy, a category that occupies its own ambivalent cultural place. Samira Kawash argues that candy in general must be understood as a specific kind of food. In the late nineteenth century, mechanized production caused a fall in the price of sugar and an ensuing rise in cheap candy—with an accompanying reassociation of the now cheap products first with women and then with children (Wendy Woloson, quoted in Kawash 17). Driven by novelty, increasingly complex candy-making machines, and a hygienic push for individual wrappings, candy in the early twentieth century became a site of moral panic, particularly concerning children as consumers. The paradigmatic case of Necco Wafers reveals their interaction. Packaged together in newly possible paper wrappers to assure customers that shopkeepers were unable to contaminate the wafers before purchase, the brand name of the New England Confectionary Company became "part of the reassurance. . . . [W]rapping, branding, and advertising were what transformed the generic 1850s catalog of candy sticks and gumdrops into the twentieth-century candy lexicon of Necco Wafers and Hershey bars" (Kawash 154). Sold cheaply to children in public spaces, candy became associated with a new form of consumerism, and the concept of "junk food" came to occupy a role in food culture similar to that of "waste" in civic culture: an unpleasant by-product of the meaningful main business of society. Paraphrasing Tim Richardson, Kawash notes that candy exists in a "culinary limbo": "Candy isn't a staple or a necessity, it isn't part of ordinary meals or food rituals, and most of the time it isn't even considered food. When it's eaten with a meal, it's given its own separate category (dessert) and when eaten at other times of day, it becomes a snack, as if calling it something else means it doesn't really count" (16). "Snack" and "dessert" function as labels to make candy a kind of food without collapsing it into any existing category—similar to the way that the category of "trash" functions to make cultural sense of waste products.

In the case of *Dubble Bubble Funnies,* the similarity of "junk food" like candy and "trash" as a category is particularly important because the *Funnies* are a kind of trash—specifically, they are disposable marketing, an inducement for consumers. The marketing of bubble gum has involved items like the *Funnies* for a very long time. From the 1930s onward (parallel to the autonomous existence of comic books), Dubble Bubble came packaged in wrappers printed with *Fleer Funnies,* a color comic strip. In 1947, the rival Topps Chewing Gum Company of New York began to sell bubble gum wrapped in comics featuring Bazooka the Atom Boy, a dual reference to weapons of the recently ended war. Bazooka was, distinctly, a superhero, who used magic gum to resolve dangerous situations. In 1949, Bazooka was redesigned as Bazooka Joe, a more distinctive character thanks partially to his eyepatch, in imitation of contemporary advertising icon "the man in the Hathaway shirt" (Topps Company, *Bazooka Joe* 55). In 1950, Fleer introduced Pud, a rotund boy in a striped shirt.

Pud first resembled the comic strip, cartoon, and comic book character Tubby. Created by cartoonist Marjorie "Marge" Buell in her *Saturday Evening Post* comic strip *Little Lulu,* Tubby was popular enough to receive his own comic book series by John Stanley from 1952 to 1962 (Horn, *100 Years* 485–86). Unlike Tubby, Pud became slimmer in the 1960s. Bubble gum companies associated themselves with numerous existing characters—at various points, Topps licensed Carl Anderson's silent newspaper strip *Henry* as well as Al Capp's *Lil' Abner,* and Topps imprint Blony Gum would reprint *Archie* strips—but, having originated in premiums, Bazooka Joe and Pud are by far the most distinctive characters to emerge from comic strips attached to gum.

Pud and Bazooka Joe are mascots, a category of fictional character taking root at the beginning of consumer culture. The majority of mascots originate from outside the product they endorse and function by creating an intertextual association between the product and the text being referenced. The issue of narratives and licensing seems to be a straightforward one when discussing examples of "endorsement," where the product can be positioned in terms of an existing narrative. An Amos 'n' Andy candy bar, for example, develops a brand from being associated with the ongoing radio and television shows, but the candy bar doesn't have an obvious relationship to any specific narrative in either show. Instead, the bar is presented as the kind of thing Amos and Andy would enjoy, as suggested by the wrapper slogan, which replicates the program's minstrel-show version of African American English to indicate that the (radio) blackface characters are the ones speaking on the packaging. There are also examples of products aggressively woven into the fabric of a narrative, such as the example of Ovaltine and the *Little Orphan Annie* radio show, made infamous by Jean Shepherd's memoirs and the film *A Christmas Story* based on them, in which the young Shepherd is incensed at the nakedness of a particular plug for Ovaltine. Ian Gordon traces this kind of fictional spokesperson and endorsement to comic strip character Buster Brown and the constellation of products that surrounded him, arguing that Brown cannot even be understood as a comic strip separate from his products: "All of his incarnations contributed to the makeup of his character, and each reinforced or advertised the others" (*Comic Strips and Consumer Culture* 51). Gordon distinguishes the licensing of Buster Brown from earlier "mascots" such as Sunny Jim, the mascot of Force cereal created in 1902, in that Brown *did* exist as a narrative rather than just an image. These distinctions point the way to understanding the different kinds of mascots who exist within consumer culture and underline the specific nature of Pud as a character who does not exist outside of marketing.

As Gordon argues, in American media in the 1920s and 1930s, the extension of commodity status to intellectual property "helped to create a national culture of consumption fixated on images" (*Comic Strips and Consumer Culture* 51). Comic strips that advertised products, and advertisements in the form of comic strips, existed in a media landscape where print media, movies, and radio were linked into a network of image consumption. The distinction between Little Orphan Annie and another intermedial character like Captain Midnight, who was created by an advertising company to feature in a radio show for the purposes of advertising Ovaltine, is negligible in terms of how their narratives circulated. For some fictional characters, particularly those who only appear in advertisements, the relationship between narrative and product is even more direct than with these two radio shows. For example, the phantasmatic supervillain Mr. Coffee Nerves, who can only be defeated by coffee substitute Postum, is essentially a typical comic character except for the branded specificity of his weakness. This kind of narrative comic ad is always constructed around the product involved, despite the form being identical to one-page comic strips. At a certain point, advertising mascots and fictional characters are distinguishable not based on what their narratives look like but based on the diegetic role of brands. As Gordon points out, "Comic books owe their existence to the success of comic-art-style advertising in the early 1930s" (*Comic Strips and Consumer Culture* 129). This is true not only of the format of American comic books but also of their style. Comic art style continues to encompass both comic books and advertising, particularly marketing in the form of comics.

What differentiates Pud and Bazooka Joe from the majority of mascots is that they are characters whose adventures are primarily circulated through products. A comparison with other premiums suggests a few important divergences. *Bugs Bunny and Buried Treasure* is a comic that was offered as a premium with Quaker Oats cereals in 1949. A small pamphlet (3 by 7 inches, roughly the size of a newspaper comic strip) consisting of seven pages glued together, the book is much longer than any Pud or Bazooka Joe adventure except the latter's 1983 *Bazooka Joe Super Fun Pad* coloring books and his assorted View-Master adventures. The story of *Bugs Bunny and Buried Treasure*, despite a superficial resemblance to 1948's theatrical short "Buccaneer Bunny," is apparently original to this publication, and contemporary newspaper ads claim that the stories are "ALL-NEW." Despite this originality, *Bugs Bunny and Buried Treasure* bears striking differences from *Dubble Bubble Funnies* in terms of its connection to other texts and to food products. Not only does the comic end with an ad for *Looney Tunes and Merrie Melodies Comics* (a comic book published by Dell), but the newspaper advertisements for the promotion also strengthen the links into other formats, connecting to the daily *Bugs Bunny* comic strip, which began in 1948. Furthermore, the actual process of obtaining the comic is another monetary exchange: as the back cover explains, "Just get a package of Quaker Puffed Wheat or Quaker Puffed Rice," fill in the blank on top of the package, and then mail it along with fifteen cents. Although Topps offered a number of premiums in exchange for wrappers, Pud and Bazooka Joe belong to a more immediate category of premium, since they come along with the product itself.

The one exception for Pud is that the character appeared in advertisements outside of *Dubble Bubble Funnies*, or perhaps it is more accurate to say that *Dubble Bubble Funnies* have been published outside of bubble gum. Pud appeared in half-page comic advertisements in 1950s comic books. In these narratives, Dubble Bubble appears in adventure stories performing much the same role that Grape-Nuts Flakes do for Volto, the Man from Mars. In most of them, the bubbles blown with Dubble Bubble allow Pud to float over a high jump, or help a friend be lifted out of a crevasse. The snapping of the bubble also replicates the sound of a blow dart in the jungle, or a gunshot. Aside from glorifying bubble gum play, sometimes the gum is simply an exchange, as when Pud pays a pirate's ransom with a case—an exchange reminiscent of the role that Hostess foods played in the famous 1970s advertisements described earlier in this book.

In one demonstrative advertising strip, Pud impresses a braggart Egyptian with an American wonder to rival the pyramids and the Sphinx: a colossal bubble that puts the Egyptian in his place and emphasizes the Americanness of Dubble Bubble bubble gum. These ads barely resembled the adventures of Pud in the comics attached to actual gum, and they eventually ceased. Furthermore, the labeling of these strips as advertisements indicates that despite their more elaborate narratives, full coloring, and larger size, they are clearly of secondary significance to the *Funnies* included with gum. The ads position the gum as the object of primary desire, followed by the printed material ("You'll like the comics . . . too!").

In this context, Pud is an example of a comic strip that is an extremely efficient premium, contained within the product it is incentivizing. Pud is a comic strip character so associated with a product that he can essentially only be encountered in that product. Pud's circulation most closely resembles another kind of premium, the collectible gum card. These cards are a version of cigarette cards, which, as Liz Moor points out (22), were part of an imperial project to provide a panorama of imperial troops, projects, and locations, a project easily translatable to the history and sports cards of a later period. Interestingly, before the 1950s innovations of the Topps company, sports cards "usually measured around two inches by two and a half inches, in the tradition of tobacco and candy cards from the 1910s and 1920s" (Jamieson 90)—the size that *Dubble Bubble Funnies* continue to be into the present. The concept of premiums would become extremely important for both major American gum companies, Fleer and Topps, particularly once the shift toward sports cards began in the 1950s (Jamieson 90–102). By the 1990s, the sports card "premiums" had economically supplanted the candy, and both companies had shifted their focus almost entirely to collectible sports cards, with Fleer being purchased by the Marvel Entertainment Group in 1992 and becoming both a significant part (roughly 50 percent) of Marvel's business and a significant producer of comic book superhero cards (Carr 41). When Marvel entered bankruptcy court in 1998, Canadian company Concord Confections purchased the Fleer Confections division (Carr 41). Concord Confections was in turn acquired in 2004 by Tootsie Roll Industries (Saunders). As its interweaving with the history of comics, candy, and sports cards demonstrates, bubble gum (as opposed to gum) has no history outside of the world of twentieth-century consumer culture, and bubble gum comics exist on a continuum with trading cards and bubble gum itself, as marketing. By contrast to trading cards, which began as marketing but became a significant business themselves, bubble gum comics remained financially subordinate to the products for which they were premiums.

Dubble Bubble Funnies can be likened both to bubble gum itself as a highly artificial object of play, and to bubble gum wrappers in the sense that they are marketing whose purpose was to brand the gum. In terms of their circulation, they can also be associated with trading cards. Trading cards have an intriguing relationship to narrative, one that reveals the narrative possibilities of candy premiums. While sports cards are nonnarrative and instead rely on ideas of completing teams, leagues, and sports, there is a tradition of stories being remediated into card form, and of original stories told in the form of trading cards. In the select materiality of narratives that come attached to candy (though in the case of cards, arguably the candy is the premium), there have been serialized narratives spread across several premiums. Topps's *Star Trek* card series of 1976 adapted several episodes of the show, incompletely and erratically but sometimes showing a suggestive correlation in the gap between cards and the advertising breaks of the original episodes (Block and Erdmann). The three original *Star Wars* films (Topps Company, *Star Wars*; *Star Wars: The Empire Strikes Back*; and *Star Wars: Return of the Jedi*) as well as *Back to the Future Part II* were also released in the form of gum cards shortly after their theatrical releases (Cracknell). In these examples, serialization was linked by paratext, such as the blurb on *Back to the Future Part II* cards: "Continued on Card #." There are even narratives native to candy. In 1965, Cadet in the United Kingdom released *Doctor Who and the Daleks* cards, which adapted the television show but told an original story, bundled with "sweet cigarettes" ("Cadet Sweets"). The American examples here used actual frames from their TV series and films, while the *Doctor Who* story consisted of painted, original illustrations with captions. Perhaps this latter example is best considered a comic book released in the form of individual panels attached to gum. Finally, the infamous *Mars Attacks* of 1962 (also Topps Company) sold itself on its own violent, sexual, and tasteless content with no tie-in to another property. The remediation of film and television into the form of bubble gum cards highlights the fragmentary nature of bubble gum narratives and the use of narrative suspense to drive collecting and continued purchases and consumption.

For bubble gum comics like Pud and Bazooka Joe, however, there is no element of serialization in the story, indicating that narrative serialization was not obligatory in the context of gum. When Bazooka's imprint Blony Gum carried Archie comics in the 1950s, the kind of Archie stories adapted were "half-page" Archie strips, already the briefest of Archie stories, which fit entirely on one piece of paper included with one piece of gum.

While longer Archie stories could have been turned into serialized narratives in gum, the Archie stories published with gum were those that most resembled Pud and Bazooka Joe. The physical affordances of candy premiums allowed for serialization, but the majority of cases seem to be completely self-contained. Furthermore, there seems to be a sharp divide between nonserial humor and serialized adventure, suggesting that, as in the *Star Trek* and *Doctor Who* cards, the purpose of splitting a narrative between the wrappers of different pieces of candy is to create cliffhangers. *Mars Attacks* is an anomaly for telling an ongoing storyline while also clearly deriving pleasure from the grotesque, dark humor of each individual card. In premium narratives, a distinct division exists between serialized and nonserialized narratives such as *Dubble Bubble Funnies*.

The division between serialized and nonserialized premiums is further reflected in their physical differences. Trading cards, packaged along with candy, are made out of different, thicker cardboard than the wrappers. Their construction distinguishes them from the materials of packaging and indicates that they are meant for preservation, since they are hardier than the packaging. Since the 1950s, trading cards have also typically been larger (2⅝ inches by 3¾ inches) than bubble gum comics, though they began as the same size (Jamieson 90). In terms of reading, the physical construction of cards promotes a protracted period of assembling the story, rather than repetitious encounters in which the "story" is meant to be discarded. Candy comics seem to invariably be printed on material that is identical with the wrapper, and in some cases (such as the comics sometimes included with lollipops) literally is the wrapper. The waxy paper narratives are materially different from the cardboard narratives.

In contrast to periodicals published at regular intervals and numbered sequentially, the only form of serialization attached to these bubble gum comics are the numbers attached to each comic. These numbers do not seem to sequence the comics in any particular order. Where trading card narratives have numbers attached to make sense of the sequence of events they portray, bubble gum comics are numbered in an altogether mysterious way that seems to only indicate the order in which they were published. The suggestion seems to be that these numbers fix the uniqueness of each comic and imply the practice of collecting—and, since it requires more purchases, marketing. The idea of collecting and exchange is important in the history of candy wrappers, including Topps and Dubble Bubble and analogous operations such as the Popsicle Pete Points attached to the popsicle sticks of Popsicle-brand popsicles. The fact that bubble gum comics could be exchanged for "prizes" indicates a further complication and enmeshment in the consumer network. Topps and Fleer offered items as "prizes," turning a purchase into a competition but also turning the wrappers of their own product, which they had already turned into premiums, into currency. Unlike Topps's card series, the original reason to collect bubble gum comics was not because they told a story but because a company would accept them in exchange for further purchases. Some stories, told in cards and attached to bubble gum, are valued as stories, but bubble gum comics are materially positioned with artistic value as an afterthought.

Some premium narratives have been salvaged and rehabilitated from their status as trash in a Barksist manner. In addition to *Mars Attacks*, the Topps *Star Trek* and *Star Wars* cards have been collected in hardcover editions by Topps in conjunction with art publisher Abrams ComicArts. So has *Dubble Bubble Funnies*' rival *Bazooka Joe*. While *Star Trek* and *Star Wars* seem to gain their prestige from the work to which they are attached, the cult status of *Mars Attacks* is related to the cultural value of original illustrator Wally Wood, along with that of penciller (and fellow comic book artist) Bob Powell and painter Norm Saunders (a former pulp cover illustrator), to say nothing of the 1996 Tim Burton film adaptation. The *Mars Attacks* hardcover contains an essay by Saunders's daughter as well as numerous sketches by Wood. The role of the individual artist in each of these cases is significant, since the recovery of premiums as valuable often follows the same procedure as in the case of Carl Barks, in which the auteuristic genius of an artist is used to grant "exceptional" or "subversive" status to a subset of examples. The role of *Maus* creator Art Spiegelman's work for Topps is epitomal: his work for Topps on *Wacky Packages* and *Garbage Pail Kids*, both card/sticker series, receives significantly more attention than the *Bazooka Joe* strips he wrote, which were printed on lollipops (Topps Company, *Bazooka Joe* 127). This fact suggests that it isn't simply the presence of candy that hampers works from considerations of value, but rather that the work itself needs to have some distance from obvious consumer culture. What unites *Mars Attacks*, *Wacky Packages*, and *Garbage Pail Kids* is an idea of subversion, of consumer culture being used perversely as a medium for distasteful, unappealing messages. By transcending the category of premium, the salvaged premiums enhance the notion that the "other" premiums are particularly valueless—we could call them the Good Premiums.

In the context of bubble gum comics, the key fact of authorship is that *Bazooka Joe* was designed by advertising artist Wesley Morse. Though nowhere near as famous, Morse's reputation has undergone a process comparable to Carl Barks's over the past three decades, one that can be seen to be directly connected to Spiegelman's own relationship with trash culture. As identified by Spiegelman (Adelman 7), Morse is essentially the only artist known to have worked on Tijuana Bibles. The existence of Morse as an author function—as an organizing narrative principle to let us see "behind the scenes"—shapes *Bazooka Joe*'s sixtieth anniversary hardcover collection. The inclusion of a memoir by Morse's son Talley Morse, linking *Bazooka Joe* to personal experiences of the artist, suggests that the name "Wesley Morse" affords the collection and celebration of the work. To further the use of the author function, the *Bazooka Joe* anniversary retrospective book contains reminiscences by many artists (such as underground cartoonists Jay Lynch, R. Sikoryak, and Howard Cruse) who worked on *Bazooka Joe* and who are recognizable from other artistic contexts. The cultural status of Bazooka Joe is higher than that of Pud, partially because Bazooka Joe can be made into a book.

By contrast to the function of Wesley Morse, for the history of Pud we have almost no information. In the beginning, Pud was illustrated in longer ads by cartoonist Ray Thompson. The signature of Thompson, a newspaper cartoonist and advertising artist who lived from 1905 to 1982, appears on many Dubble Bubble advertisements starring Pud. It's unclear if Thompson also wrote and drew *Dubble Bubble Funnies*, and whether he did or not, who designed the characters. Thompson's papers remain in the archives of Syracuse University, and the status of Fleer's archive is unknown. If *Bazooka Joe* represents trash that can be recuperated by association with such notable figures as Spiegelman, Morse, and Cruse, Pud has very little cultural capital. Because *Bazooka Joe* can be easily fit into a continuity with the more acclaimed and well-known work of its contributors, it is recuperated in a way that is extraordinarily difficult for Pud. While *Bazooka Joe* made a return from the trash through the operations of nostalgia and the association of several famous creators, Pud remains in the cultural sphere of garbage.

GARBAGE AND COMICS

The divergent fates of *Bazooka Joe* and *Dubble Bubble Funnies* indicate two historically diachronic ways of considering comic books. *Bazooka Joe* is representative of former "low art" that is now considered valuable, making it the exceptional bubble gum comic. Over the first century of their existence, comic books have been figured differently from bubble gum comics. Despite their origins as premiums deeply embedded in consumerism, they have been, as a form of art, recovered from the trash heap (Beaty, *Comics versus Art* 18). In some cases this has been due to collectors valuing comics for rarity rather than artistic value: ironically, the rarest professional comics are editions printed exclusively and assembled hastily to secure copyright, known as "ashcans" because of their intended purpose of being destroyed immediately after serving their purpose of securing copyright. The role of the archetypal story of now valuable comic book collections being thrown out—usually by oblivious mothers—is instructive in understanding the historical use of the concept of trash in establishing the value of comics. In other cases, it has been publishers or academics setting a text as having literary or historical value. The transformation of comic books into cultural capital is a well-trodden path. Comics' imitation of older forms, most notably the novel in the creation of the "graphic novel," has proven to be a viable way to increase the cultural capital of comics. *Dubble Bubble Funnies*, intended to always be thrown out, still exists in an unsalvaged state.

In their analysis, although Steven Heller and Anne Fink identify food packaging as "the least experimental and probably the most conservative of any graphic design form" (4), they also identify a 1980s–1990s style of packaging they call "Post Modern" in which older styles of packaging or other art are sampled to indicate a self-awareness (18). In the case of the packaging style of *Dubble Bubble Funnies*, the style resembles Heller and Fink's description of 1950s supermarket brands: "bold gothic type, loud primary colors, and friendly (often goofy) trade characters and mascots" (10). This "Post Modern" strategy in packaging can be likened to the same move as the "graphic novel," making it all the more notable that bubble gum comics packaging seems to evoke sincere nostalgia rather than a self-awareness, though as we will see, the comics themselves are frequently quite self-aware.

Complicating this case is comics' history of being considered trash itself. A rhetoric of trash exists in discussions of comics, usually as "other" to the subject being discussed. For example, in his 1971 history of comics, fan Les Daniels's introduction is followed by a caricature of underground cartoonist the Mad Peck proclaiming "Well folks, like the man says above, comics are swell! Unfortunately, they are mostly printed on sleazy paper that falls apart in fifteen years" (Daniels x) as an explanation for Daniels's hardcover collection of comics. This use of "trashy" rhetoric often appears to sympathetic historians to define a portion of comics, typically the majority. For example, responding to the infamous anticomics claims of Fredric Wertham, historians George Perry and Alan Aldridge disagree but add the revealing compromise that "many shady publishing houses were undoubtedly putting out quantities of sordid rubbish" (168). Wertham, probably the most important public figure in the comics-as-trash rhetoric of the 1950s, was one contributing factor in the creation of the Senate Subcommittee on Juvenile Delinquency's investigation into comic books, which the subcommittee described in terms of hygiene: a mission to ensure that the comics placed before children at every newsstand "are clean, decent, and fit to be read by children" (US Congress 27). Figures within the comic industry adopted this rhetoric: contemporaneously, Helen Meyer of Dell Comics claimed that "[w]e abhor horror and crime comics. We would like to see them out of the picture because it taints us" (quoted in Nyberg 77). The rhetoric of trash also existed for comics creators. The attitude that, in the words of historian David Hajdu, comics were "a diversion that may serve a purpose for a time but is best abandoned before too long" (193), could also be expressed with the same rhetoric of rubbish put forth by Daniels, Perry and Aldridge, the Senate subcommittee, and Meyer. Of course this rhetoric also reflects the material fact that as ephemera, the majority of comics and comic books were literally trashed. From cartoonists considering their comics to be fish wrapping (as newspaper cartoonist Al Capp humorously did), to fans admitting that most comics are rubbish, to politicians insisting that comics be clean and not tainted, the evaluative words used here indicate a midcentury conversation in which people with a variety of relationships to comics, from fans to politicians, could agree that there was something trashy (and not booky) about comics, a move that eventually had to be undone by salvage.

The status of being disposed of and then recovered, a process that comic books underwent mostly successfully as they became a respectable art form and cultural capital and that bubble gum comics have mostly failed to undergo, is pivotal to the complicated concept of trash in a consumer culture such as twentieth-century America. Histories and theories of trash (and the related but sometimes distinct concepts of garbage, refuse, and waste) locate the key moment in the history of American trash as the late nineteenth and early twentieth centuries. It is linked to the rise of consumerism, or the transformation of American society into a consumer culture. As John Tomlinson points out, while humans in all cultures consume, the stakes in the idea of "consumer culture" and "consumerism" are "a culture whose *central preoccupation* seems to be that of consuming" (122). While the material roots of the "consumer revolution" that created a consumer culture in the West go back to the practices of the wealthy in late eighteenth-century western Europe (Strasser 4), the cultural backdrop of these changes is somewhat mysterious. Whatever the cause, Western societies in the nineteenth century saw a dramatic rise in production and consumption, and the remnants of both activities (Scandura 18–19).

In this context, the concept of trash evolved from the Victorian concept of "dust," which described the residue inevitably accumulated by urban spaces (Strasser 6). The common profession of the dustman revealed that "dust" still had some potential value, and the exigence of dust was that it must be sifted by dustmen for this value. "During the forty or so years around the turn of the twentieth century, mass production and mass distribution created unprecedented quantities of trash that disturbed private citizens and plagued city administrations" (Strasser 17). Anxieties connected to increasing urban density and mass production replaced dust with the newer concept of "trash" as a specifically harmful buildup. Piles of trash were figured "as menaces to public health and as public eyesores" (120). Influenced by the then popular miasmic theory of hygiene, Western society largely thought of trash as corrosive to the health of a community. This theory involved a shift in exigence: where dust had to be sifted, trash had to be relocated to a space separate from the community. This imperative has a moral dimension. "Trash" is not merely physically distasteful and dangerous but creates demands to be removed, and to fail to address this miasma is to morally fail the community (Strasser 121). In contrast to dust, trash defines value in the same way that dirt defines cleanliness. Trash is the remainder or waste of value. Bubble gum comics, for example, are literally the waste of the practice of consuming bubble gum.

Trash functions as waste in the context of consumer culture. In such a culture, trash is the remainder of consumption, most obviously including packaging because packaging is a component of marketing. Paper is particularly significant in discourses of trash because of its use in packaging and other forms of marketing. As Susan Strasser points out, "marketing produced its own ephemera" (171). Tadeusz Sławek theorizes two kinds of waste, both of which apply to consumer trash. According to Sławek, one kind of waste is the undesirable by-product of production itself. This "waste" is "a barely tolerated by-product of making which is hidden on the far margins of society" (10). The other kind of waste is the inevitable shadow of everything that is produced in a consumer society: "The ever increasing rate of production hides in itself a dark heart of the un-productive: objects must be disposable, must be made in such a way so that either technologically (due, for instance, to poor quality materials and planned obsolescence) or culturally (due to insistent pressures of advertisement) they will not only 'use themselves up' rapidly becoming their own waste, but they will also tend to concentrate our attention upon their process of getting used-up" (11). Bubble gum wrapping and *Dubble Bubble Funnies* are the second kind of waste. Both these kinds of waste trouble us culturally because, as Sławek suggests, "in the culture centered upon things they move within a sphere which borders both upon NOTHING and SOMETHING" (10). The significance of waste is precisely that it is carried away rather than destroyed: "To become a part of waste does not mean to be annihilated, to undergo the process of *Vernichtung* ['annihilation' or 'destruction'], but to obtain a strange mode of existence suspended between being and not being" (10–11). Rather than an industrial by-product, trash specifically is a consumer by-product. It is required by a consumer culture, but it questions the basic precepts of value that underpin such a culture. Packaging is in this "strange mode of existence" because it consists of manufactured objects that are perceived to have no value but are essential to the value of consumer products. The bubble gum comic, like candy, exists in Sławek's "strange mode of existence" because it is simultaneously garbage as well as a valued item to be collected.

Conceiving of trash as something that operates between modes of existence might seem to exclude projects that seek value in trash, such as a literary analysis of *Dubble Bubble Funnies*. However, Anna Chromik-Krzykawska points out a key feature of modern rehabilitations of trash: "What is considered dirty/useless/out of place by a modern discourse is first excluded and marginalized, but then there is a strong imperative to reclaim it into the circuit of usefulness. This process requires, however, certain exorcising procedures which will deprive the excessive of its transgressive qualities" (106). This exorcism and revaluation, which requires a separation from the sphere of order (typically, the city), consists of a "mark of order and purposefulness," which Chromik-Krzykawska exemplifies by the "rational, sophisticated machinery of sewers" (106). While her example is sewage, I would suggest that "trash" undergoes a similar process in the space of the garbage can or dumpster, and the garbage dump or landfill. Chromik-Krzykawska points out how Sławek's "strange mode of existence" allows for some trash to move out of the category of trash and back into the realm of value. In her historical analysis of the modernist dump, Jani Scandura locates this impulse in progressive narratives of modernism, particularly the US government's Depression-era efforts at reclamation and salvage. Paying attention to the affect of "refuse," Scandura finds that trash is subject to ambivalence even on a theoretical level, casting "depressive modernity" against "progressive modernity" and describing the same division as Sławek in terms of being on a borderland between Lacanian ideas of the symbolic and the real (13). Trash's unceasing ambivalence comes from the fact that capitalist America needed trash to be created: as Scandura points out, the culture of 1930s America is where the marketing philosophy of "progressive obsolescence" was invented (19). Trash implies ideas of depression and failure, as well as opposing concepts such as productivity and recovery, but the category of trash never resolves the tension between these two ideas.

In the case of bubble gum comics, the materiality of the comics always invokes the condition of trash even when they are valued by a mark of order and purposefulness. When *Bazooka Joe* comics were collected into a hardcover reprint book, giving them considerable order and purpose as well as upscaling those comics as cultural capital, anxiety about the concept of trash was not silenced (indeed, the concept of trash is inescapable in the assorted text pieces about the comics). Despite the fact that this chapter functions as a collection and a kind of salvage of *Dubble Bubble Funnies*, it can't fully bring Pud into the realm of value in the way that Chromik-Krzykawska suggests. Ultimately, no analysis of comics can treat comics entirely as trash, any more than it can fully take trash out of the equation. In an attempt to understand *Dubble Bubble Funnies*, the possibilities are limited by an awareness of their unchallenged status as trash.

A number of particular historical trends intersect to put bubble gum comics in the category of trash, but one of the most notable is the discourse around marketing. The key historical moment for consumerism is the decades surrounding the beginning of the twentieth century, making this the key moment in the history of trash and also in the history of marketing. Liz Moor locates the first "rise of the brand" to the late nineteenth century, when contemporary developments in manufacturing, printing, transportation, and nationalism made it possible and desirable for consumers to recognize the same, uniform products no matter where they were. Such packaging, to Moor, constitutes a national imagining, analogous to Benedict Anderson's understanding of that other nineteenth-century paper ephemera, the newspaper. However, Moor's work is among the few that discuss branding critically without being reductive of marketing's project. Less critical overviews tend to portray marketing as the straightforward manipulation of consumers, often using the language of violence. This is particularly the case when discussing the characters and narratives attached to products associated with children. For example, Norma Odom Pecora writes on media convergence: "What has happened more recently is the acceleration of the process and the takeover of all aspects of children's play and imagination" (153). *Dubble Bubble Funnies*, as marketing associated with children, are difficult to read without bringing in the mark of order and purpose, namely a critique of consumerism.

It is a commonplace to see consumer culture, and especially marketing, as a despicable deception practiced on the weak-minded and vulnerable. In one revealingly mixed metaphor, critic Leslie Savan claims that "advertising now infects just about every organ of society, and wherever advertising gains a foothold it tends to slowly take over, like a vampire or a virus" (1). But marketing is not a simple command that is obeyed wherever it is heard, and more recently scholars have objected to the specific idea that consumers are simply victims of advertising. Ed Schiffer points out that "if advertising were completely successful at inscribing the consumer, it would not insist on depicting him/her as an at least potentially oppositional force" (290–91): aside from the possibility of lack of comprehension, advertising theory also includes the concept of Agent Knowledge. "Rather than a target consumer passively receiving messages, the target is an active receiver, interpreter, and responder to advertising messages" (Nelson and Chang 174). Indeed, what happened to Richie Rich's brand is an example of what marketing theorist Stephen Brown calls "cannibalization" or "dilution" in which "additional products or services or branches can undermine existing products" (184). Feminist scholar Ellen Seiter points out that critiques of consumer culture often either focus on consumers who are literally female or children, or they feminize or infantilize all consumers. For example, the subtitle of Benjamin Barber's 2008 book *Consumed* promises to address "How Markets Corrupt Children, Infantilize Adults, and Swallow Citizens Whole." Seiter argues persuasively that while consumer culture should be actively criticized, women and children are not simply its helpless victims (41), while Daniel Thomas Cook uses anthropological research to unveil how discourse over children's attachment to commercials is a symptom of parental anxiety over children's subjectivity (118). Marketing for children's products such as bubble gum is widely culturally understood to be noxious, which has particular consequences for the dismissal of *Dubble Bubble Funnies*.

A related element of consumer critiques, essentially the same as the infantilizing rhetoric described above, is a (usually implicit) concern that the bodies of consumers will become fat. Michele Simon recounts controversy between health advocates about whether cartoon characters should be used to advertise food at all, or should be used to advertise only healthy food (139), essentially a controversy over whether manipulation or fatness is ethically worse for children. Even more subtle discourses still imply that the stakes in consumerism are the bodies of consumers: attempting to define "junk food," Robert Albritton, for example, declares that it is "of course a colloquialism, but . . . one that can be given a very precise meaning. It is food that is extremely high in sugars, fats and salts, or what are often called 'empty calories.' Of course, the 'junkiness' of foods is a matter of degree" (3). While this definition of junk food illuminates Albritton's purpose in critiquing the capitalist food system, it does not acknowledge that the "junk" in food discourse functions very similarly to Sławek's concept of "trash" precisely in defying classification. To complicate this final category of rhetoric involved in marketing critiques, the notion of fat and fat bodies is culturally constructed and historically contingent: as Laura Fraser points out, American culture came to figure the previously pleasant notion of "fat" as a health risk in the same period in which "dust" became "trash," as part of the same discourse of hygiene. Fraser is skeptical of appeals to the objective meaning of fat, noting that turn-of-the-century "physicians came to believe that they were able to arrive at an exact measure of human beings; they could count calories.... But when the plump figure fell from fashion, physicians found new theories to support the new fashion" (13). Most critical discourses about marketing are excessively simple, preferring to adopt one culturally contingent category (usually childhood, fat, or as Samira Kawash points out, femininity) in order to critique another (consumerism or capitalism more generally). As John Tomlinson points out in his analysis of cultural imperialism, many critiques that are overtly hostile to the problems of contemporary Western society trade in "a mistrust of the satisfactions of the body over the 'spirit'" (124), and thus replicate a prevalent binary of Western culture. As Tomlinson's comment implies, it's difficult to read marketing texts like *Dubble Bubble Funnies* because there is already a deceptively simple and problematic widespread understanding of marketing in consumer culture. It would be easy to "take bubble gum comics seriously" by simply noting that they are clearly part of consumerism, which is bad.

Janice Radway developed a metacritique similar to Tomlinson's in her 1984 analysis of romance novels. Noting the widespread metaphor of ingestion and consumption when conceiving of participants in mass culture, Radway finds that these kinds of readers "are understood to be helpless in the face of ideology" (6). In her understanding, clichéd critiques wind up doing worse than failing to illuminate the culture:

> Like many other mass-culture critics, these students of the romance finally produce their explanations simply by positing a desire in the reading audience for the specific meaning they have unearthed, a meaning that they then declare to have been there from the start. (7)

Radway also notes that the repetitive messages and recurring readings of a text indicate to critics "a more insistent need to receive [the message] again and again" (19). By contrast, Radway calls for a focus on the way that "various groups appropriate and use the mass-produced art of our culture" (222). In her reasoning, this activity reveals that consumer culture is not an uncomplicated transmission of messages down from the corporate heights, but rather an ongoing negotiation between many parties. While Radway's readers are women whom she sees seeking to oppose a dissatisfying patriarchal culture, the children who read *Dubble Bubble Funnies* have their own reasons to feel ambivalent about mass culture and their own negotiation with that culture.

While Radway's critique relies on the distinction between readings of the text (whether performed by her or by her informants) and the patterns of the text's consumption, the case of Pud presents a challenge to this method. It is very difficult to distinguish between Pud and Dubble Bubble. Pud is not an existing character endorsing a product. For many decades, his texts have had no official circulation outside packaging, and they have never existed outside of marketing—except when traded back and forth by consumers after purchase, or found as discarded garbage. Whatever the text of Pud says, and whatever meanings readers can find in it, the physical circulation of Pud has largely determined the reception of *Dubble Bubble Funnies*: namely as hardly being a text at all. The feature that makes *Dubble Bubble Funnies* waste in the Sławek sense is that it both is and is not text. The undeniable fact of Pud's bounded existence as a part of a brand associates him closely with the realm of marketing and not with the realm of literature. Whether Savan and Barber are right to figure consumers as childlike victims, they indicate a common view that makes it difficult to see *Dubble Bubble Funnies* as a text. Indeed, it is much easier to see it as trash, because trash requires no systematic, methodical reading.

Material affordance complicates this matter by allowing for *Dubble Bubble Funnies* to be detached and to circulate outside purchases. *Dubble Bubble Funnies* are not actually printed on the packaging of Dubble Bubble bubble gum. They are included within the packaging and are usually attached to, rather than a part of, the wrapper. There is a historical distinction between texts included *with* a product and texts printed *on packaging*. The earliest comic books in the modern format were designed explicitly as premium versions of comic strips, to be offered to customers as an incentive to choose those retailers over others. When they became self-contained items, a shift in the 1930s that coincided with the idea that comic books should contain original material unavailable anywhere else, comic books became advertisements for premiums of other kinds. By being included with packaging, *Dubble Bubble Funnies* becomes the specific kind of text Gordon calls, following marketing language, a premium.

Pud is difficult for theories of comics because the materiality of *Dubble Bubble Funnies* aggressively confronts the reader with the reader's participation in a particularly disreputable and unvirtuous sphere of consumer culture. Furthermore, what is undeniable about Pud threatens to taint the status that comics have acquired by being the subject of academic analysis. Comics come from a realm of consumerism that is infantilized and certainly figured as viscerally unhealthy in the same terms as candy. Unhelpfully, if we want to treat comics as art, Pud reminds us that the two exist in the same cultural place of kids' commodities. The concepts of art and literature provide us with ways to study comics aside from being trash, but this pretense doesn't work with Pud. The material conditions of Pud and Pud's circulation are extraordinarily difficult to overlook. To study *Dubble Bubble Funnies* is a confrontation with the part of comics that we easily refuse from the literary conversation. This trashy negotiation between candy, comics, and consumerism forms the backdrop for understanding what happens in the text of *Dubble Bubble Funnies*, the premium comics, which are about negotiating consumption.

A BUCKET OF COMICS

Reviewing the 175 *Dubble Bubble Funnies* contained in my one-kilogram bucket, it is immediately apparent that the *Funnies*, due to their brief length, strongly resemble a subject for which a critical apparatus does exist, namely newspaper comics strips. Many of the observations regarding Ernie Bushmiller's *Nancy* in Paul Karasik and Mark Newgarden's intensive study of one *Nancy* strip hold true for the *Funnies*, including their economy of imagery, plot, characterization, words, and structure.

To begin with the recurring structures of the *Funnies*, some consist of one panel. In the strip shown in figure 4.1 (#9), reading from right to left and top to bottom, the composition is balanced roughly between Pud and Bigfoot, with Pud's remark in the center, balanced with the campfire. Pud, whether familiar from other strips or not, is the more mundane element, just as the campfire is also mundane compared to what Pud is saying. This single panel has a rough vertical asymmetry between the more banal Pud and the legendary Bigfoot, as well as a less pronounced diagonal asymmetry. We interpret these "events" as taking place simultaneously, and humor arises from the inclusion of the bizarre into a standard scenario. The juxtaposition is spatial, because this is a single panel.

In some cases, the *Funnies* contain two panels. These, the most common *Funnies* configuration, are always formed with a vertical gutter. The *Funnies* can also have three panels, always created with one horizontal gutter and one vertical one. Gutters, the space in between panels, have been imagined as the construction that encourages the reader to infer what has happened in between two images in a process theorist Scott McCloud calls "closure" (63)—in the current discussion, they might also remind us that a literal gutter's purpose is to convey refuse away from the site of its waste to the sewer, which carries it farther away; a gutter clears its surrounding space.

Figure 4.1. *Dubble Bubble Funnies* #9.

The horizontal line between the first two panels of #25 implies a different function: not only is it a thin line with no space between images, but it is obviously different from the vertical gutter elsewhere in the strip. Readers may find panels divided by only a line to "feel" closer together when juxtaposed with the break of a gutter. Since time passes between the first two panels, and the characters take actions (Pud walking away to catch Daisy's pitch, Daisy winding up) between the two kinds of gutters, it's difficult to understand the distinction between them.

Sometimes, *Dubble Bubble Funnies* have four panels. Four panels can be created with even panels, each a quarter of the strip, or by the subdivision of a quarter panel. In the comics from around 2017, #22 is the only example with this configuration, but there were no copies in my particular bucket. The two-panel structure is predominant in the complete set of sixty *Funnies*, as well as in the random sampling in my bucket. The structure with two even panels divided vertically seems unusually significant, since even *Funnies* with more than two panels preserve the gutter running vertically through the strip. Even an evenly divided four-panel strip such as *Funny* #29 only uses black lines horizontally and a white gutter vertically. The structure is notable because it has a discernible effect on the joke style of *Dubble Bubble Funnies*.

Figure 4.2. *Dubble Bubble Funnies* #39.

See #17, another strip not included in my bucket. This joke appears to not require the first panel at all, since the information in that panel (Pud's friend Daisy and the childlike pictures beside Pud's self-portrait) is also present in the second panel. It's easy to imagine a single-panel version, which, like the Bigfoot strip (#9) discussed above, would balance elements on opposite sides of the image. However, the way this joke is structured in the two-panel form suggests a pause between panels, and the use of a second panel rather than part of a single panel to display a new idea creates a rhythm to this joke, in what I see as the familiar rhythm of *Dubble Bubble Funnies*. Two-panel strips bear a common structure that is best understood as a separated set-up and punch line. Because *Dubble Bubble Funnies* are physically very small, compositions are often repeated between panels, as seen in two near-identical panels (figure 4.2).

Two-panel strips sometimes have only minute visual variations between panels, though another comedic technique makes use of significant differences between panels. In terms of repetition, three- and four-panel strips always have at least two almost identical panels.

A panel that takes up one-fourth of the available space is five-eighths of an inch tall and at most one and one-eighth of an inch wide, suggesting that

Figure 4.3. *Dubble Bubble Funnies* #38.

repetitive composition is a useful tool for reader comprehension. *Dubble Bubble Funnies* participate in artistic and narrative techniques common in newspaper comic strips: single-panel strips usually derive humor from the reader's assumptions about what happened just before or just after the scenario depicted, while two-panel strips use the second panel to subvert expectations raised by the first or to explain the mystery of the first panel. In their work on Bushmiller's *Nancy* newspaper strip, Karasik and Newgarden center the idea of the "gag," a brief joke or narrative, and report the workings of Bushmiller's artistic theory. Bushmiller, as described by Karasik and Newgarden, would begin with "the snapper" (67)—the last panel of the strip, often a surreal image—and work backward to explain how it came about, creating a gag out of the journey to the strip's narrative destination. This concept is useful when looking at Pud's most frequent structure, the two panels.

For example, in *Dubble Bubble Funnies* #38 (figure 4.3), Pud's second-panel comment does the work of explaining his pricing to Daisy, and his comment functions as an explanation of the mystery raised by the first panel, of Pud's extremely expensive lemonade. The *Funnies* most commonly present one of two joke formulas. In the first, a common situation or figure of speech invoked in the first panel is followed by an absurd result, as in #46.

In the other variety of joke (such as #38), a puzzling image in the first panel is followed by an explanation. Both techniques are present in newspaper strips. Robert Harvey explains this latter technique in the context of a *FoxTrot* strip by Bill Amend: the panels "become a sort of puzzle which is explained by the last panel" (131). This is an apt description of *Funny* #2. The mystery-or-puzzle joke is significantly less common than the absurd-result joke in my bucket of *Dubble Bubble Funnies*.

The *Funnies*, similar to strips like Bushmiller's *Nancy*, have very little plot. As Karasik and Newgarden observe, "Emotional depth, social comment, plot, internal consistency, and common sense were all merrily surrendered in Bushmiller's universe to the true function of a comic strip as he now unrelentingly saw it: to quickly and efficiently trip the 'gag reflex' of his readership on a daily basis" (62). Most characters (including Pud) are typically unnamed, and most strips minimize narrative even within the events they recount. For example, #9, the Bigfoot panel, affirms this paradigm by using an unseen narrative for humor: as in many single-panel newspaper "strips," the joke is the implicit events that take place before those narrated, so the reader is compelled to imagine an outlandish series of earlier events that resulted in the depicted situation. The assumption is that whatever series of events led to Pud roasting marshmallows with the mysterious primate is the funniest element of the joke in the reader's imagination. The fact that *Dubble Bubble Funnies* are a sequence of randomly distributed strips not connected to each other emphasizes the limits of their narrative, since if they told a tale spread over dozens of comics, the reader might never encounter all the constituent parts. In bubble gum comics, the same logic of the newspaper strip's extreme ephemerality is at work, but even more emphatically. Karasik and Newgarden make this point about *Nancy*: "Like every last one of them, it was intended to be read once, discarded with the rest of the newspaper at the end of the day, and forgotten" (72). Although narrative can be sustained over a period of time in newspaper strips, since a reader may be assumed to read the same newspaper every day, it is also the case that a strip needs to be able to stand alone as a coherent event. That is, a reader should be able to pick up a newspaper and more or less engage with a strip without background information. A consumer of Dubble Bubble may or may not read the *Funnies* and may or may not chew gum every day; the *Funnies* thus operate within a discontinuous narrative (things that happen to Pud), without being part of a story per se. The purpose of *Dubble Bubble Funnies* is not to tell stories but rather to circulate gags.

This purpose is further defined by a noticeably limited number of jokes. The highly formulaic nature of *Dubble Bubble Funnies* is enhanced by the extreme repetition of the comics collectively. In 175 random comics unevenly selected from 60 possibilities, some comics repeat many, many times. In this close to random distribution, outré elements such as Pud meeting Bigfoot or posing as a superhero seem underlined by the banal subject matter of most strips.

As the two major categories of jokes—the mystery and the absurd result—suggest, Pud primarily traffics in irony in the sense of the pointedly unexpected. *Funny* #46, where Pud becomes a human pizza, and #25, where a humble Pud asks Daisy to teach him how to throw hard, are representative of this trend. It might be the case that the *Funnies*' writers are aware of the presumption that these comics are deeply unfunny, and are using irony and outré elements to play with expectations raised by the specific example of *Dubble Bubble Funnies*. In the less realistic strips, it seems likely that the writers are playing on the perception that the *Funnies* are bound to banality. In the more realistic, ironic strips, the jokes frequently play on the perception of Pud as a generic boy.

Worth noting briefly is *Dubble Bubble Funnies*' eccentric approach to coloring; while past bubble gum comics (notably *Bazooka Joe*) appear to have used a variety of four-color printing processes, modern *Dubble Bubble Funnies* use only shades of pink, red, and blue over a white background. Although identifying Pud as a representation of a white person might make sense for a variety of reasons (including earlier iterations of the character where it is unambiguous; see the Egypt ad), his skin is literally a garish pink and notably *not* the blank white of the paper. A variety of *Bazooka Joe* comics localized for sale in Africa decades ago recolored the main character's skin to be brown; it is difficult to imagine the same decision in the lurid, tinted world of twenty-first-century *Dubble Bubble Funnies*. Ultimately, the coloring of *Dubble Bubble Funnies* is clearly indebted to the brand rather than to realism or representational traditions, quoting the color of the packaging (which itself quotes the bright pink color of the gum). It's another way in which the art has been determined by consumerism, with intriguing results.

In terms of Pud's character, this play with assumptions leaves him an ambiguous figure of ironic masculinity, the last major category of Pud jokes. Pud blends the character of the boy prankster, familiar in comic strips from Buster Brown onward, with irony. The irony is one of an incompetent prankster invested in an aggressive masculine identity. *Funny* #56 is an ironic take on the genre of the masculine superhero, as "Pud the Protector" is positioned as a persona associated with an embarrassing childhood phase. In #25, the ball-throwing strip, if Pud were a different generic character such as an overweight boy (as Pud was in the 1950s), and were to be beaten by a girl at

Figure 4.4. *Dubble Bubble Funnies* #47.

sports (another "coin-of-the-realm" truism and sexist stereotype), the joke could be seen as idealizing the (absent) fit masculine body rather than subverting the character's chauvinism. The distinction indicates a tendency in *Dubble Bubble Funnies* to make Pud the object of humor, raising the question of whether he is meant to be an audience role model. Not all *Funnies* are ironic, meaning that some *Funnies* present unsubverted sexism. Pud is not entirely a role model in these strips, but he is also not an entirely ironic figure.

As in *Nancy*, where the characters have no particular consistent attributes, this inconsistency suggests that these strips have little to no purpose beyond the frivolous gag. Various morals and imperatives—turn the lights off when they're not in use (#39), ask even girls to help when they're better than you (#25)—are raised, but their weight is lightened by the strip's lack of consistency. What unites the inconsistent *Dubble Bubble Funnies* is their overwhelming structural predictability. If the first panel has Pud being cocky, the second panel will twist this idea and present a moral; if the first panel presents a moral, the second will twist this message into subversion. What stands out in Pud is less the messages than this structure, which is particularly noticeable in the context of the relative sameness of the *Funnies*. While the jokes in Pud are more often at the expense of his pranks and his

Figure 4.5. *Dubble Bubble Funnies* #11.

arrogance, those character traits essentially only exist to set up punch lines, or to provide them.

In terms of motifs, in my particular bucket the most common *Funny* was #47 (figure 4.4). In this example of the "absurd result" joke, while the raccoons are visible in the first panel, the strip delves into the fantastical by presenting the raccoons as speaking (and using human body language). The chiasmus structure whereby Pud turns from a human in the foreground into a faceless shape in the background, and the raccoons go from animal faces to human-like speakers, underlines both the similarities (the raccoons are also speaking, and speak about food as humans do) and the differences (food humans might reject could be considered a feast by animals). The subjective value of trash when considered from outside Pud's taste is humorously exaggerated into the difference between raccoons and humans. Whatever Pud's mother said in response to Pud's remark is unimportant compared to the raccoon view on the situation.

The second most common *Funny* in my bucket was #11 (figure 4.5). Here, Pud's comment indicates a desire for more bubbles, and the second panel indicates that he got what he wanted, to an absurd degree. In the first panel, bubbles (of soap, but looking identical to bubble gum in the *Funnies*) are already overflowing a bathtub, a situation magnified to absurdity in the second panel. Some features of this strip seem intended to have it make sense within the milieu of the *Funnies* (Pud's bathing suit and to some extent his hat, but also his speaking his plans out loud to an inanimate object), but other details are clearly for humorous purposes, such as Pud attributing the desire for more bubbles to Mr. Ducky. The second panel also requires the reader's imagination by not showing whoever is yelling "Pud" and what might be happening to them as the house overflows with bubbles. Here, the absurd result is an astonishing surplus of bubbles.

The third most common *Funny* in my bucket is #20, in which Daisy has a tea party with Pud's dog. With thirty-nine, thirty, and seventeen instances, respectively, *Funnies* #47, #11, and #20 account for nearly one-half of the entire bucket. Conversely, the five rarest (with each appearing only once in my bucket) include #9 (Pud's encounter with Bigfoot) and #27. *Funny* #27 combines the "absurd result" joke with the ironic undercutting of the banal dialogue in the first panel, emphasizing that reading the first dialogue literally ("what you want") produces, with Pud, an absurd stack of boxes. Pud's comment in the second panel further emphasizes this with understatement: he only "thinks" that this column of junk food taller than himself is everything he needs.

The distribution appears random in the sense that frequency doesn't emphasize any particular themes (Pud's refusal of "healthy" food, for example, is the subject of both the most frequent and the rarest comics in the bucket), though rarer structures could be minimized by it: of the three possible single-panel strips, only two appeared in my bucket, and each of them only once. As Gerald Saul notes of an uncut sheet of *Funnies*, each printed sheet contains eighty-one comics, meaning that there aren't an even number of *Funnies* produced—since there are sixty possible strips, twenty-one of them are printed twice and are thus twice as common, though of course each bucket is entirely random within this parameter. Combining this information with the observation that the gum is more likely encountered one piece at a time suggests that Pud is subject to a more extreme version of the readings in *Watchmen*'s serial printing: the themes of *Dubble Bubble Funnies* exist depending entirely on the reader's material encounter with installments. Every observation about the "themes" of Pud's gags is contingent on encountering them: a reader might never encounter Pud's misogyny being subverted, or see Pud skateboard, and equally a reader might theoretically only ever see Pud roast marshmallows with Bigfoot, leading to three different visions of the character. As Bushmiller once commented of *Nancy*, "Ninety per cent of my strips are just individual gags without any theme tying them together," an estimate Karasik and Newgarden call conservative (62). This simplicity became more pronounced in the strip's history, for "although Bushmiller's true audience was composed of anyone within reach of a newspaper, he came to slant *Nancy*, he once said, 'for the gum chewers'" (66).

The subject of gum itself appears throughout *Dubble Bubble Funnies*. Six of the series of sixty strips are centered around bubble gum. Only two of these appeared in my bucket: #2 (where bubble gum is fed to animals) and #54.

In #54, the overflowing result of Pud's decision (reminiscent of the soap bubbles in #11) is the punch line because of the characters' aghast anticipation of what is about to happen when the bubble bursts. Despite bursting bubbles being the key innovation of bubble gum in 1928, the joke here is that Pud was intending instead to create the (ridiculous) bubble gum soup. *Funny* #54 subverts the "absurd result" formula by setting up an absurd intended result and then showing a result that is more realistic (while still not being realistic). Where #11 showed us the absurd extent of Pud's desire for more bubbles, this strip asks us to imagine what happens to Pud and Daisy next, imagining the inevitable given the improbable setup.

A reader might encounter four other *Dubble Bubble Funnies* about bubble gum. Considering that the *Funnies* can safely assume that their readers consume bubble gum, it seems worth noting that, of these six *Funnies*, three portray gum being used incorrectly, from the absurd visions of a forest of animals blowing bubbles and Pud's immense stovetop bubble to the more mundane #13, where realism intervenes to spatter Pud's bubble over his face. The remaining three, #50, #12, and #14, portray impossible uses of gum, with the final panel a "snapper" as Bushmiller would have dubbed it. Bubble gum appears incidentally in a few other strips.

It also appears incidentally in #25. Bubble gum, and even the particular properties of bubble gum as opposed to any other kind of treat, can be significant without being the focus of the joke in the *Funnies*. In #36, a bubble gum–based dare could be based on any candy, but in #28, the property of gum to stick to hands (and hair) is an important feature of the (four-panel, and thus longest) narrative. *Funnies* #10 and #25 both portray characters incidentally blowing bubbles, but in neither case does bubble gum serve any even minor narrative role. However, in light of a visual narrative, it's worth pointing out that bubble gum is a candy whose use can be portrayed visually with remarkable efficiency, not even requiring multiple panels to establish what's happening. In #25 and #28, bubble gum use is portrayed with a transparent pink bubble floating over a character's mouth. Since #25 isn't about gum in any sense, it seems believable that the gum is simply gratuitous, adding nothing *but* a self-reflexive reminder to the reader about the usage of the product to which *Dubble Bubble Funnies* is attached. The visual portrayal of #10 is more in line with the common rendering of gum chewing: to wit, Pud's cheek is portrayed as inflated (as it is in #12, #14, and #50), so not just the bubble but the blowing of the bubble is represented. Gum is also unnecessary to the joke of #10, but the portrayal of gum chewing as a process draws attention to the idea of sequence.

In #50, in the first panel Pud declares that he is going to blow a bubble in cold weather. Part of this strip (Pud's mention of cold weather) is redundant given the visual information, indicating that the *Funnies* try to minimize the need to reread a given strip for visual clues. The mystery of the early panels, or the snapper of the last panel, is not meant to be a protracted mystery but a mystery resolved immediately, especially considering that *Dubble Bubble Funnies* are so physically small as to be difficult not to take in at a glance. Consider what must happen between panels in #50: Pud blows a bubble, which attains an impressive size (the same size as Pud's head, in fact), then freezes solid, and then partially shatters. Telling this story in four panels (the seeming maximum) could portray more stages in this sequence, but the decision to make the story two panels emphasizes the juxtaposition between Pud's boasting and his ironic comeuppance. The style of *Dubble Bubble Funnies* makes the sequence of events mostly irrelevant. *Dubble Bubble Funnies*, even when they are about gum, aren't concerned with narratives about gum or the practice of using bubble gum, instead emphasizing the spectacle of the bubble. *Funny* #10 is instructive because it artistically renders the practice of bubble blowing. In the context of the joke, Pud giving Daisy a picture of himself for a birthday present, the fact that the picture includes Pud blowing a bubble is self-reflexive in another way, suggesting that Pud's role as mascot is at absurd odds with his portrayal as an ordinary person. The picture-within-a-picture suggests a self-reflexive way to read the other portrayals of blowing bubbles in the series, namely as a self-conscious representation of the very product bound up in *Dubble Bubble Funnies*. It could be argued that *Dubble Bubble Funnies* is simply taking the opportunity to remind the reader of gum at all times, but this is manifestly untrue. Not only do other strips focus on foods unrelated to Dubble Bubble, but some strips seem to swerve away from mentions of bubble gum. An example is #27, where Pud picks out a stack of junk food at a store. In this case, not only would bubble gum being one of Pud's purchases not disrupt the joke, it would undermine the point of *Dubble Bubble Funnies* if they were meant to be unironic portrayals of Concord Confections' desired consumer behavior.

As would be expected of sixty joke narratives set in the twenty-first-century industrialized world, characters are often portrayed in the act of consuming products. *Funny* #38, about Pud's lemonade stand, is particularly interesting in the material context of bubble gum comics (and not only because it mysteriously contains a self-reflexive Fun Fact). The strip fits into the gag pattern described above of a mystery in the first panel resolved in the second. Although one suspects that this could also be a single-panel strip, two panels means that there's a panel where Pud's tremendously overpriced lemonade exists without explanation or doubt from passersby. Clearly, the point of this strip is that marking up the price of lemonade severely doesn't make it taste any better.

Funny #38's message about the overpriced lemonade is far from ironic when applied to Dubble Bubble itself. Could there be a more appropriate message than "price doesn't equal quality" for a comic strip found only wrapped around a piece of gum that retails for 10¢ per piece? Encountering this same message in different consumer contexts would change its implications. A reader encountering this joke for free, for example spray-painted on the side of a public wall, would take it differently than if it were an enormously expensive oil painting. In the context of cheap bubble gum, and *Dubble Bubble Funnies'* printing on paper that is literally the same as the wrapping it comes in, the message seems inextricably connected to the related concepts of marketing and its construction of value. If they weren't attached to a product, and specifically bubble gum, these themes wouldn't seem as significant; for one thing, the theme of candy wouldn't register as marketing.

The marketing/theme of consumption interacts with the theme of Pud's wastefulness, as in #11, where he floods the house with bubbles from a bubble bath. In #11, the joke is the extent of Pud's excess (structurally, the same joke as #27). In #39, where Pud is told to turn the lights off when he's not using them, the joke shares some thematic similarities. Told to "help the planet" in this way, Pud says that he hopes this rule doesn't apply to scary movie night. Because the first panel involves Pud being told a moral about consumerism, the standard structure of *Dubble Bubble Funnies* requires Pud's response to be irreverent. Another strip, #48, presents a similar structure of asserting a moral about consumerism (and trash disposal) but instead uses the two-panel structure to present Pud as incompetent.

The suggestion in #48, that Pud is the reason that care should be taken with waste disposal, and this unbeknown to himself, unites several other strips, making Pud and the consumer's relationship to waste a textual theme. *Dubble Bubble Funnies*, though presenting Pud's antics for our amusement, makes it possible to see them ironically, particularly in light of other strips—again, a highly contingent possible reading. The small size of *Dubble Bubble Funnies*, the simple structure of the drawing, the material style of their circulation, and the product and pricing they are circulated with all combine to indicate that the themes of *Dubble Bubble Funnies* are endlessly ambivalent because they aren't supposed to be coherent. The suggestion is not that one should collect all sixty *Funnies* because only then will a reader learn the "real" message of *Dubble Bubble Funnies*. Like *Nancy*, the characters in the *Funnies* are not intended to display consistent traits. In the case of these gum comics, the matters that recur are given a new significance not only because Pud, like Nancy, is disposable and intended to convey gags, but also because, unlike newspaper strips, *Dubble Bubble Funnies* are packaging. The material form of *Dubble Bubble Funnies* is not just ephemeral paper but wastepaper, making the comics' ambivalent portrayal of consumerism unusually fraught. As the Nahua figure Tlazōlteōtl incarnated purity and trash in the form of an ambivalent entity, making her association with the food-that-is-junk (gum) entirely appropriate, *Dubble Bubble Funnies* are ambivalent about the way bubble gum is for, and is not for, consumption.

This trashy status has enormous significance for comics as a whole. In his history of the comic book subculture, Matthew Pustz points out that "although there is a history of comics as collectors' items, the extreme commodification of the hobby is fairly recent. In the golden age of comics, comic books were ephemera" (14). Part of the value of old comics is the unspoken fact that their ephemerality meant that the majority were removed from circulation—most comic books have literally been trashed. As mass-produced consumer items, few comics begin as truly rare, and the majority become rare thanks to surviving the subsequent incursions of becoming garbage. Not just printed to be thrown out, this scarcity is intimately related to the fact that comic books were and are rarely printed to survive for long periods—and to the practice of returning unsold comics for pulping, necessary to maintain prices low enough to be in the reach of children. The idea of trash is important to the culture of comics because, as an absence, it defines the value of the present objects, making them existing copies rather than just copies. This dynamic also extends to define the value of exceptional comics as departures from the mass of disposable trash. As Ian Gordon says of the enormously esteemed *Maus*, "It is the very ubiquity of comics that gives *Maus* its narrative power. Which is to say, without Mickey Mouse there would be no *Maus*" (*Comic Strips and Consumer Culture* 157), a remark that is less direct but equally true when applied to *Dubble Bubble Funnies* and any comic valued as a book. Just as ads are not simply impositions that interfere with the "real" stories of Carl Barks, and the hostile reading of Richie Rich is not really a misreading, the idea of trash is not simply a tragic flaw in the materiality of comics or an impediment to studying them. Instead, it is a consequence and a reminder of comics' deeply embedded history in twentieth-century American consumer culture. The existence of bubble gum comics demonstrates that comics are, in an important way, like bubble gum wrappers.

Epilogue

COMIC BOOKS AND THEIR READERS

Speaking of his time owning and operating a comic book store in downtown Cleveland from 1978 through 1989, comic book writer Tony Isabella remarks: "My most enthusiastic customers for Richie Rich comics were middle-aged black women" (4). To Isabella, the seeming contradiction between "this most Aryan of comics characters" whom "no one short of Donald Trump should be able to relate to" and his customers prompted him to ask these women about the appeal:

> These ladies loved their Richie Rich comics on two levels. First, and most obviously, they absolutely got and relished the humor of the absurd displays of wealth seen on virtually every page of every Richie Rich story. It was fantasy wealth and not something to be envied in the slightest. More importantly, they loved that all that money meant very little to Richie. What was important to Richie were the same things that were important to them: family and friends. (Isabella 4)

They saw themselves in Richie and Richie in themselves. In this tantalizing and all-too-rare record of how people *read* comics, we can see the ideology that resolves the racial and class distinctions alluded to by Isabella: the higher value placed on friends and family than on material wealth. Isabella introduces his most intriguing customers by cataloging his varieties of customers, including his favorites, "workers who came from both sides of the city to buy the comic books that were, in many cases, . . . their favorite form of relaxation. . . . Harvey was publishing over a dozen Richie Rich comics and digests every month and these ladies were buying them by the fistful" (3). As any perusal of Robert Darnton's communication circuit would remind us, these transactions are not simply interactions between readers and the makers of Richie Rich: Harvey Comics and Isabella himself occupy important stations along that circuit as publisher and bookseller, respectively. They also remind us that Darnton, in his famous essay "What Is the History of Books?," concludes that the experiences of readers are the most difficult to reconstruct or access.

Since its origins in the Annales school of social history, book history has sought to connect case studies of publications, authors, and retailers to the overall culture in which those case studies took place. As Régis Debray notes, because "historians of ideas . . . having tended to concentrate on textual analysis, those who take up sociocultural history have, in place of that, turned more recently to the history of the book" (112), but he also records that book historians like Darnton now wish to move from the history of ideas to the history of communication, and that "it becomes necessary to move from the history of ideas to that of meaning if we want to take into account the broad spectrum of all flows of information that can circulate, in both directions, between the man in the street and the Great Author, taking such forms as pamphlets, rumors, songs, common reports, tracts, lampoons, caricatures, word of mouth, leaflets, and satires" (112)—the milieu of the early modern equivalents of the comic book. Comic books, precisely because they have occupied the same strata of value as Debray's examples, have an understudied role to play in histories of the book.

In that context, it is particularly meaningful that the portrayal of material value in comic books is confused by the materiality of those texts. I would never argue, in the face of evidence, that *instead* of seeing Richie Rich as an unsympathetic, smug monster, readers actually saw him as a good-hearted fantasy adventurer wryly plagued with wealth. Instead, both readings coexist and are given emphasis by some material contexts—actual *readers* of Richie Rich such as Isabella's customers (who, after all, sought out a comic book store to acquire their material) would be much more likely to see Richie as an intentionally ironic figure for whom wealth is not ultimately very important; readers who were reached by the ramifications of Ernie Colón's realization that money gets boringly repetitive. On the other hand, readers primarily aware of Richie as an iconic brand would perhaps only see him reveling in wealth for decades on end (on supermarket shelves no less), and be more inclined to see the character as a caricature of the undeserving wealthy. In the case of Barks's Uncle Scrooge McDuck, the change has been chronological: a reader encountering "Back to the Klondike" in the handsome Fantagraphics hardcover of 2012 is primed to appreciate the story as a moral model for Scrooge's prizing of love above money—within reason. It was entirely possible for a reader in 1953 to see the story that way, but it was a little less likely thanks to the poor quality of the 1953 printing; and this is all to say nothing of the 1977 printing, in which ads emphasize how far the reader is from Scrooge's position. With millions of readers, even a slight adjustment to possible interpretations is consequential. For *Watchmen* and *Dubble Bubble Funnies*, meaning is at stake, and while *Watchmen* is in the custody of a publisher deeply invested in forging a psychological-historical classic that stands above the genre, the other ways to read *Watchmen* still exist. *Dubble Bubble Funnies* has not yet had the fortune to be revalued by its publisher or by fans, but even so it has meaning. As unshakable as some sort of sticky substance on the bottom of a shoe, the *Funnies* are a kind of memento mori for comics studies as it confidently walks the streets with head held high: Pud saying "even in Academia, there am I."

What does this argument say about twentieth-century American comics, and about the *mentalité* from which these comics originated? As Pierre Bourdieu posited in *Distinction*:

> Intellectuals and artists have a special predilection for the most risky but also most profitable strategies of distinction, those which consist in asserting the power, which is peculiarly theirs, to constitute insignificant objects as works of art or, more subtly, to give aesthetic redefinition to objects already defined as art, but in another mode, by other classes of class fractions (e.g., kitsch). In this case, it is the manner of consuming which creates the object of consumption, and a second-degree delight which transforms the "vulgar" artifacts abandoned to common consumption, Westerns, strip cartoons, family snapshots, graffiti, into distinguished and distinctive works of culture. (279)

What a study of the varied fortunes of material comic books reveals is that not just any "strip cartoon" can be turned into distinguished and distinctive works of culture—the vulgar artifact must have an ambiguous value in the first place, and that ambiguity must be altered as part of this redefinition. In other words, the unfixed portrayal of value within comic books, such as Barks's ambivalent Scrooge or *Watchmen*'s investment in street-level comics, is precisely what has allowed comic books to be the subject of their enormous value transformation in American culture since the 1950s. If Pud ever becomes a hardcover, it will present the strip as having value, and not just the price of the hardcover book.

At the same time, ambiguous values are not enough. In much the same way that the transformation of comic books has prompted the remediation of comics into the new form of the graphic novel, maintaining a textual message while radically altering the material context, the messages of some comics have left them unable to remediate with anything like the same level of success. Bourdieu's strategy of distinction has not functioned for *Richie Rich* or *Dubble Bubble Funnies*, and it is difficult to imagine that it could. The difference between these case studies no doubt has something to do with corporate ownership (Warner Bros.' DC Comics division and Disney's partners Dell and Western, as against the defunct Harvey and the smaller Tootsie Roll Industries), but more to do with reading practices. A major difficulty for this study has been the enormous paucity of information about how texts have been read. As any book historian would suggest with a survey of comics studies, and as many comics scholars have suggested, significantly more work is needed on how people bought and read comics.

As another example, journalist Ryan Holmberg describes a very different *Richie Rich* encounter from Isabella's in his article about the rental bookstores—circulating libraries—of Mumbai. Noting that these rental comics are often physically repaired and refurbished by the owner, Holmberg detects in this material an element of satire: "In place of the wealthy and ingenuous blonde cartoon kid, the covers of some *Richie Rich* issues now feature images of wealthy white people taken from luxury advertisements in British fashion and lifestyle magazines. The 'Richie Rich' scrawled on these new covers, sometimes more than once, seems as much a description of the cover images as the content inside." What if a reader came to Richie as an emanation from another country (and indeed, not just *any* other country, but the precise colonizing reason for the presence of English-language comic books, as Shilpa Davé points out [130]), an ambassador clad in photographs of wealthy Britons?

From a book history perspective, the horizon of comics readership seems to stretch on forever. The readers described by Isabella and Holmberg inhabit worlds different from my own, but looking at the works in question enables some imaginary reconstruction of how they might have been read by their purchasers. And beyond. Secondary and tertiary readers, and readers further removed from purchasers—it begins to feel that in this parent/child/sibling/friends economy, the answer to a variety of puzzlements might yet remain. In writing this book, I came across many, many allusions to Richie Rich in rap music, from Kool G Rap's statement in 1992's "Crime Pays" that violent criminals are striving to become Richie Rich, to the Insane Clown Posse's apocalyptic invocation of judgment for everyone from Richie Rick [*sic*] to Charlie Cheap in 2009's "Bang! Pow! Boom!" The branding of the character is so excellent that he still survives as shorthand for the materially successful life, without the satirical layer I describe above (although the concept of "the Black Richie Rich" is an intriguing recurring trope). The Insane Clown

Posse's lyrics in particular brought me up short: in some ways, my entire point in this book is that, from comic books to comics studies, Richie Rich necessarily implies the existence of Charlie Cheap.

Beyond this book's implications for comics studies, I believe that because of comics' specific history as an integral part of consumer culture, their material form has a relevance to the history of the book at large. Comic books are a rare example of a cultural category that has, within living memory, become a somewhat abject physical form that is the source of texts regarded enormously well by critics and audiences. Comics have as a category undergone a serious shift in cultural capital (in Bourdieu's term), yet this shift has accompanied a large-scale change in physical format. Considering that one of the major debates in book history is precisely the nature of large-scale cultural change, a shift as unusual as that of comics, taking place within print culture but recently enough to be reconstructed by the diligent application of book history methods, resonates with the field's major concerns.

Adrienne Resha argues that around 2012, American comics entered the Blue Age, defined at least partially by the role of the "immaterial" digital: guided reading technology, social media and fandom, and digital comics. In the Blue Age, physical comics continue to exist and indeed are "associated with value and status" (Resha 71), but they now define half of a tense relationship with the digital. This tension is far from abstract: as Resha correctly points out, the Blue Age is also defined by conflict on many levels between traditional and nontraditional audiences, as defined along many axes of identity, a conflict easily mapped to the material/digital divide. This book is solidly concerned with traditional comics in that sense but heavily dwells on the construction of those comics as having value and status that is profoundly historically contingent. On the other side of the shift in the value of the comic book, it makes sense to see Carl Barks and *Watchmen* as traditional stalwarts, and they often are used as such—but they didn't start as texts for traditional fans, and the texts didn't arrive in the Blue Age without many incarnations in between. Arguably, Richie Rich and *Dubble Bubble Funnies* didn't make it into the 2020s at all, except as subjects of nostalgia. A serious look at the material lives of "traditional" comics, and particularly how other values have always been present, can only add to this story by pointing out that the "traditional" comic book has its own complex history, one that does not have to end as the intractable nemesis of the Blue Age. To paraphrase Isabella, Richie Rich was never exclusively the character of rich white boys.

A great many of the comics discussed here are no longer cheap, yet the reason they are now expensive has everything to do with what happened to cheap comics. The thrown-out collection, the newsstand purchase read through to tatters, the pulped returns, the candy wrapper, the fish-wrap newspaper, the supermarket racks, the taped covers, the gas station giveaways, the back covers folded in, the floppies folded to fit in a back pocket: the value of comics, not only the mint copies and complete runs but the Good Artists and the Greatest Graphic Novels, is defined by necessarily absent trash. The same is true in comics studies.

NOTES

INTRODUCTION: COMICS AND BOOKS

1. David M. Earle argues that the influence of dime novels on pulp magazines is overstated, pointing to the context of other, more popular all-fiction magazines (8).

2. Controversy continues around this historiography. See Kunka for the more tangled 1960s–1970s history of the term and concept.

CHAPTER 1: BACK TO "BACK TO THE KLONDIKE": BOOK HISTORY AND CULTURAL SALVAGE

1. Zoë Smith's article on CYMK processes and representations of Black skin serves as a strong reminder that whiteness (of the paper, and of cartoon skin) is insidiously invisible in considering only four colors as contributing to meaning on the page.

CHAPTER 3: MONEY, MONEY, MONEY: READING RIcHIE RIcH

1. The "Harvey Girls" merit significantly greater attention than they have yet received. Kathy Merlock Jackson and Mark Arnold, in their overview of Harvey's kid comics, argue that the (anomalous in an industry-wide historical context) female characters are more significant to understanding Harvey Comics than Richie Rich, while Michelle Ann Abate's chapter on Little Audrey makes a compelling argument for that specific character's complexity. Christopher Hayton and Janardana Hayton point out the sadly unusual racial politics of the series. These characters were adapted into a Netflix animated series in the late 2010s, in which both Casper and Richie Rich eventually appeared.

2. The permutations outside the bounds of house style could intriguingly resemble both AI art generation and the work of visual artist Jess, who made collages out of the Dick Tracy comics of Chester Gould, but most notably Mark Newgarden's Nancy permutations in his 1986 work for *RAW* magazine, "Love's Savage Fury."

3. The series *Richie Rich & Jackie Jokers*, spotlighting Richie's "showbiz" friend Jackie, frequently parodied movies and, in issue #8 (January 1975), included "Dr. Jackie and Mr. Hide," a parody of the Robert Louis Stevenson novel and film adaptations.

4. The most significant US publisher and group of titles to have not shifted away from newsstand distribution is Archie Comics, demonstrating that business success continued to be possible in that market through the 1990s.

WORKS CITED

Abate, Michelle Ann. *Funny Girls: Guffaws, Guts, and Gender in Classic American Comics*. UP of Mississippi, 2018.
Adelman, Bob. *Tijuana Bibles: Art and Wit in America's Forbidden Funnies, 1930s–1950s*. Simon and Schuster, 2005.
Adin, Mariah. *The Brooklyn Thrill-Kill Gang and the Great Comic Book Scare of the 1950s*. Praeger, 2015.
Albritton, Robert. *Let Them Eat Junk: How Capitalism Creates Hunger and Obesity*. Pluto Press, 2009.
Anderson, Benedict. *Imagined Communities: Reflections on the Origin and Spread of Nationalism*. Verso, 1983.
Anderson, John C., and Bradley Katz. "Read Only Memory: *Maus* and Its Marginalia on CD-ROM." *Considering "Maus": Approaches to Art Spiegelman's "Survivor's Tale" of the Holocaust*, edited by Deborah R. Geis, U of Alabama P, 2003, pp. 159–74.
Andrae, Thomas. *Carl Barks and the Disney Comic Book: Unmasking the Myth of Modernity*. UP of Mississippi, 2006.
Arnold, Mark, editor. *The Best of the Harveyville Fun Times!* Fun Ideas Productions, 2006.
Arnold, Mark. "A Family Affair: The Harvey Comics Story." *Comic Book Artist*, no. 19, June 2002, pp. 18–39.
Arnold, Mark. *The Harvey Comics Companion*. BearManor Media, 2017.
Ault, Donald. *Carl Barks: Conversations*. UP of Mississippi, 2003.
Ayres, Jackson: "The Integrity of the Work: Alan Moore, Modernism, and the Corporate Author." *Journal of Modern Literature*, vol. 39, no. 2, Winter 2016, pp. 144–66.
Banham, Rob. "The Industrialization of the Book, 1800–1970." *A Companion to the History of the Book*, edited by Simon Eliot and Jonathan Rose, Wiley-Blackwell, 2007, pp. 273–90.
Barber, Benjamin R. *Consumed: How Markets Corrupt Children, Infantilize Adults, and Swallow Citizens Whole*. W. W. Norton, 2007.
Baring-Gould, William S., editor. *The Annotated Sherlock Holmes*, by Arthur Conan Doyle. Clarkson N. Potter, 1967.
Barks, Carl. *The Best of Uncle Scrooge and Donald Duck* #1. Gold Key, 1966.
Barks, Carl. *The Carl Barks Library of Walt Disney's Uncle Scrooge*, 1952–1958, set III, *Uncle Scrooge, 1–20*. Another Rainbow, 1984.
Barks, Carl. *Four Color* #456. Dell, 1953.
Barks, Carl. *Gladstone Comic Album* #4. Gladstone, 1987.

Barks, Carl. *Only a Poor Old Man*. Fantagraphics Books, 2012.
Barks, Carl. *Uncle Scrooge* #22. Dell, 1955.
Barks, Carl. *Uncle Scrooge* #142. Gold Key, 1977.
Barks, Carl. *Walt Disney's Uncle Scrooge Adventures in Color* #2. Gladstone, 1996.
Barnes, David. "Time in the Gutter: Temporal Structures in *Watchmen*." *KronoScope*, vol. 9, nos. 1–2, May 2009, pp. 51–60.
Barrier, Michael. *Funnybooks: The Improbable Glories of the Best American Comic Books*. U of California P, 2015.
Barrier, Michael, and Martin Williams. *A Smithsonian Book of Comic-Book Comics*. Smithsonian Institution Press, 1982.
Beaty, Bart. *Comics versus Art*. U of Toronto P, 2012.
Beaty, Bart. *Twelve-Cent Archie*. Rutgers UP, 2015.
Beaty, Bart, and Benjamin Woo. *The Greatest Comic Book of All Time: Symbolic Capital and the Field of American Comic Books*. Palgrave Macmillan, 2016.
Beaty, Bart, and Benjamin Woo. What Were Comics? Whatwerecomics.com.
Becker, Romain. "Telling *The Killing Joke*: How Editorial Intent Co-Constructs a Comic." *Comicalités*, April 1, 2021, https://journals.openedition.org/comicalites/5754.
Belk, Russell W. "Material Values in the Comics: A Content Analysis of Comic Books Featuring Themes of Wealth." *Journal of Consumer Research*, vol. 14, no. 1, June 1987, pp. 26–42.
Bell, Blake, and Michael J. Vassallo. *The Secret History of Marvel Comics*. Fantagraphics Books, 2013.
Benson, John. "Silver Threads among the Mold." *Alter Ego*, vol. 3, no. 89, Oct. 2009, pp. 3–12.
Blake, Brandy Ball. "*Watchmen*: The Graphic Novel as Trauma Fiction." *ImageTexT*, vol. 5, no. 1, 2009, https://imagetextjournal.com/watchmen-the-graphic-novel-as-trauma-fiction/.
Block, Paula M., and Terry J. Erdmann. *Star Trek: The Original Topps Trading Card Series*. Abrams ComicArts, 2013.
Boscagli, Maurizia. *Stuff Theory: Everyday Objects, Radical Materialism*. Bloomsbury, 2014.
Bourdieu, Pierre. *Distinction: A Social Critique of the Judgement of Taste*. Translated by Richard Nice, Routledge, 2010.
Brake, Laurel. *Print in Transition, 1850–1910: Studies in Media and Book History*. Palgrave, 2001.
Brienza, Casey. "Books, Not Comics: Publishing Fields, Globalization, and Japanese Manga in the United States." *Publishing Research Quarterly*, vol. 25, no. 2, June 2009, pp. 101–17.
Brown, Stephen. *Brands and Branding*. Sage, 2016.
Browne, Ray B., editor. *Popular Culture and the Expanding Consciousness*. John Wiley and Sons, 1973.
Bugs Bunny and Buried Treasure. Warner Bros., 1949.
Cabarga, Leslie, editor. *Harvey Comics Classics*, vol. 2, *Richie Rich: The Poor Little Rich Boy*. Dark Horse Books, 2007.
"Cadet Sweets: Doctor Who and the Daleks." *The Keys of Marinus*, *Doctor Who*. BBC, 2010.
Carr, David. *Candymaking in Canada: The History and Business of Canada's Confectionery Industry*. Dundurn Group, 2003.

Carvell, Tim. "How One Man Spooked Universal." *Fortune*, Dec. 29, 1997, p. 48.
Chartier, Roger. "The Practical Impact of Writing." *The Book History Reader*, edited by David Finkelstein and Alistair McCleery, Routledge, 2006, pp. 118–42.
Chromik-Krzykawska, Anna. "Reusing or Refusing? Waste in the Discourse of Wastelessness." *Rubbish, Waste and Litter: Culture and Its Refuse/als*, edited by Tadeusz Rachwał, Wydawnictwo SWPSA Academica, 2008, pp. 102–12.
Ciemcioch, Mark. "Marvel for Kids: Star Comics." *Back Issue*, vol. 1, no. 77, Dec. 2014, pp. 65–74.
Colón, Ernie. "The Importance of Being Ernie." Interview by Jon B. Cooke. *Comic Book Artist*, no. 19, June 2002, pp. 74–78.
Cook, Daniel Thomas. "Children's Subjectivities and Commercial Meaning: The Delicate Battle Mothers Wage When Feeding Their Children." *Children, Food and Identity in Everyday Life*, edited by Allison James, Anne Trine Kjørholt, and Vebjørg Tingstad, Palgrave Macmillan, 2009, pp. 118–27.
Cook, Roy T., and Aaron Meskin. "Comics, Prints, and Multiplicity." *Journal of Aesthetics and Art Criticism*, vol. 73, no. 1, Winter 2015, pp. 57–67.
Corrigan, Timothy, and Patricia White. *The Film Experience: An Introduction*. 2nd ed., Bedford/St. Martin's, 2009.
Cracknell, Ryan. "A Brief History of *Back to the Future* Trading Cards." Beckett Collectibles, May 6, 2018, https://www.beckett.com/news/back-to-the-future-trading-cards/.
Daniels, Les. *Comix: A History of Comic Books in America*. Bonanza Books, 1971.
Danky, James, and Denis Kitchen. *Underground Classics: The Transformation of Comics into Comix*. Harry N. Abrams, 2009.
Darnton, Robert. "What Is the History of Books?" *The Broadview Reader in Book History*, edited by Michelle Levy and Tom Mole, Broadview Press, 2015, pp. 231–50.
Davé, Shilpa. "Spider-Man India: Comic Books and the Translating/Transcreating of American Cultural Narratives." *Transnational Perspectives on Graphic Narratives: Comics at the Crossroads*, edited by Shane Denson, Christina Meyer, and Daniel Stein, Bloomsbury, 2013, pp. 127–43.
Davis, Kenneth C. *Two-Bit Culture: The Paperbacking of America*. Houghton Mifflin, 1984.
Davis, Paul. *The Lives and Times of Ebenezer Scrooge*. Yale UP, 1990.
DC Entertainment Essential Graphic Novels and Chronology 2015. DC Comics, 2015.
DC Entertainment Graphic Novel Essentials and Chronology 2014. DC Comics, 2014.
DC Essential Graphic Novels 2016. DC Comics, 2016.
DC Essential Graphic Novels 2017. DC Comics, 2017.
DC Essential Graphic Novels 2018. DC Comics, 2018.
Debray, Régis. *Transmitting Culture*. Translated by Eric Rauth, Columbia UP, 2000.
DiCesare, Catherine R. *Sweeping the Way: Divine Transformation in the Aztec Festival of Ochpaniztli*. UP of Colorado, 2009.
Dietrich, Bryan. "The Human Stain: Chaos and the Rage for Order in *Watchmen*." *Extrapolation*, vol. 50, no. 1, March 2009, pp. 120–44.
Dittmar, Jakob F. "Experiments in Digital Comics: Somewhere between Comics and Multimedia Storytelling." *Comics Forum*, March 14, 2015, https://comicsforum.org

/2015/03/14/experiments-in-digital-comics-somewhere-between-comics-and-mult imedia-storytelling-by-jakob-f-dittmar/.

Dittmer, Jason. "The Tyranny of the Serial: Popular Geopolitics, the Nation, and Comic Book Discourse." *Antipode*, vol. 39, no. 2, March 2007, pp. 247–68.

Donahue, Dick. "Paperback Bestsellers/Trade." *Publishers Weekly*, March 16, 2009, p. 19.

Dorfman, Ariel, and Armand Mattelart. *How to Read Donald Duck: Imperialist Ideology in the Disney Comic*. Translated David Kunzle, International General, 1975.

Doyle, Larry, and Angelo DeCesare. "Richie Riche." *National Lampoon*, Dec. 1991, pp. 45–51.

Duin, Steve, and Mike Richardson. *Comics: Between the Panels*. Dark Horse Books, 1998.

Duke, Judith S. *Children's Books and Magazines: A Market Study*. Knowledge Industry Publications, 1979.

Earle, David M. "The Pulp New Deal: Audience, Popular Front Politics, and the Pulps as a Socially Democratic Form." *Journal of American Culture*, vol. 44, no. 1, March 2021, pp. 6–21.

EC Comics. *The EC Archives: The Haunt of Fear*, vol. 3. Comixology. Dark Horse Books, 2016.

Eichenwald, Kurt. "Recent Casper Popularity Doesn't Show Big Picture." *New York Times*, June 11, 1995, nytimes.com/1995/06/11/business/investing-it-street-smarts-recent -casper-popularity-doesn-t-show-big-picture.html.

Eisenstein, Elizabeth L. *The Printing Press as an Agent of Change*. Cambridge UP, 2005.

Eisner, Will. *Comics and Sequential Art*. Poorhouse Press, 1985.

Erwin, Brent E., et al. *Richie Rich #1*. Comixology. Ape Entertainment, 2013.

Exner, Eike. *Comics and the Origins of Manga: A Revisionist History*. Rutgers UP, 2022.

Fantagraphics. "The Complete Carl Barks Library." https://www.fantagraphics.com/ collections/the-complete-carl-barks-library.

Feiffer, Jules. *The Great Comic Book Heroes*. Dial Press, 1965.

Feldman, Michael. "How Men's Magazines Got to the Masses." *The History of Men's Magazines from 1900 to Post-WWII*, edited by Dian Hanson, Taschen, 2004.

Flagg, Gordon. "Another Look at: *Watchmen*." *Booklist*, March 1, 2009, p. 34.

"Fleer Closes Philadelphia Plant." *Candy Industry*, vol. 12, no. 160, Dec. 1995.

Fraser, Laura. "The Inner Corset: A Brief History of Fat in the United States." *The Fat Studies Reader*, edited by Esther Rothblum and Sondra Solovay, New York UP, 2009, pp. 11–14.

"The Fuddleduck Diggins." *Donald Duck* #125. Gold Key, 1969.

Gabaccia, Donna R. "As American as Budweiser and Pickles? Nation-Building in American Food Industries." *Food Nations: Selling Taste in Consumer Societies*, edited by Warren Belasco and Philip Scranton, Routledge, 2002, pp. 175–90.

Gabilliet, Jean-Paul. *Of Comics and Men: A Cultural History of American Comic Books*. Translated by Bart Beaty and Nick Nguyen, UP of Mississippi, 2010.

Gardner, Jared. *Projections: Comics and the History of Twenty-First-Century Storytelling*. Stanford UP, 2012.

Garvey, Ellen Gruber. "Out of the Mainstream and into the Streets: Small Press Magazines, the Underground Press, Zines, and Artists' Books." *Perspectives on American Book*

History: Artifacts and Commentary, edited by Scott E. Casper, Joanne D. Chaison, and Jeffrey D. Groves, U of Massachusetts P, 2002, pp. 367–402.

Gaskell, Philip. *A New Introduction to Bibliography*. Oak Knoll Press, 2009.

Gearino, Dan. *Comic Shop: The Retail Mavericks Who Gave Us a New Geek Culture*. Swallow Press, 2017.

Genette, Gérard. *Paratexts: Thresholds of Interpretation*. Translated by Jane E. Lewin, Cambridge UP, 1997.

Ghosal, Torsa. "Books with Bodies: Narrative Progression in Chris Ware's Building Stories." *Storyworlds: A Journal of Narrative Studies*, vol. 7, no. 1, Summer 2015, pp. 75–99.

Gibbons, Dave. *Watchmen: Artifact Edition*. IDW Publishing, 2014.

Gibbons, Dave. *The Watchmen Portfolio*. DC Comics, 1988.

Gibbons, Dave, et al. *Watching the Watchmen*. Titan Books, 2008.

Gluckson, Robert. "The Big Boy's Comic Book." *The History of Men's Magazines from 1900 to Post-WWII*, edited by Dian Hanson, Taschen, 2004.

Gordon, Ian. *Comic Strips and Consumer Culture, 1890–1945*. Smithsonian Institution Press, 1998.

Gordon, Ian. "Culture of Consumption: Commodification through *Superman: Return to Krypton*." *Critical Approaches to Comics: Theories and Methods*, edited by Matthew J. Smith and Randy Duncan, Routledge, 2012, pp. 157–66.

Goulart, Ron. *The Adventurous Decade: Comic Strips in the Thirties*. Arlington House, 1975.

Goulart, Ron. *Comic Book Encyclopedia: The Ultimate Guide to Characters, Graphic Novels, Writers, and Artists in the Comic Book Universe*. HarperCollins, 2004.

Goulart, Ron. *Great American Comic Books*. Publications International, 2001.

Grand Comics Database. "Watchmen." https://www.comics.org/issue/43793/.

Greenberger, Robert. "Comic Books Examine Themselves." *Watchmen* #1, by Alan Moore and Dave Gibbons, Millenium Edition, DC Comics, 2000.

Groening, Matt. "Behind the Laughter." *The Simpsons*, season 11, episode 22, Fox, May 21, 2000.

Groening, Matt. "Three Men and a Comic Book." *The Simpsons*, season 2, episode 21, Fox, May 9, 1991.

Groensteen, Thierry. "Definitions." *The French Comics Theory Reader*, edited by Ann Miller and Bart Beaty, Leuven UP, 2014, pp. 93–114.

Grossman, Lev. Review excerpt on book cover. *Watchmen*, by Alan Moore and Dave Gibbons, DC Comics, 2014.

Hague, Ian. *Comics and the Senses: A Multisensory Approach to Comics and Graphic Novels*. Routledge, 2014.

Hajdu, David. *The Ten-Cent Plague: The Great Comic-Book Scare and How It Changed America*. Picador, 2009.

Harris-Fain, Darren. "Watchmen." *Critical Survey of Graphic Novels: Heroes and Superheroes*, vol. 2, edited by Bart H. Beaty and Stephen Weiner, Salem Press, 2012, pp. 622–26.

Harvey, Alan. "Harvey Shame." *Animation World Magazine*, vol. 5, no. 6, Sept. 2000, awn.com/mag/issue5.06/5.06pages/5.06letters.php3.

Harvey, Robert C. *Children of the Yellow Kid: The Evolution of the American Comic Strip.* Frye Art Museum, 1998.

Hatfield, Charles. *Alternative Comics: An Emerging Literature.* UP of Mississippi, 2005.

Hayles, N. Katherine. "How We Read: Close, Hyper, Machine." *The Broadview Reader in Book History,* edited by Michelle Levy and Tom Mole, Broadview Press, 2015, pp. 491–510.

Hayles, N. Katherine. "Print Is Flat, Code Is Deep: The Importance of Media-Specific Analysis." *Poetics Today,* vol. 25, no. 1, Spring 2004, pp. 67–90.

Hayton, Christopher J., and Janardana D. Hayton. "In the Minority: Constructions of American Dream Childhood in 1950s–Early 1960s *Little Audrey* Comics." *Picturing Childhood: Youth in Transnational Comics,* edited by Mark Heimermann and Brittany Tullis, U of Texas P, 2017, pp. 48–69.

Hedges, Joseph. *Wild Times: An Oral History of WildStorm Studios.* Esposito and Hedges, 2017. http://www.wildstormoralhistory.com/.

Heer, Jeet, and Kent Worcester, editors. *Arguing Comics: Literary Masters on a Popular Medium.* UP of Mississippi, 2004.

Heller, Steven, and Anne Fink. *Food Wrap: Packages That Sell.* Graphic Details, 1996.

Hensley, Tim. *Wally Gropius.* Fantagraphics Books, 2010.

Herman, Lenny, et al. *Royal Roy. Star Comics All-Star Collection,* vol. 1, Marvel Comics, 2009, pp. 50–95.

Herman, Lenny, et al. *Top Dog. Star Comics All-Star Collection,* vol. 1, Marvel Comics, 2009, pp. 96–164.

Hindman, Sandra L. Introduction. *Printing the Written Word: The Social History of Books, circa 1450–1520,* edited by Sandra L. Hindman, Cornell UP, 1991, pp. 1–18.

Hoberek, Andrew. *Considering Watchmen: Poetics, Property, Politics.* Rutgers UP, 2014.

Holmberg. Ryan. "Poor Little Rich Boys: The Art of the Mumbai Circulating Library." *Comics Journal,* Nov. 18, 2013, http://www.tcj.com/poor-little-rich-boys-the-art-of-the-mumbai-circulating-library/.

Holtz, Allan. *American Newspaper Comics: An Encyclopedic Reference Guide.* U of Michigan P, 2005.

Horn, Maurice. *100 Years of American Newspaper Comics.* Gramercy Books, 1996.

Horn, Maurice. *The World Encyclopedia of Comics.* Chelsea House, 1999. 7 vols.

Howsam, Leslie. *Old Books and New Histories: An Orientation to Studies in Book and Print Culture.* U of Toronto P, 2006.

Hughes, Jamie A. "'Who Watches the Watchmen?' Ideology and 'Real World' Superheroes." *Journal of Popular Culture,* vol. 39, no. 4, July 2006, pp. 546–57.

Hunter, Beatrice Trum. "The Evolution of Chewing Gum." *Consumers' Research,* Oct. 2003, pp. 18–23.

Hutton, Robert. "A Mouse in the Bookstore: *Maus* and the Publishing Industry." *South Central Review,* vol. 32, no. 3, Fall 2015, pp. 30–44.

IDW Publishing. "Dave Gibbons' Watchmen Artifact Edition HC." www.idwpublishing.com/product/dave-gibbons-watchmen-artifact-edition-hc/.

Insane Clown Posse. "Bang! Pow! Boom!" *Bang! Pow! Boom!* Psychopathic Records, 2009.

Isabella, Tony. "Ghosts, Witches, Giants, Devils, Dogfaces, Zillionaires and Other Friends: The Harvey Comics Legacy." *The Best of the Harveyville Fun Times!*, edited by Mark Arnold, Fun Ideas Productions, 2006, pp. 3–4.
Itzkoff, Dave. "Behind the Mask." *New York Times Book Review*, Nov. 20, 2005, www.nytimes.com/2005/11/20/books/review/behind-the-mask.html.
Itzkoff, Dave. Review excerpt on book cover. *Watchmen*, by Alan Moore and Dave Gibbons, DC Comics, 2014.
Jackson, Kathy Merlock, and Mark D. Arnold. "Baby-Boom Children and Harvey Comics after the Code: A Neighborhood of Little Girls and Boys." *ImageTexT*, vol. 3, no. 3, 2007, https://imagetextjournal.com/baby-boom-children-and-harvey-comics-after-the-code-a-neighborhood-of-little-girls-and-boys/.
Jacobson, Sid. "Sid's Kids: The Harvey Years." Interview by Bill Matheny. *Comic Book Artist*, no. 19, June 2002, pp. 40–56.
Jacobson, Sid. "You Could Get Away with Murder!" Interview by John Benson. *Alter Ego*, vol. 3, no. 89, Oct. 2009, pp. 24–40.
James, Allison, Anne Trine Kjørholt, and Vebjørg Tingstad, editors. *Children, Food and Identity in Everyday Life*. Palgrave Macmillan, 2009.
Jamieson, Dave. *Mint Condition: How Baseball Cards Became an American Obsession*. Atlantic Monthly Press, 2010.
Janocha, Bill. "Créme de la Kremer." Interview with Ken Selig, Warren Kremer, and Grace Kremer. *Comic Book Artist*, no. 19, June 2002, pp. 56–67.
Jenkins, Henry. "The Cultural Logic of Media Convergence." *International Journal of Cultural Studies*, vol. 7, no. 1, March 2004, pp. 33–43.
Jenkins, Henry. "Should We Discipline the Reading of Comics?" *Critical Approaches to Comics: Theories and Methods*, edited by Matthew J. Smith and Randy Duncan, Routledge, 2012, pp. 1–14.
Jensen, Jeff. Review excerpt on book cover. *Watchmen*, by Alan Moore and Dave Gibbons, DC Comics, 2014.
Jensen, Jeff. "*Watchmen*: An Oral History." *Entertainment Weekly*, Oct. 21, 2005, http://ew.com/books/2005/10/21/watchmen-oral-history/.
Jesser, Dave, and Matt Silverstein, creators. "The One Wherein There Is a Big Twist, part 1." *Drawn Together*, season 1, episode 7, Double Hemm and Rough Draft Studios, 2004.
Johanningsmeier, Charles. "The Industrialization and Nationalization of American Periodical Publishing." *Perspectives on American Book History: Artifacts and Commentary*, edited by Scott E. Casper, Joanne D. Chaison, and Jeffrey D. Groves, U of Massachusetts P, 2002, pp. 311–38.
Johns, Geoff, and Ethan Van Sciver. *Absolute Green Lantern: Rebirth*. DC Comics, 2010.
Johnston, Rich. "How Watchmen Will Be Annotated—And Remind You about Vietnam." *Bleeding Cool*, March 16, 2017, https://www.bleedingcool.com/2017/03/16/how-watchmen-will-be-annotated-and-remind-you-about-vietnam/.
Juricevic, Igor, and Alicia Joleen Horvath. "Analysis of Motions in Comic Book Cover Art: Using Pictorial Metaphors." *Comics Grid: Journal of Comics Scholarship*, vol. 6, no. 1, 2016, p. 6, https://www.comicsgrid.com/article/id/3532/.
Juvenal. *The Satires*. Translated by Niall Rudd, Oxford UP, 2008.

Kahn, Michael Alexander, and Richard Samuel West. *What Fools These Mortals Be! The Story of Puck, America's First and Most Influential Magazine of Color Political Cartoons.* IDW Publishing, 2014.

Karasik, Paul, and Mark Newgarden. *How to Read Nancy: The Elements of Comics in Three Easy Panels.* Fantagraphics Books, 2017.

Kashtan, Aaron. *Between Pen and Pixel: Comics, Materiality, and the Book of the Future.* Ohio State UP, 2018.

Kashtan, Aaron. "Digital Comics and Material Richness." *Comics Forum*, July 12, 2013, https://comicsforum.org/2013/07/12/digital-comics-and-material-richness-by-aaron-kashtan/.

Kashtan, Aaron. "My Mother Was a Typewriter: *Fun Home* and the Importance of Materiality in Comics Studies." *Journal of Graphic Novels and Comics*, vol. 4, no. 1, 2013, pp. 92–116.

Katz, Bill. *Dahl's History of the Book.* 3rd English ed., Scarecrow Press, 1995.

Kawash, Samira. *Candy: A Century of Panic and Pleasure.* Farrar, Straus and Giroux, 2013.

Keating, Erin M. "The Female Link: Citation and Continuity in *Watchmen*." *Journal of Popular Culture*, vol. 45, no. 6, March 2012, pp. 1266–88.

Kidman, Shawna. *Comic Books Incorporated: How the Business of Comics Became the Business of Hollywood.* U of California P, 2019.

Kimmerle, Beth. *Candy: The Sweet History.* Collectors Press, 2003.

Kirkpatrick, Robert J. *From the Penny Dreadful to the Ha'Penny Dreadfuller: A Bibliographical History of the Boys' Periodical in Britain, 1762–1950.* British Library; Oak Knoll Press, 2013.

Kirtz, Jaime Lee. "Computers, Comics and Cult Status: A Forensics of Digital Graphic Novels." *Digital Humanities Quarterly*, vol. 8, no. 3, 2014, http://www.digitalhumanities.org/dhq/vol/8/3/000185/000185.html.

Klaehn, Jeffery. "An Interview with Chris Ryall, Chief Creative Officer and Editor-in-Chief of IDW Publishing." *Journal of Graphic Novels and Comics*, vol. 7, no. 1, January 2016, pp. 88–92.

Klinger, Leslie S., editor. *Watchmen Annotated*, by Alan Moore and Dave Gibbons, DC Comics, 2017.

Knowlton, Timothy W. "Filth and Healing in Yucatan: Interpreting Ix Hun Ahau, a Maya Goddess." *Ancient Mesoamerica*, vol. 27, no. 2, Fall 2016, pp. 319–32.

Koch, Shelley L. *A Theory of Grocery Shopping: Food, Choice and Conflict.* Berg, 2012.

Konstantinou, Lee. "Watching Watchmen: A Riposte to Stuart Moulthrop." *Electronic Book Review*, Jan. 25, 2012, https://electronicbookreview.com/essay/watching-watchmen-a-riposte-to-stuart-moulthrop/.

Kool G. Rap and DJ Polo. "Crime Pays." *Live and Let Die.* Cold Chillin' Records, 1992.

Korda, Andrea. *Printing and Painting the News in Victorian London: "The Graphic" and Social Realism, 1869–1891.* Routledge, 2015.

Kremer, Warren. "Strange Things Went On in Those Days." Interview by John Benson. *Alter Ego*, vol. 3, no. 89, Oct. 2009, pp. 41–55.

Krieger, Todd. "Getting Rich off 'Richie's' Trademark." *Daily Breeze* (Torrance, CA), Dec. 18, 1994, p. D1.

Krugman, Dean M., and Jameson L. Hayes. "Brand Concepts and Advertising." *Advertising Theory*, edited by Shelly Rodgers and Esther Thorson, Routledge, 2012, pp. 434–48.

Kunka, Andrew J. "*A Contract with God*, *The First Kingdom*, and the 'Graphic Novel': The Will Eisner/Jack Katz Letters." *Inks: The Journal of the Comics Studies Society*, vol. 1, no. 1, Spring 2017, pp. 27–39.

Lacayo, Richard, and Lev Grossman. "Books: 10 of TIME's Hundred Best Novels." *Time*, Oct. 17, 2005, content.time.com/time/magazine/article/0,9171,1118375,00.html.

Lee, Stan. "Stan Lee: 1974." Interview by Jay Maeder. *Alter Ego*, vol. 3, no. 74, Dec. 2007, pp. 36–46.

Lefévre, Pascal. "Mise en Scène and Framing: Visual Storytelling in *Lone Wolf and Cub*." *Critical Approaches to Comics: Theories and Methods*, edited by Matthew J. Smith and Randy Duncan, Routledge, 2012, pp. 71–83.

Levitz, Paul. *75 Years of DC Comics: The Art of Modern Mythmaking*. Taschen, 2017.

Levitz, Paul. Inside cover note. *Watchmen* #1, by Alan Moore and Dave Gibbons, Millennium Edition, DC Comics, 2000.

Levy, Michelle, and Tom Mole. *The Broadview Introduction to Book History*. Broadview Press, 2017.

Lil' Romeo. "Richie Rich." *Gametime*. No Limit Records, 2002.

Lopes, Paul. "Growing Up: The Popular Genre Strategy in Transforming Mainstream Comic Books." American Sociological Association Annual Meeting, San Francisco, August 2004.

Lyles, William H. *Putting Dell on the Map: A History of the Dell Paperbacks*. Greenwood Press, 1983.

Lyons, Martyn. *A History of Reading and Writing in the Western World*. Palgrave Macmillan, 2007.

Manovich, Lev, Jeremy Douglass, and William Huber. "Understanding Scanlation: How to Read One Million Fan-Translated Manga Pages." *Image and Narrative*, vol. 12, no. 1, 2011, pp. 206–28.

Marcus, Leonard S. *Golden Legacy: The Story of Golden Books*. Golden Books, 2007.

Margerum, Eileen. "The Case for Sunny Jim: An Advertising Legend Revisited." *Sextant: The Journal of Salem State College*, vol. 12, nos. 1–2, Fall 2001–Spring 2002, https://web.archive.org/web/20080604161845/http://www.salemstate.edu/sextant/volXII_2/SEXT-essay-sunny-jim.htm.

Marschall, Rick, and Warren Bernard. *Drawing Power: A Compendium of Cartoon Advertising, 1870s–1940s*. Fantagraphics Books; Marschall Books, 2011.

Mash Out Posse. "Get the Fuck Outta Here." *Mash Out Posse*. Family First, 2004.

Mathews, Jennifer P. *Chicle: The Chewing Gum of the Americas, from the Ancient Maya to William Wrigley*. U of Arizona P, 2009.

McCloud, Scott. *Understanding Comics: The Invisible Art*. HarperCollins, 1994.

McDonnell, Patrick, et al. *Krazy Kat: The Comic Art of George Herriman*. Harry N. Abrams, 2004.

McNeal, James U. *On Becoming a Consumer: Development of Consumer Behavior Patterns in Childhood*. Butterworth-Heinemann, 2007.

Meskin, Aaron, and Roy T. Cook, editors. *The Art of Comics: A Philosophical Approach.* Wiley-Blackwell, 2012.

Meyer, Christina. "Serial Entertainment/Serial Pleasure: The Yellow Kid." *Media of Serial Narrative*, edited by Frank Kelleter, Ohio State UP, 2017, pp. 74–89.

Miettinen, Mervi. "Past as Multiple Choice: Textual Anarchy and the Problems of Continuity in *Batman: The Killing Joke*." *Scandinavian Journal of Comic Art*, vol. 1, no. 1, Spring 2012, pp. 5–25.

Millington, Michael P. "Paneling Rage: The Loss of Deliberate Sequence." *Crossing Boundaries in Graphic Narrative: Essays on Forms, Series and Genres*, edited by Jake Jakaitis and James F. Wurtz, McFarland, 2012, pp. 207–18.

Moor, Liz. *The Rise of Brands.* Berg, 2007.

Moore, Alan. "The Alan Moore Interview." Interview by Barry Kavanagh. *Blather*, Oct. 17, 2000, http://www.blather.net/projects/alan-moore-interview/.

Moore, Alan, and Dave Gibbons. *Absolute Watchmen*, Absolute Edition. DC Comics, 2005.

Moore, Alan, and Dave Gibbons. *Les Gardiens*, tome 3. Éditions Zenda, 1988.

Moore, Alan, and Dave Gibbons. *Watchmen.* DC Comics, 2014.

Moore, Alan, and Dave Gibbons. *Watchmen* #1, Millennium Edition. DC Comics, 2000.

Moore, Alan, and Dave Gibbons. *Watchmen* #1–12. DC Comics, 1986–1987.

Moore, Alan, and Dave Gibbons. *Watchmen Collector's Edition.* DC Comics, 2016.

Moore, Alan, and Dave Gibbons. *Watchmen: International Edition.* DC Comics, 2008. https://www.dccomics.com/graphic-novels/watchmen-1986/watchmen-international-edition.

Moore, Alan, and Dave Gibbons. *Watchmen Noir.* DC Comics, 2016.

Moore, Alan, and Dave Gibbons. *Watchmen: The Deluxe Edition.* DC Comics, 2013.

Morton, Drew. "'Watched Any Good Books Lately?' The Formal Failure of the *Watchmen* Motion Comic." *Cinema Journal*, vol. 56, no. 2, Winter 2017, pp. 132–37.

Moses, Geoffrey. "'What a Life!' Carl Barks' Donald Duck as Nervous Modern." *International Journal of Comic Art*, vol. 12, no. 1, Spring 2010, pp. 288–301.

Mosley, Walter. *Maximum FF: A Visual Exegesis of Fantastic Four #1*, by Stan Lee and Jack Kirby. Marvel Enterprises, 2005.

Mott, Frank Luther. *A History of American Magazines, 1741–1930*, vol. 3. Belknap Press of Harvard UP, 1958.

Mougin, Lou. "Thrilling Harvey Heroes." *Comic Book Artist*, no. 19, June 2002, pp. 88–96.

Murray, Padmini Ray. "Behind the Panel: Examining Invisible Labour in the Comics Publishing Industry." *Publishing Research Quarterly*, vol. 29, no. 4, Dec. 2013, pp. 336–43.

Nasaw, David. *The Chief: The Life of William Randolph Hearst.* Houghton Mifflin, 2001.

Nead, Lynda. *The Haunted Gallery: Painting, Photography, Film c. 1900.* Yale UP, 2007.

Nelson, Michelle R., and Chang Dae Ham. "The Reflexive Game: How Target and Agent Persuasion Knowledge Influence Advertising Persuasion." *Advertising Theory*, edited by Shelly Rodgers and Esther Thorson, Routledge, 2012, pp. 174–87.

"New Trump Hotel on Central Park." *New York Times*, Jan. 19, 1997, nytimes.com/1997/01/19/travel/new-trump-hotel-on-central-park.html.

Noakes, Richard. "*Punch* and Comic Journalism in Mid-Victorian Britain." *Science in the Nineteenth-Century Periodical: Reading the Magazine of Nature*, edited by Geoffrey Cantor et al., Cambridge UP, 2004, pp. 91–122.

Nolan, Michelle. *Love on the Racks: A History of American Romance Comics*. McFarland, 2008.
Nyberg, Amy Kiste. *Seal of Approval: The History of the Comics Code*. UP of Mississippi, 1998.
Orbán, Katalin. "A Language of Scratches and Stitches: The Graphic Novel between Hyperreading and Print." *Critical Inquiry*, vol. 40, no. 3, Spring 2014, pp. 169–81.
Parent, Dan, and Fernando Ruiz. *Die Kitty Die: Hollywood or Bust*. Comixology. Chapterhouse Comics, 2017.
Parille, Ken. "Friendly Ghosts and Comics Form." *Comics Journal*, Feb. 14, 2013, http://www.tcj.com/friendly-ghosts-and-comics-form/.
Pearson, David. *Books as History: The Importance of Books beyond Their Texts*. Rev. ed., British Library; Oak Knoll Press, 2012.
Pecora, Norma Odom. *The Business of Children's Entertainment*. Guilford Press, 1998.
Perry, George, and Alan Aldridge. *The Penguin Book of Comics*. Penguin Books, 1971.
Petrie, Donald, director. *Richie Rich*. Warner Bros., 1995.
Piatti-Farnell, Lorna. "'For God's Sake, Cover Yourself': Sexual Violence, Disrupted Histories, and the Gendered Politics of Patriotism in *Watchmen*." *Journal of Graphic Novels and Comics*, vol. 8, no. 3, April 2017, pp. 238–51.
Pizzino, Christopher. *Arresting Development: Comics at the Boundaries of Literature*. U of Texas P, 2016.
Pogrebin, Robin. "52-Story Comeback Is So Very Trump: Columbus Circle Tower Proclaims That Modesty Is an Overrated Virtue." *New York Times*, April 25, 1996, nytimes.com/1996/04/25/nyregion/52-story-comeback-so-very-trump-columbus-circle-tower-proclaims-that-modesty.html.
Polley, Jason S. "Watching the Watchmen, Mediating the Mediators." *Literature Compass*, vol. 10, no. 8, Aug. 2013, pp. 593–604.
Post, Howard. "Howie's Hot Stuff." Interview by Chris Knowles and Jon B. Cooke. *Comic Book Artist*, no. 19, June 2002, pp. 80–85.
Priego, Ernesto. "On Cultural Materialism, Comics and Digital Media." *Opticon1826*, no. 9, Autumn 2010, pp. 1–3.
Pustz, Matthew J. *Comic Book Culture: Fanboys and True Believers*. UP of Mississippi, 1999.
Quattro, Ken. "The Ken Quattro Interview." *Will Eisner: A Spirited Life*, by Bob Andelman, deluxe ed., TwoMorrows Publishing, 2015, pp. 23–28.
Radway, Janice A. *Reading the Romance: Women, Patriarchy, and Popular Literature*. U of North Carolina P, 1984.
Ray, Alice. "Who Translates the Translation? (Re)traduire les héros marginaux d'Alan Moore." *TranscUlturAl*, vol. 8, no. 2, 2016, pp. 42–67.
Redclift, Michael. *Chewing Gum: The Fortunes of Taste*. Routledge, 2004.
Reitberger, Reinhold, and Wolfgang J. Fuchs. *Comics: Anatomy of a Mass Medium*. Little, Brown, 1972.
Resha, Adrienne. "The Blue Age of Comic Books." *Inks: The Journal of the Comics Studies Society*, vol. 4, no. 1, Spring 2020, pp. 66–81.
Richie Rich #219. Harvey Comics, 1986.
"Richie Rich Finds a Friend." *Time*, Sept. 25, 1989, p. 57.

Rifkind, Candida. "The Biotopographies of Seth's *George Sprott (1894–1975)*." *Material Cultures in Canada*, edited by Thomas Allen and Jennifer Blair, Wilfrid Laurier UP, 2015, pp. 225–46.

Roberts, Garyn G. "Understanding the Sequential Art of Comic Strips and Comic Books and Their Descendants in the Early Years of the New Millennium." *Journal of American Culture*, vol. 27, no. 2, June 2004, pp. 210–17.

Robinson, Jerry. *The Comics: An Illustrated History of Comic Strip Art.* G. P. Putnam's Sons, 1974.

Rockwell, Geoffrey, and Stéfan Sinclair. *Hermeneutica: Computer-Assisted Interpretation in the Humanities.* MIT P, 2016.

Rodgers, Shelly, and Esther Thorson, editors. *Advertising Theory.* Routledge, 2012.

Round, Julia. "'Is This a Book?' DC Vertigo and the Redefinition of Comics in the 1990s." *The Rise of the American Comics Artist: Creators and Contexts*, edited by Paul Williams and James Lyons, UP of Mississippi, 2010, pp. 14–30.

Ryall, Chris, and Scott Tipton. *Comic Books 101: The History, Methods and Madness.* Impact Books, 2008.

Sanders, Joe Sutliff. "How Comics Became Kids' Stuff." *Good Grief! Children and Comics: A Collection of Companion Essays*, edited by Michelle Ann Abate and Joe Sutliff Sanders, Ohio State University Libraries, 2016, pp. 9–28.

Sassienie, Paul. *The Comic Book: The One Essential Guide for Comic Book Fans Everywhere.* Chartwell Books, 1994.

Saul, Gerald. "Amazing Pud Delivery." *Blogspot*, Aug. 23, 2017, https://geraldsaul.blogspot.ca.

Saunders, John. "Tootsie Roll Buys Dubble Bubble." *Globe and Mail*, Sept. 1, 2004, https://www.theglobeandmail.com/report-on-business/tootsie-roll-buys-dubble-bubble/article1140310/.

Savan, Leslie. *Sponsored Life: Ads, TV, and American Culture.* Temple UP, 1994.

Scandura, Jani. *Down in the Dumps: Place, Modernity, American Depression.* Duke UP, 2008.

Schenk, Ramon. "Hey, Who Took That?!" *Alter Ego*, vol. 3, no. 89, Oct. 2009, pp. 82–83.

Schiffer, Ed. "'Fable Number One': Some Myths about Consumption." *Eating Culture*, edited by Ron Scapp and Brian Seitz, State U of New York P, 1998, pp. 288–97.

Schilling, Peter, Jr. *Carl Barks' Duck: Average American.* Uncivilized Books, 2014.

Schulz, Charles M. *Snoopy and the Red Baron.* Holt, Rinehart and Winston, 1966.

Scott, Sharon M. *Toys and American Culture: An Encyclopedia.* Greenwood, 2010.

Seiter, Ellen. *Sold Separately: Parents and Children in Consumer Culture.* Rutgers UP, 1995.

Selig, Ken. "Come Back When You Learn How to Draw." Interview by Jim Amash. *Alter Ego*, vol. 3, no. 89, Oct. 2009, pp. 56–66.

@ShaynessMac. "Donald Trump is Richie Rich 50 years later #debate." Twitter, Oct. 9, 2016, 7:16 p.m., twitter.com/ShaynessMac/status/785302977976213506.

Shelley, Percy Bysshe. *The Selected Poetry and Prose of Shelley.* Introduction and notes by Bruce Woodcock. Wordsworth Editions, 2002.

Simon, Joe. "Harvey Gets Simonized." Interview by Jon B. Cooke. *Comic Book Artist*, no. 19, June 2002, pp. 86–87.

Simon, Michele. *Appetite for Profit: How the Food Industry Undermines Our Health and How to Fight Back.* Nation Books, 2006.

Sławek, Tadeusz. "The Vase and Broken Pieces: Productivity and the Margin of Waste." *Rubbish, Waste and Litter: Culture and Its Refuse/als*, edited by Tadeusz Rachwał, Wydawnictwo SWPSA Academica, 2008, pp. 9–29.
Smith, Craig. "Motion Comics: Modes of Adaptation and the Issue of Authenticity." *Animation Practice, Process and Production*, vol. 1, no. 2, June 2012, pp. 357–78.
Smith, Matthew J., and Randy Duncan, editors. *The Secret Origins of Comics Studies*. Routledge, 2017.
Smith, Zoë. "4 Colorism: The Ashiness of It All." *Inks: The Journal of the Comics Studies Society*, vol. 4, no. 3, Fall 2020, pp. 340–56.
Smolderen, Thierry. "Graphic Hybridization, the Crucible of Comics." *The French Comics Theory Reader*, edited by Ann Miller and Bart Beaty, Leuven UP, 2014, pp. 47–61.
Spiegelman, Art. *MetaMaus*. Pantheon, 2011.
Spiegelman, Art. "Putting Out the Garbage." *Garbage Pail Kids*, by the Topps Company. Abrams ComicArts, 2012, pp. 6–10.
Spiegelman, Art. "Wacky Days." *Wacky Packages*, by the Topps Company. Abrams ComicArts, 2008, pp. 6–8.
Steedman, Carolyn. *Dust: The Archive and Cultural History*. Rutgers UP, 2002.
Stein, Daniel. "'Mummified Objects': Superhero Comics in the Digital Age." *Journal of Graphic Novels and Comics*, vol. 7, no. 3, 2016, pp. 283–92.
Stewart, Bhob. "Bubbling Over." *Bazooka Joe and His Gang*. Topps, 2013.
Strasser, Susan. *Waste and Want: A Social History of Trash*. Henry Holt, 1999.
Stuller, Jennifer K. "Second Wave Feminism in the Pages of *Lois Lane*." *Critical Approaches to Comics: Theories and Methods*, edited by Matthew J. Smith and Randy Duncan, Routledge, 2012, pp. 235–51.
Svensson, Patrik. *Big Digital Humanities: Imagining a Meeting Place for the Humanities and the Digital*. U of Michigan P, 2016.
Tinker, Emma. "Manuscript in Print: The Materiality of Alternative Comics." *Literature Compass*, vol. 4, no. 4, July 2007, pp. 1169–82.
Tomlinson, John. *Cultural Imperialism: A Critical Introduction*. Johns Hopkins UP, 1991.
Topps Company. *Bazooka Joe and His Gang*. Abrams ComicArts, 2013.
Topps Company. *Mars Attacks*. Abrams ComicArts, 2012.
Topps Company. *Star Wars: The Original Topps Trading Card Series*, vol. 1. Abrams ComicArts, 2015.
Topps Company. *Star Wars: The Empire Strikes Back; The Original Topps Trading Card Series*, vol. 2. Abrams ComicArts, 2016.
Topps Company. *Star Wars: Return of the Jedi; The Original Topps Trading Card Series*, vol. 3. Abrams ComicArts, 2016.
Travis, Trysh. "Print and the Creation of Middlebrow Culture." *Perspectives on American Book History: Artifacts and Commentary*, edited by Scott E. Casper, Joanne D. Chaison, and Jeffrey D. Groves, U of Massachusetts P, 2002, pp. 339–66.
United States, President's Special Review Board. *Report of the President's Special Review Board, February 26, 1987*. Government Printing Office, 1987.
Unser-Schutz, Giancarla. "Developing a Text-Based Corpus of the Language of Japanese Comics (*Manga*)." *Corpus-Based Studies in Language Use, Language Learning, and*

Language Documentation, edited by John Newman, Harald Baayen, and Sally Rice, Rodopi, 2011, pp. 213–38.

US Congress. Senate. Subcommittee to Investigate Juvenile Delinquency. *Interim Report: Comic Books and Juvenile Delinquency*, 84th Long., 1st Sess., 1955. Greenwood Press, 1969.

Van Ness, Sara J. *"Watchmen" as Literature: A Critical Study of the Graphic Novel*. McFarland, 2010.

Varma, Sandeep K. "Quantum *Bhangra*: *Bhangra* Music and Identity in the South Asian Diaspora." *Limina*, vol. 11, 2005, pp. 17–27.

Walker, Brian. *The Comics before 1945*. Harry N. Abrams, 2004.

Walsh, John A. "Comic Book Markup Language: An Introduction and Rationale." *Digital Humanities Quarterly*, vol. 6, no. 1, 2012, https://www.digitalhumanities.org/dhq/vol/6/1/000117/000117.html.

Wardle, D. B. *Document Repair*. Society of Archivists, 1971.

Weiner, Robert G. "Educating about Comics." *The Secret Origins of Comics Studies*, edited by Matthew J. Smith and Randy Duncan, Routledge, 2017, pp. 12–30.

Wernick, Andrew. *Promotional Culture: Advertising, Ideology and Symbolic Expression*. Sage, 1991.

Wilde, Lukas R. A. "Distinguishing Mediality: The Problem of Identifying Forms and Features of Digital Comics." *Networking Knowledge*, vol. 8, no. 4, July 2015, 1–14.

Williams, Paul. *Dreaming the Graphic Novel: The Novelization of Comics*. Rutgers UP, 2020.

Williams, Paul, and James Lyons, editors. *The Rise of the American Comics Artist: Creators and Contexts*. UP of Mississippi, 2010.

Williams, Raymond. *Television: Technology and Cultural Form*. Routledge, 2004.

Wolf-Meyer, Matthew. "The World Ozymandias Made: Utopias in the Superhero Comic, Subculture, and the Conservation of Difference." *Journal of Popular Culture*, vol. 36, no. 3, Jan. 2003, pp. 497–517.

Wolk, Douglas. *Reading Comics: How Graphic Novels Work and What They Mean*. Da Capo Press, 2007.

Woo, Benjamin. Review of *Considering "Watchmen": Poetics, Property, Politics*, by Andrew Hoberek. *Cinema Journal*, vol. 56, no. 2, Winter 2017, pp. 151–55.

Wright, Bradford W. *Comic Book Nation: The Transformation of Youth Culture in America*. Johns Hopkins UP, 2001.

Würth, Kiene Brillenburg. "Posthumanities and Post-Textualities: Reading *The Raw Shark Texts* and *Woman's World*." *Comparative Literature*, vol. 63, no. 2, 2011, pp. 119–41.

Yezbick, Daniel F. "Ridiculous Rebellion: George L. Carlson and the Recovery of *Jingle Jangle Comics*." *The Rise and Reason of Comics and Graphic Literature: Critical Essays on the Form*, edited by Joyce Goggin and Dan Hassler-Forest, McFarland, 2010, pp. 25–41.

Youngquist, Paul. "Stats of Exception: Watchmen and Nixon's NSC." *Postmodern Culture*, vol. 23, no. 2, Jan. 2013, https://www.pomoculture.org/2015/07/08/stats-of-exception-watchmen-and-nixons-nsc/.

INDEX

Abrams ComicArts, 79, 124
Absolute Editions, 50, 62–66, 74–76
advertising: and bubble gum comics, 120–21, 130–31; in *Uncle Scrooge*, 27, 29–32, 34–35; for *Watchmen*, 52–53, 67
album (format), 38, 50, 55–56, 112
Amazon.com, 4, 79
American News Company, 25
annotations, 69, 77–78
Another Rainbow, 36–37
Arnold, Mark, 85, 95
Artifact Editions, 51, 73–75
Artist's Editions, 41–42, 74
Association of Comics Magazine Publishers (ACMP), 14, 46. *See also* Comics Code Authority

Barks, Carl, 4–5, 19–22, 36–43, 54, 74, 113
Barks, Garé, 41–42
Batman, 15, 49, 70, 50, 63–65
Bazooka Joe, 114, 118, 120, 124–25, 130, 139. *See also* Topps Company
Beaty, Bart, 14, 21, 47, 57, 100, 125
binding: hardcover, 36, 38, 47, 75–76; history of, 3, 10, 11; stapled, 3, 7, 23–24, 43, 52, 76; trade paperback, 43, 50, 53
Blue Age of Comics, 152
Bonfire of the Vanities, The (Wolfe novel), 99
book history, 6–18, 19–48, 81, 148–53
branding: candy, 117, 130–31; comic book, 12, 16, 23–24, 61; readers and, 149–51; *Richie Rich*, 82–96, 104–12
Buell, Marjorie "Marge," 85, 118
Bushmiller, Ernie, 134, 137, 142–43

Cadet Sweets, 122
cards, 31, 34, 121–24. *See also* Cadet Sweets; Fleer Corporation; Topps Company
cartoons, 8–9, 84–85, 89, 96, 98, 109
Casper the Friendly Ghost, 82, 84–85, 88–89, 93, 98
Celestial Arts, 36
cheapness, 6–7, 14, 25, 80, 151; cheap food, 117, 145. *See also* value
Colón, Ernie, 84, 88–89, 92–95, 100, 101, 107, 109, 111–12, 149. *See also* Richie Rich
coloring, 8–10, 26–27, 29, 38–39, 64–66, 139. *See also* Daigle-Leach, Susan; Higgins, John; Tommaso, Rich
Comics Code Authority, 14–15, 46–47, 87–89. *See also* Comics Magazine Association of America (CMAA)
Comics Magazine Association of America (CMAA), 46–47, 87. *See also* Association of Comics Magazine Publishers (ACMP); Comics Code Authority
Concord Confections, 113, 121. *See also* Fleer Corporation; Tootsie Roll Industries
Craig, Chase, 38
Crisis on Infinite Earths (Wolfman and Perez limited series), 58, 63, 80

Daigle-Leach, Susan, 39, 41. *See also* coloring
Davis, Paul, 101–3
DC Comics, 5, 13, 30, 49, 66–68, 69–72, 74, 75–76, 77, 78, 80–81, 151. *See also* National Allied Publications

169

INDEX

Dell Publishing: history of, 11, 14, 120, 127, 151; publishers of Disney comics, 23–25, 27, 43, 46; rivals to Harvey Comics, 85. *See also* Golden Books; Gold Key Comics (Western Publishing imprint); Western Printing and Lithographing Company

Dick Tracy (Chester Gould comic strip), 23, 83, 84

Die Kitty Die (Parent and Ruiz limited series), 98

Disney, 21, 151

distribution: bookstores, 61; direct market, 15–16, 53, 95, 110, 148; newsstand, 11–13, 24–25, 39, 46, 154n4; tension between digital and direct market, 152–53. *See also* American News Company

Doyle, Larry, 99

Dunbier, Scott, 63, 74

editing, 38, 43–44, 63, 83–86, 95, 107. *See also* Craig, Chase; Dunbier, Scott; Jacobson, Sid; Lee, Stan

Éditions Zenda, 55–56

Eisner, Will, 15, 22

ephemera, 7, 25, 127–30, 138, 146

Famous Studios, 84–85

Fantagraphics, 39–44

Fantastic Four, 13, 79

Fleer Corporation, 115, 116, 118, 121, 123, 125

food, 6, 30–32, 113–20, 131, 141–46

Fuddleduck, Rufus, 45–46

Gabor, Zsa Zsa, 99

Gandalf Products Company, 30–35

Gibbons, Dave, 5, 15, 49, 52–57, 66–69, 74–78. *See also Watchmen* (Moore, Gibbons, and Higgins limited series)

Glad, Gloria, 90–91, 97

Gladstone Publishing, 38–39

glut: love, 86; New Kids on the Block, 96; as publishing strategy, 12, 82–83; Richie Rich, 93–96, 105; superheroes, 12

Golden Books, 30. *See also* Western Publishing

Goldie, Glittering, 19, 32–33, 35–37

Gold Key Comics (Western Publishing imprint), 26–30, 46

Goodman, Martin, 83–84

Gordon, Ian, 97, 119–20, 133, 146

graphic novel: concept of, 70–73, 80–81, 126, 150; history of, 15–17, 49, 52–54

Graphitti Designs, 56–58, 70, 75–76, 78

"Great Comic Book Scare" of 1947–1955, 14, 46, 87–89. *See also* Association of Comics Magazine Publishers (ACMP); Comics Code Authority; Comics Magazine Association of America (CMAA); US Senate Subcommittee on Juvenile Delinquency (1953–1955); Wertham, Fredric

Harvey, Alfred, 82–84, 94–95

Harvey Comics, 5, 82–87, 88, 89, 92, 93, 94–96, 97, 103, 105, 107, 109, 110, 111, 112, 148, 151. *See also* Harvey, Alfred; Jacobson, Sid; Montgomery, Jeff

Higgins, John, 5, 15, 49–50, 64–65, 74, 76–77. *See also* coloring; *Watchmen* (Moore, Gibbons, and Higgins limited series)

Hostess (food brand), 30–32, 35, 44, 120

Hot Stuff, 88–89

IDW Publishing, 41–42, 73–75

Insane Clown Posse, 151

Iran-Contra, 54–55

Iron Man, 31, 32, 35

Isabella, Tony, 148–52

Ix Hun Ahau, 115

Jacobson, Sid, 86, 95, 112

Jippes, Daan, 38–39

Johns, Geoff, 64

Juvenal (poet), 54

Kodansha Limited, 78

Kool G Rap, 151

INDEX

Kremer, Warren, 88, 94, 109, 112. *See also* Richie Rich

Lee, Stan, 13, 83
lettering, 41, 56. *See also* Barks, Garé
Levitz, Paul, 62, 80
Lindelof, Damon, 72
Lodge, Veronica, 100
Lynde, Paul, 99

Marvel Comics, 30–31, 52–53, 79, 83, 94–96, 121. *See also* Goodman, Martin; Lee, Stan; Timely Comics
McDuck, Scrooge, 19–20, 28–29, 32–35, 37, 43–46, 100–101. *See also* Barks, Carl
Meltzer, Brad, 64
Meyer, Helen, 127. *See also* Dell Publishing
Montgomery, Jeff, 95–96
Moore, Alan, 5, 15, 49–58, 61, 64–65, 68. *See also Watchmen* (Moore, Gibbons, and Higgins limited series)
Morse, Wesley, 124–25
Mosley, Walter, 79
motion comics, 68–69, 79

National Allied Publications, 11–12, 83. *See also* DC Comics; Wheeler-Nicholson, Malcom
Nevins, Jess, 77
newspapers, 8–12, 118, 127, 130, 143; underground, 15

1 Central Park West (Trump International Hotel and Tower), 97

pamphlet (format), 3, 6–7, 11, 17, 34–35, 149
paper: Baxter, 50; low-quality, 3, 7, 25–26, 35, 52–53, 65, 95; wrappers, 113, 128, 139. *See also* pulp
Peanuts (Schulz comic strip), 14, 40, 99
publishing. *See* Goodman, Martin; Harvey, Alfred; Jacobson, Sid; Levitz, Paul; Meyer, Helen; Montgomery, Jeff; Wheeler-Nicholson, Malcom

Pud, 6, 113, 114, 115, 118, 119, 120–21, 122–23, 125, 130, 133–34, 135, 136, 137, 138–42, 143, 144–46, 150
pulp, 7, 11–13, 24–26, 146, 153. *See also* paper

Resident Evil 3: Nemesis, 62
Richie Rich, 4, 5, 82, 83–84, 85, 87, 88–95, 96–101, 102–3, 104–6, 107–12, 148–53; 1994 film, 96; 2015 TV series, 96–97

slipcase, 36, 51, 56, 62–63, 65, 75–76
Spiegelman, Art, 15, 40, 49, 124–25, 146
St. John Publications, 85

Taschen, 80
Teen-Age Dope Slaves, 87
Thompson, Ray, 125
Tijuana Bibles, 124
Timely Comics, 13, 86. *See also* Marvel Comics
Tintin (Hergé bande-dessinée), 92, 111–12
Titan Books, 59–61
Tlazōlteōtl, 115–16, 146
Tommaso, Rich, 41. *See also* coloring
Tootsie Roll Industries, 113, 121, 151. *See also* Concord Confections
Topps Company, 114, 118, 120–24. *See also* Bazooka Joe
trash, 6, 49, 113, 114, 118, 124, 125–30, 131–32, 133, 134, 141, 146–47, 153
Trump, Donald, 97–102, 111, 148
tzictli (chicle), 115–16

US Senate Subcommittee on Juvenile Delinquency (1953–1955), 3, 14, 87, 126–27. *See also* "Great Comic Book Scare" of 1947–1955

value, 4; changing, 152; high, 5, 39, 42, 49, 73–75; low, 6–7, 141. *See also* cheapness; trash

Watchmen (Moore, Gibbons, and Higgins limited series), 4, 5, 49–55, 56, 57, 58,

59–62, 63, 64, 65–69, 70, 71–72, 73, 75–77, 78, 79, 80–81; motion comic, 68–69; 2009 film, 67–69

Wertham, Fredric, 87, 126

Western Printing and Lithographing Company, 23–25, 40–43, 151. *See also* Dell Publishing; Golden Books; Gold Key Comics (Western Publishing imprint); Whitman Publishing

Wheeler-Nicholson, Malcolm, 11–12. *See also* publishing

Whitman Publishing, 10, 30, 23. *See also* Western Printing and Lithographing Company

ABOUT THE AUTHOR

Photo by Aspen Zettel

Dr. **Neale Barnholden** is an instructor at the University of Alberta in Edmonton, and is originally from Vancouver, British Columbia. His research is primarily concerned with the farrago of comics and consumer culture—from intermedial brands like the Addams Family to the long shadow of pulp. He can be found by searching his extremely distinctive name.

www.ingramcontent.com/pod-product-compliance
Lightning Source LLC
Chambersburg PA
CBHW022023220426
43663CB00007B/1185